THE COMPLEXITY OF AUTISM SPECTRUM DISORDERS

Since its first identification, autism spectrum disorder (ASD) has presented myriad challenges of diagnosis and classification. Our understanding has evolved from a cluster of diagnostic categories (Asperger's, autism, and pervasive development disorder) to the current continuum of autism spectrum disorder. Meanwhile, we have progressed from debating the validity of the diagnosis to considering it a modern epidemic. This evolution has drawn attention across a variety of fields, including the neurosciences, education, forensics, and behavioral health. While new research accumulates, there remains a lack of conceptual and practical clarity about what ASD is, how specific diagnoses might be delineated, and what we can do to understand and manage the complexity of individuals on the spectrum. In understanding ASD, one size does not fit all—families, schools, and clinicians all need a multi-faceted engagement with the specifics they encounter. This text opens a critical dialogue through which students, researchers, and clinicians can challenge their ideas about what it means to work with the unique presentations of individuals on the Spectrum. It provides education, clinical expertise, and personalization to the lives influenced by the ever-changing dynamics of autism spectrum disorder.

Michael Wolff, PsyD, ABPdN, is a clinical psychologist and board-certified neuropsychologist. He is the co-founder of Behavioral Resources And Institute for Neuropsychological Services (BRAINS).

Bradley Bridges, LMSW, is an outpatient counselor providing therapy to children, adolescents, and young adults at BRAINS. He specializes in challenges associated with ASD, providing services for clients, parents, and professionals.

Thomas Denczek, LMSW, has been practicing for 25 years. Mr. Denczek has experience with children and families in residential, community mental health, in-home, and outpatient care settings. He is also an advocate for those with ASD.

THE COMPLEXITY OF AUTISM SPECTRUM DISORDERS

Edited by Michael Wolff, Bradley Bridges, and Thomas Denczek

Routledge
Taylor & Francis Group

NEW YORK AND LONDON

First published 2019
by Routledge
711 Third Avenue, New York, NY 10017

and by Routledge
2 Park Square, Milton Park, Abingdon, Oxon, OX14 4RN

Routledge is an imprint of the Taylor & Francis Group, an informa business

© 2019 Taylor & Francis

Library of Congress Cataloging-in-Publication Data
Names: Wolff, Michael, 1975- editor. | Bridges, Bradley, 1979-
    editor. | Denczek, Thomas, 1966- editor.
Title: The complexity of autism spectrum disorders / edited by
    Michael Wolff, Bradley Bridges, Thomas Denczek.
Description: New York, NY : Routledge, 2019. | Includes
    bibliographical references and index.
Identifiers: LCCN 2018016221 | ISBN 9781138316621 (hb :
    alk. paper) | ISBN 9781138316638 (pb : alk. paper) | ISBN
    9780429454646 (eb)
Subjects: | MESH: Autism Spectrum Disorder
Classification: LCC RC553.A88 | NLM WS 350.8.P4 | DDC
    616.85/882—dc23
LC record available at https://lccn.loc.gov/2018016221

ISBN: 978-1-138-31662-1 (hbk)
ISBN: 978-1-138-31663-8 (pbk)
ISBN: 978-0-429-45464-6 (ebk)

Typeset in Bembo
by Swales & Willis Ltd, Exeter, Devon, UK

CONTENTS

CONTRIBUTORS

D. J. Bernat is currently pursuing a doctoral degree in school psychology from Ball State University with a dual focus in neuropsychology and counseling.

Amy Caffero-Tolemy, PsyD, is a licensed clinical psychologist at Verdant Oak Behavioral Health, where she provides therapy and conducts psychological assessments. Her areas of specialty include forensic studies, developmental disorders, and substance abuse.

Susan Cleghorn, DrOT, OTRL, CAPS, is Assistant Professor of Occupational Science & Therapy at Grand Valley State University. Her clinical practice, teaching, and scholarship include global and domestic health promotion, sensory motor spaces in schools, and home and community accessibility.

Liane Holliday-Willey, EdD, is a psycholinguist, autism advocate, developmental delays consultant, international bestselling author, and keynote speaker, who shares her personal experience as a woman diagnosed with autism and as a researcher working with universities and the Department of Defense. Her work focuses on educating and supporting females with autism from the diagnostic stage through self-advocacy in relationships, employment, and personal security.

Shaunna Kelder, DrOT, OTRL, is Assistant Professor of Occupational Science and Therapy at Grand Valley State University and lead professor of pediatric practice course content. Her expertise is in school-based and acute inpatient pediatric OT and Sensory Integration intervention for ASD and ADHD.

Mira C. Krishnan is a board-certified neuropsychologist specializing in lifespan development. She is co-chair for the Committee for Transgender People

& Gender Diversity of the Society for the Psychology of Sexual Orientation and Gender Diversity, a Division of the American Psychological Association.

Rochelle Manor, PhD, is a neuropsychologist and the co-founder of BRAINS. She earned her master's and PhD at Ball State University with a dual cognate in Neuropsychological Assessment and Marriage & Family Therapy. She splits her time between neuropsychological evaluations and overseeing daily operations of BRAINS.

Cassandra E. Marschall is a School Psychologist Education Specialist providing educational services in Indianapolis, focusing on emotion regulation, mindfulness, and preventative interventions.

Erin Matlosz, PsyD, is a fully licensed Clinical Psychologist and Doctoral level Board Certified Behavior Analyst at BRAINS. She specializes in the assessment and treatment of developmental and behavioral disorders.

Janine D. Mator is a doctoral student in human factors psychology at Old Dominion University. Her research interests focus on human-computer interaction, particularly simulation-based training.

Jennifer Maurer, PsyD is a clinical neuropsychologist with a pediatric focus in the assessment of neurodevelopmental disorders at BRAINS. She completed her doctorate in counseling psychology with a specialization in neuropsychology at Carlow University.

Paige Mission, PhD, is a Pediatric Neuropsychology Postdoctoral Fellow at the University of Wisconsin-Madison Hospital and Clinics and American Family Children's Hospital

Diana Osipsov, LMSW, is a clinical therapist specializing in early childhood development, with a focus in trauma, anxiety, ASD, and emotional/behavioral dysregulation. Diana is pursuing a PhD in Infant and Early Childhood Development with emphasis in Mental Health and Developmental Disorders.

Thomas J. Overly, LMSW, is the co-founder and CEO of Promena VR and the Founder of VR Therapy and Counseling Center.

Jesse E. Piehl, PhD, is a clinical neuropsychologist at BRAINS, working with pediatric populations with a variety of developmental, behavioral, and medical complications. He completed a PhD in school psychology with a specialization in neuropsychology at Ball State University.

Mary S. Rozendal, PhD, is an educational therapist and Director of EnCourage Institute. She provides developmental, behavioural, and educational therapy for children with autism and other learning challenges, and advocacy for parents navigating the school IEP process.

Richard Solomon is a board-certified developmental pediatrician specializing in autism spectrum disorders with over 25 years' experience. He uses a developmental, relationship-based approach that embraces the uniqueness of the child in the context of his/her family. He created the PLAY Autism Intervention (PLAY Project).

Stefany Tucker is an applied behavior analysis technician working directly with individuals diagnosed with autism spectrum disorder. She is currently pursuing credentialing to become a board-certified behavior analyst. She has experience developing educational and behavioral systems of support for children and adolescents in the school setting.

Lauren Vetter, MS, OTRL, is an Adjunct Professor of Occupational Science & Therapy at Grand Valley State University and occupational therapist at The Center for Childhood Development. Her clinical practice and teaching focuses on the pediatric population, specifically children with developmental, motor, and social-emotional challenges.

Christina Warholic, PsyD, is a clinical neuropsychologist at BRAINS working primarily with a pediatric population. She has a special interest in working with children with developmental disorders secondary to genetic conditions and histories of prematurity and prenatal exposure. She completed her doctorate at Chestnut Hill College.

Nalova Westbrook, PhD, is Assistant Professor of Education at Calvin College. Her areas of expertise include emergent literacy, content literacy, media literacy, English Language Learning, and Universal Design for Learning.

1

THE EVOLUTION OF AUTISM SPECTRUM DISORDER

Michael Wolff and Rochelle Manor

Historical Timeline

In 1943, Dr. Leo Kanner, psychiatrist, discussed 11 children who seemed to be more isolated and who had also demonstrated an obsessive desire for sameness. He referred to these children as being autistic and suggested it would be important to further research in terms of the biological basis and effect of autism. In 1944, Hans Asperger described children that he had also referred to as autistic, but seemed to have higher perceptual reasoning/nonverbal intelligence and had a tendency to use broader vocabulary appropriately. Through the 1950s and 1960s, autistic spectrum disorder children were commonly thought to have a form of childhood schizophrenia. Attribution was often given to this being caused from schizophrenogenic mothers, who were not always accessible to their children. Finally, in the 1970s, autism started to become better researched and started to be differentiated on the biological basis of the disorder.

Research started to recognize a variation in brain development. In DSM-III (Diagnostic and Statistical Manual for Mental Disorders) (1980), the first description of autism was finally articulated. The DSM-III distinguished autism from childhood schizophrenia: children with an autism spectrum disorder do not often endorse auditory or visual hallucinations in childhood. Clinically, there can be some distortion, discussed later in their development, where they might have difficulty separating reality from fantasy. However, their beliefs are not necessarily delusional in nature, though there is an atypicality to their belief structure. Rather, those with autism are persistent in their ideas and areas of focus. And behaviors, although repetitive in nature, are not necessarily varied and bizarre (like behaviors commonly demonstrated in schizophrenia). However, similarities between autism and childhood schizophrenia would be the changes in self-care or lack of concern for self-care. There can also be social isolation and distancing that is commonly associated with schizophrenia or autism, as it was initially defined.

In 1987, the DSM-III revised provided a checklist for delineating autism from other disorders. And, in DSM-IV and DSM-IV TR (text revision), there was an expansion to include autism and Asperger's into the diagnostic cluster. The delineation between autism from Asperger's persisted until publication of DSM-V (APA, 2013).

Complications of diagnostic differentiation:

Autism and Asperger's have many overlapping qualities. Both sets of diagnostic criteria reiterate that there needs to be a developmental delay in social skills, repetitive behavior, focal areas of interest, challenges with communication, and delays in activities of daily living. Autism and Asperger's should not be better accounted for by conditions like Rett syndrome or childhood disintegrative disorder.

While autism and Asperger's both include many of the same features, the biggest differentiation that was made (in DSM-IV) was that in Asperger's there would typically not be a clinically significant delay in language. Further, Asperger's individuals tended to have higher cognitive abilities, would more routinely develop age-appropriate self-help skills, would be more likely to make gains in adaptive functioning, and, therefore, may not stand out as much as those with autism in their classroom or the general environment. They seem to be more curious and socially interested, but could still not easily fit in with their cohort. Yet, similar to autism, individuals with Asperger's would struggle with social interaction, have repetitive behaviors, and the disturbance would cause clinically significant impairment in social, occupational, or other important functional domains.

DSM-IV also proposed the diagnosis of a pervasive developmental disorder unspecified. This would be considered because there is a significant overlap between autism, Asperger's, and other pediatric developmental delays that could not be better delineated between just autism and Asperger's. "PDD-NOS [i.e., not otherwise specified]" was more of an umbrella term that would encompass many children developing broad spectrum developmental delays, even if they did not possess all the criteria of autism or Asperger's.

Again, delineating the differences between autism and Asperger's is important, but language is a broad category and may not be the best factor to consider between these two diagnoses. There have been multiple iterations stating that individuals with autism have speech delays and those with Asperger's do not. However, Dr. Tony Atwood suggests that individuals with Asperger's will likely experience speech and language delays, but this should not include phonological or other articulation disorder, and there also needs to be broader consideration of the social context of the speech and language deficit. Unfortunately, using this language, results in more confusion regarding the delineation between an Autism Spectrum Disorder and a social (pragmatic) language disorder. According to historical diagnostic contexts, Asperger's is more difficult to "tease apart" from a Social Language Disorder. Both have at their core a social language deficit and associated social/emotional challenges as a result of the difficulty communicating in social context, but in Asperger's there should be accompanying focal interests and repetitive behavior(s). In clinical relevance, we see more individuals with social pragmatic disorders, who struggle in courses like English Language Arts, philosophy, and the social sciences. Social language problems also contribute to greater difficulty in larger group interactions, whereas small group discussions are not as troublesome. And, there needs to be vigilance, as those with social language struggles many also develop obsessive qualities, the need for routine, may avoid social interaction, can become rigid and demonstrate very similar patterns to ASD (particularly Asperger's) as a way to compensate for their struggles. This is why discussions in overseas blogs and educational sites have commonly associated Semantic Pragmatic Disorder in the cluster of diagnoses under the umbrella of the autism continuum (see www.spdsupport.org.uk/). Semantic Pragmatic Disorder was recognized overseas well before the idea of a social (pragmatic) language disorder was included in the DSM here in the US.

This is again functionally meaningful, as an individual with autism may lack content in speech and require more recurrent prompting or may lack functional communication altogether. However, an individual with Asperger's more commonly can talk. In fact, individuals with Asperger's may share extensive ideas about their areas of interest and other details, but still not come to the point in order to engage in interactive communication. Using the DSM-V (which does not distinguish between autism and Asperger's), it is challenging to differentiate an individual who is higher functioning like Asperger's from an individual with autism. Rather, the family would have to understand what their child with an autism spectrum disorder Level I from Level III severity specifier would mean for them now and in the future. The categorization is nonspecific and easily confusing. These qualities are quite similar, as they are both likely to require significant support not only in childhood, but progressing into adulthood as well. Essentially, what would have previously been considered a low functioning Asperger's individual could also be considered a high functioning individual with autism. While this latter point is somewhat esoteric considering that the ASDs have been combined under the umbrella of an autism spectrum disorder, I believe it is still important that consideration be made to provide the best diagnostic clarity for families. In these domains where it is hard to differentiate, the prior diagnosis of PDD, NOS would be appropriate. Consistent with medical disorders, approximately 25% of children are not easily able to be captured in one medical category. This would be similar to what we would likely see with autism spectrum disorders—if we continue using the current International

Classification of Diseases (ICD) model, where differentiation remains possible for autism, Asperger's, pervasive developmental disorder, unspecified and Social Pragmatic Communication Disorder. The differential, as best as possible, is very consistent with the medical classification for diseases, and then leads to the discourse of treatment options with better specificity. It leaves the obvious question. Why wouldn't everyone, particularly clinicians, want this specificity?

Clinical Research

Subsequent to DSM-IV, clinical research began to search for specific delineations that researchers and other clinicians could prove; better defining each presentation of symptoms. The goal was to try to better understand the sensitivity and specificity between autism, Asperger's and PDD-NOS. This became a highly contentious line of research, with universities, clinicians, and families all having strong opinions regarding whether each diagnosis was distinct or to include all ASD-like qualities under one broader umbrella.

Throughout this time, the Centers for Disease Control also began to demonstrate epidemic rates of autism spectrum disorders. In 2000, 1 in 150 children had been diagnosed with some type of an autism spectrum disorder; by 2012, 1 in 68 children, typically males, were being diagnosed with an autism spectrum disorder; and, further, between 2006 and 2008, 1 in 6 children in the United States had demonstrated developmental disabilities ranging from mild disabilities, such as speech and language delays, to more serious difficulties with intellectual disability, cerebral palsy, and autism.

Still, there continues to be debate pointing to other diagnoses that could also influence the diagnostic prevalence rates for autism spectrum disorders. For example, at this point, the Diagnostic and Statistical Manual does not endorse central auditory processing disorder (CAPD) as a mental health condition. However, the American Speech and Hearing Association has endorsed the diagnosis and the ICD-10 includes the delineation of CAPD versus other communication and ASD diagnoses.

Additional Variables and Considerations

Semantic Pragmatic

For the first time, DSM-V also separated a condition (that had been recognized overseas as a Semantic Pragmatic Disorder) into a new diagnostic category— referred to as Social (Pragmatic) Communication Disorder. In this diagnosis, there are more persistent difficulties in the social use of language—whether this is in using verbal or nonverbal cues. It was thought that this diagnosis could be effectively diagnosed as separate from the autism spectrum disorder (ASD) now clustered into one condition, rather than autism, Asperger's, and PDD-NOS.

When there were three domains/diagnoses of ASD, there were two primary criteria that had to be met: (1) significant deficit in social communication and social interaction across multiple contexts; and (2) restrictive, repetitive patterns of behavior, interests, or activities. So, when Social Pragmatic Communication disorder did not have restrictive behaviors and ASD did, the differentiation was clear. Any nuances between autism, Asperger's, and PDD were thought to be eliminated under that structure.

Nonverbal Learning Disorder

The concept of a nonverbal learning disorder (NLD) is another highly debated diagnosis. There is extensive literature published in this area. Further, universities are starting to demonstrate that different neurological patterns might be associated with differentiating autism, Asperger's, and NLD (see Michigan State University: https://msutoday.msu.edu/news/2013/shedding-new-light-on-learning-disorders/).

Social Language Disorder

The concept of social language disorders is also a unique function. Historically, a Semantic Pragmatic Disorder would also have been included in the umbrella, but then it was split from ASD. I anticipate that these factors will continue to gain resource attention and effective differentiation from an individual with an ASD.

Sensory Processing Disorder

The last is probably the most debatable of all diagnoses, and that is the broader description of sensory processing disorders. I think it is clear that all medical and behavioral health professionals recognize that children can struggle with sensory deficits, but invariably these seem to be connected with other medical or mental health conditions. A neurological exam will test sensory functions. Individuals may be sensory-seeking, sensory-avoidant, or may demonstrate a combination of all sensory-seeking and -avoidance behavior. These disorders can affect unilateral sensory areas or any combination involving touch, taste, texture, sight, sound, and smell. Many individuals on the spectrum also demonstrate clumsiness and it is not uncommon for there to be toe-walking, which could again relate to a sensory deficit or other medical factors. Yet, identifying children with sensory processing concerns apart from other ASD symptoms is still debated.

Early Onset

In all iterations of diagnostics, symptoms have to be present earlier in development. There is recognition that symptoms could be masked by learned strategies in later life. The symptoms would still need to have a clinically significant impairment in social, occupational, or other important areas of functioning. The DSM-V also included: (1) whether there is accompanying intellectual impairment, language impairment, or other medical or genetic factors that may be associated with the ASD; and (2) severity levels (Level I, which would require support, to Level III, where the person would require very substantial support for functioning.)

Medical and Congenital Overlap

A majority of countries, including the United States, consider several medical and congenital disorders that are commonly implicated in children who demonstrate autism spectrum disorders. These disorders commonly include: the Fragile X syndrome, Landau-Kleffner, Rett syndrome, childhood disintegrative disorder, and Williams syndrome. Several of these conditions can be diagnosed most effectively via the use of genetic testing. Landau-Kleffner is an epileptic condition. Many individuals with Landau-Kleffner demonstrate autistic behavior such as social withdrawal, insistence on sameness, and have language deficits. Children with Landau-Kleffner more often demonstrate a regressive pattern where language skills may progress neurotypically developing at first, but then decline appreciably between the ages of 3 and 7. An EEG is needed to delineate the epileptic pattern; otherwise, these children mimic autism.

Intellectual Disability

In the research prior to the publication of DSM-V, a plethora of material had been completed. Again, opinions were easily divided, but, in general, it was believed that professionals cannot easily and accurately differentiate autism from Asperger's or other ASD-like conditions. The general belief was that, by combining the conditions under one umbrella, there would be fewer false positives (Frazier, 2012). Yet, in the Frazier literature, it was suggested that females may be more commonly missed by the "relaxed DSM criteria." There was a stronger emphasis on social attributes and in early development; females may not demonstrate as many symptoms as a result of their higher likelihood to demonstrate early interaction. McPartland, Reichow, and Volkmar (2012) and Mazurek et al. (2017) suggested that there seemed to be higher specificity, but lower sensitivity for Asperger's and PDD-NOS if a cutoff IQ of 70 was used. Looking at individuals who had an IQ of over 70 seemed to increase the ability to specify Asperger's as opposed to autism. Huerta, Bishop, Duncan, Hus, and Lord (2012) also denoted that most individuals diagnosed with an autistic spectrum disorder by DSM-IV criteria would still remain eligible for the diagnosis of autism or Asperger's, but would simply be placed under the umbrella of ASD. As such, there would be no change in general prevalence rates or epidemiological concern. This seems to be consistent with what is being demonstrated by the Centers for Disease Control statistics. In fact, the latest available statistics that have been published, for between 2014 and 2016, demonstrate rise in the percentage of the US population demonstrating an autistic spectrum disorder: from 2.24% to 2.76% (Zablotsky, Black, & Blumberg, 2017).

Intellectual disabilities had demonstrated a slight decline, but other developmental delays were all demonstrating increases in prevalence rates. Reading the broad base of literature since the publication of the DSM-V in 2013, some individuals continue to argue that the umbrella of autism spectrum disorder has assisted in decreasing diagnostic rates, while others would suggest that it has become even easier for individuals to fit into the autism spectrum disorder umbrella. Frazier (2012) suggests that the new criteria may reduce some false positives but, more importantly, could improve early awareness of unique ASD-like symptoms to improve early intervention access, which in the long run should decrease societal costs as a whole. Ultimately, there may be a rise in early diagnoses, but with early intervention the overall costs will decline.

Clinical Opinion Regarding the Importance of ASD Delineation

In my opinion, and that of the clinical group that I work with, it is important, as best as possible, to provide diagnostic accuracy for individuals and families. Some have argued that, as a result of DSM-V, differentiating the ASD diagnoses is an antiquated methodology. And yet, at this point in time, ICD-10 continues to delineate the diagnoses. Considering that the ICD-10 is used for electronic health code billing, the specificity remains relevant. Further, treatment should be different, depending on functional skills and adaptive needs.

Let's take the example of cancer. Most of the time, types of cancer can be effectively differentiated by histology study, and further information can be gleaned through additional radiological studies. However, in some cases, histology studies might demonstrate a mixed profile, radiologic imaging does not provide the clarification, and, as such, medical professionals have to make a judgment call on which treatment protocol to use to optimize treatment planning and outcome. The same argument could easily be used in many other medical conditions, including seizures, typology of concussion disorders, neoplasms, and many other neurological conditions. Extensive time, effort, and funds are used to try to garner the most accurate diagnosis. As a result of diagnoses in Western culture, the belief is that diagnostic clarity leads to more effective decision-making, treatment options, and predicting eventual outcome.

The same argument remains valid with autism spectrum disorder. I will readily concede that the literature presents a compelling case to suggest that it is not always possible to delineate autism from Asperger's—in which case, many of these children would eventually be diagnosed as PDD-NOS. However, even if only a fraction of the population can be more effectively and accurately diagnosed, effort should be taken to do so. When families hear the classic diagnosis of an autism spectrum disorder, they do not have a clear understanding of what this means. However, when a professional is able to tell the family that their child is autistic, there is the assumption that their child will struggle to relate to them emotionally, will have pervasive developmental delays, is likely to require support that extends into adulthood, and there is a higher likelihood of long-term care support even if they are able to live independently. This would be true if they were low to high functioning autistic.

Being diagnosed with Asperger's, on the other hand, would typically suggest that the child has a social interest, but does not know how to fit in easily with the social group. They are more likely to have higher intellectual capacity, work-related interest, and may not only have splinter skills, like individuals with autism, but are more likely to use these splinter skills toward some type of functional purpose. They are seen as having skill useful in the workforce environment (some jobs are now posting that they are actively seeking individuals with an Asperger's diagnosis). These individuals are commonly sought for jobs in computer programming, software development, engineering, and architecture. Nonetheless, individuals are starting to see the unique attributes that can be demonstrated more commonly with Asperger's, due to social interest and stronger relative ability to work with others.

The more accurate the diagnosis can also lead to additional specificity regarding treatment. Many states in the US have identified applied behavioral analysis (ABA) as a primary intervention strategy for individuals with an autism spectrum disorder. I would agree that this is accurate on many accounts, particularly when the diagnosis is more classic autism (as described by Kanner). However, some individuals with the diagnosis of Asperger's may not require the depth of service and there may not need to be the intensity of ABA, but other social groups, communication skills training through speech and language services, OT supports, and other lines of therapy that could be less intensive may be just as effective, if not more so, depending on the nature of the case. Essentially, one size does not fit all, and there are many treatment opportunities that demonstrate effective outcomes.

Further, the pejorative nature of delineating mild to moderate or severe manifestation of symptoms has been suggested. The DSM-V has essentially maintained this concept, but has changed the language—from mild, moderate to severe to severity Level I, Level II or Level III—to clarify symptom and functional severity. This is exactly the same concept that there was before, and, in fact, using the level system is more consistent with what might be found in medical terminology where there might be stages of pathology, to grade severity.

I think, in this case, that the DSM has effectively captured the importance of recognizing severity level, but has softened the language. Families who may take offense at the severity ratings need to be reminded that this specificity helps to support the intensity of services that may be needed to work with their child or other family member. It is not meant as a socially judgmental factor, but rather as a treatment-intensity opinion. The severity rating demonstrates to their insurance carrier the need for either more or less intensive services, and may also clarify the likelihood of outcome for the future, so that planning can then be focused, not only for the months or years ahead, but also on thinking into the extended future. This is imperative, as many families may be able to access disability trust funds, may start investigating alternative living arrangements either in their community or where they may be able to find these supports. There may be ancillary supports for disability, secondary insurance funding through Medicaid (or, if there are medical complications, through a children's special healthcare fund), or access other granting opportunities. As a clinician, it is important to emphasize that the severity rating level is not a reflection of family care or effort in supporting their family member. Rather, it is a treatment specificity that can support predictive outcome and a quick reference for the level of intensity for necessary services.

Overall, we disagree with the change in the DSM-V that "lumps" all individuals under one ASD umbrella. I can certainly respect the literature that outlines the challenges in always differentiating between autism, Asperger's, and PDD-NOS. However, consistent with the parallel medical community, there are often challenges in diagnostic clarity. Many times medical conjecture initially leads to the most common obvious consideration, then it starts treatment, and, depending on response to treatment, advances further delineation, continuing to provide further clarity and treatment options. I support a similar consideration for behavioral healthcare providers. All too often, time and energy are not invested as effectively in diagnostic clarification. Unfortunately, this can lead to unnecessary, ineffective, and sometimes harmful treatment for individuals.

Diagnostic specificity, as best as can be provided, can help provide better and more accurate care. It is certainly more than appropriate in non-acute care demands to take time to figure out the diagnosis, rather than "lumping everything under one umbrella." This will still not be a perfect circumstance (consistent with what is demonstrated by medical health colleagues), but the advantage appears to outweigh any potential disadvantages.

I will also recognize, from a psychiatric point of view, that medications may not fundamentally change according to whether the diagnosis is autism, Asperger's, or PDD-NOS. However, behavioral treatment approaches and predictive outcome can be more informed by using the clearest diagnostic specificity that is available. And, with the current ICD-10, it is still relevant and diagnostically accurate to differentiate autism spectrum disorders as best as possible.

References

American Psychiatric Association. (2013). *Diagnostic and Statistical Manual of Mental Disorders* (5th ed.). Washington, DC: American Psychiatric Association. retrieved from https://doi.org/10.1176/appi.books.9780890425596

Frazier, T., Youngstrom, E., Speer, L., Embacher, R., Law, P., Constantino, J., Findling, R., Hardan, A., & Eng, C. (2012). Validation of Proposed DSM-5 Criteria for Autism Spectrum Disorder. *Journal of American Academy for Child and Adolescent Psychiatry*, *51*(1), 28–40. doi:10.1016/j.jaac.2011.09.021

Huerta, M., Bishop, S., Duncan, A., Hus, V., & Lord, C. (2012). Application of DSM-5 Criteria for Autism Spectrum Disorder to Three Samples of Children with DSM-IV Diagnoses of Pervasive Developmental Disorders. *American Journal of Psychiatry*, *169*, 1056–1064.

McPartland, J., Reichow, B., & Volkmar, F. (2012). Sensitivity and Specificity of Proposed DSM-5 Diagnostic Criteria for Autism Spectrum Disorder Running Head: DSM-5 ASD. *Journal of American Academy for Child and Adolescent Psychiatry*, *51*(4). 368–383. doi:10.1016/j.jaac.2012.01.007

Mazurek, M., Lu, F., Symecko, H., Butter, E., Bing, N., Hundley, R., Poulsen, M., Kanne, S., Macklin, B., & Handen, B. (2017). A Prospective Study of the Concordance of DSM-IV and DSM-V Diagnostic Criteria for Autism Spectrum Disorder. *Journal of Autism and Developmental Disorders*, *47*(9), 2783–2794.

Zablotsky, B., Black, L., & Blumberg, S. (2017). *Estimated Prevalence of Children With Diagnosed Developmental Disabilities in the United States, 2014–2016*. U.S. Department of Health and Human Services, Centers for Disease Control and Prevention, NCHS Data Brief. No. 291, November 2017.

2

DIFFERENTIAL DIAGNOSIS

Jennifer Maurer and Christina Warholic

Introduction

The primary goal of assessment is differentiation to drive treatment. In the case of autism spectrum disorders, differential diagnosis is essential to increase the likelihood that the child or individual receives the adequate intervention and services in line with evidence-based models of treatment. Differential diagnosis, or the dissemination of symptoms into clusters to formulate an accurate diagnosis, is a careful practice in the very young. Children who experience delays in the typical developmental trajectory frequently present for assessment with several characteristics that could cause concern for autism but may also relate to disorders of early childhood, including those of a speech, motor, cognitive, medical, and genetic variety. Rapid advancements in technology and the field of developmental psychology have aided in the process of differential diagnosis, which can dramatically alter the prognosis and the course of the child's life in a positive manner. This chapter seeks to briefly explain the recent evolution of ASD diagnosis as defined by diagnostic and coding manuals to provide a broad understanding of the assessment process and the complicated nature of robust differentiation. Understanding the complexity of differential diagnosis related to autism spectrum disorders will contribute to further advancement in the field of psychology, increase the early and accurate detection of developmental disorders, enhance access to early intervention, and minimize the chance of misdiagnosis.

Diagnostic Manuals and Autism Spectrum Disorder

The primary diagnostic manual of mental health in the United States has been the *Diagnostic and Statistical Manual of Mental Disorders* (DSM), now in its fifth edition (American Psychiatric Association, 2013). Outside of the United States, other countries rely on the International Classification of Diseases (ICD), which is established by the World Health Organization, now in its tenth edition and under revision (World Health Organization, n.d.). The criteria for ASD have varied and the differences have been debated, from minor to major. Some could argue that text revisions struggle to keep up with the scientific advances in the field of ASD, specifically. It will be important for practitioners to remain engaged in the conversation and future criteria proposals. In the last DSM revision, researchers posed data to emphasize the importance of differentiation and need to standardize the criteria of ASD. Wilson et al. (2013) investigated whether ASD diagnostic outcome varied in intellectually capable adults with ASD depending on the criteria of the DSM-IV-TR, DSM-5, and ICD-10R. Their findings were the following:

> Of those diagnosed with an ASD using ICD-10R, 56 % met DSM-5 ASD criteria. A further 19 % met DSM-5 criteria for Social Communication Disorder. Of those diagnosed with Autistic Disorder/Asperger Syndrome on DSM-IV-TR, 78 % met DSM-5 ASD criteria. Sensitivity of DSM-5 was significantly increased by reducing the number of criteria required for a DSM-5 diagnosis, or by rating "uncertain" criteria as "present", without sacrificing specificity. Reduced rates of ASD diagnosis may mean some ASD individuals will be unable to access clinical services.

Utilization and Coding

In clinical practice, it is essential to understand coding and ethical standards. Our first ethical responsibility to the client is to provide the most accurate diagnosis that is substantiated during the evaluation process and meets the associated criteria put forth by the chosen manual and conceptual framework. Another ethical responsibility of the provider is to ensure accurate coding for billing and the associated treatment interventions to follow. Unbeknownst to many mental health clinicians who readily use the DSM, the codes provided in the DSM are actually derivatives of the ICD, with a relatively consistent crosswalk in coding from one manual to another (e.g., 300.00 in DSM-IV-TR and ICD-9 referred to Anxiety Disorder Not Otherwise Specified). As described previously, the revision of ICD-9 to ICD-10 brought about a revolution in the coding system that was adopted by many parts of the world and by the United States by the deadline of October 1, 2015 (Centers for Medicare & Medicaid Services, 2015). While there were many new codes added to the ICD-10 that were not previously recognized in the ICD-9, many diagnostic codes from the DSM-IV-TR were maintained, despite no longer being recognized in the DSM-5.

It is essential for the clinician to understand the coding mechanisms and standards used by the insurance companies, as they have always recognized the

ICD codes of diagnostics. Therefore, the DSM-5 also reflected this reinvention of the previous coding system and formally adopted the numbering system found with the ICD, already in use by medical practitioners but not necessarily knowingly by many mental health clinicians. This critical change in diagnostic coding brought about glaring differences and presented a new dilemma in the need for cross-referencing and correspondence between primary diagnostic manuals, the DSM and ICD.

This leads to a field-wide discussion regarding which should be the governing diagnostic manual and how best to uphold that first responsibility, diagnostic clarity. If a clinician strictly adheres to the DSM-5, they are largely subjected to a smaller class of diagnostic labels insofar as autism spectrum disorders are concerned. Given that the DSM-5 has subsumed the previously recognized diagnoses under the broader category of autism spectrum disorders, the clinician may lack a certain specificity; yet they are still providing clinical accuracy and expertise within the guidelines of the DSM. Presently, clinicians utilizing the ICD-10R as their diagnostic manual of choice continue to have access to codes that were previously recognized by former versions of the DSM. Many clinicians prefer the capability of using this level of specificity and also uphold the suggested first and second responsibilities to the client (e.g., diagnostic accuracy, ethical coding/labeling for billing and treatment purposes). However, it is also of importance to recognize the ongoing pursuit of examining and defining the critical differences between autism, Asperger's syndrome, pervasive developmental disorder, and the like. This remains a controversial and widely debated area in the field of psychology and one which will have direct ramifications on future evolutions of diagnostic manuals.

The Assessment

Assessment Preparation: The Clinical Interview

The wide range of presenting concerns presents a unique challenge to the assessing clinician. Individuals and families report a variety of symptoms affecting many domains of functioning; including, but not exclusive to, attention, concentration, mood, behavior, social, sensory processing, and executive functioning deficits. The importance of tracking symptom onset and severity is paramount in the initial intake process when determining the need and reason for assessment. Specific details regarding the young child's development progress, including gains, regression, and stagnation, are important when considering the possibility of an autism spectrum disorder. This information sets the stage for the comprehensive exam to follow. The goal of the initial intake interview should be to obtain a detailed history from the family or individual combined with external records and sources that provide a global picture of the individual. It is only with this information that an adequate assessment can be completed with the ability to yield a formal diagnosis and associated recommendations.

The clinical interview is the first step in developing a battery to adequately address the symptoms endorsed by the individuals and identified by the clinician. The battery is created with the individual's symptoms in mind but also incorporates the concerns and considerations of the clinician based on their clinical judgment. At this point, necessary consultations with other disciplines may also be determined by the clinician (e.g., speech, occupational, physical therapy).

Assessment Standards for Autism Spectrum Disorders

The assessment of autism spectrum disorders typically includes a myriad of providers from several disciplines. In pediatric cases, a developmental pediatrician, pediatric psychologist, or neuropsychologist often compiles a comprehensive report which combines data from multiple sources. Other contributing evaluators may include a speech pathologist and/or occupational therapist. The assessment standards listed below are written from the perspective of a neuropsychologist. A neuropsychologist seeks to consider how brain-based dysfunction contributes to cognition, mood, and behavior.

The comprehensive neuropsychological evaluation should seek to assess several areas of functioning according to the Houston Conference Guidelines. In 1997, representatives of the Boards of Clinical Neuropsychology convened in Houston, Texas, and finalized standards, education, and practice within the field of clinical neuropsychology (Ardila, 2002). Many neuropsychologists adopt a flexible battery which is tailored to appropriately address the referral question but also allow for adjustment of the battery to address unforeseen challenges. By comparison, a standardized highly structured battery often includes administration of full test protocols regardless of the referral question and presenting symptoms. A lengthy, standardized battery may not be feasible or appropriate in the allotted time provided for the assessment and may not include the tests needed to examine skill deficits identified within the course of the assessment. The neuropsychologist must monitor the fatigue effect and frustration tolerance of their client and adjust the battery appropriately. In this case, a flexible battery helps to mitigate these challenges that threaten the client's effort and stress tolerance, which is critical when evaluating for autism spectrum disorders, given that younger children are at high risk for resistance, intolerance, and loss of motivation and effort. A flexible battery may include abbreviated versions of larger, lengthier test protocols while also maintaining the validity and integrity of the measures. The neuropsychologist may also select several subtests of larger protocols to disseminate a specific skill and then determine any other necessary evaluation in that area.

As mentioned previously, assessing autism spectrum disorders also requires consultation from other disciplines. Though children with high functioning autism spectrum disorders, like Asperger's syndrome, do not always show speech/language delays, they can show functional deficits in communication. Fine and gross motor deficits as well as sensorimotor processing can also benefit from assessment. A comprehensive evaluation should frequently include a neuropsychological assessment in addition to these consultations to best understand the areas of deficits within the person, given the variability in symptom presentation in each person with a potential ASD diagnosis. In conjunction with standardized tests and other consultations, the clinician should also collect information from parents, teachers, and others in the community to gain a broad perspective of the individual's functioning across environments. The ability to observe the child amongst peers is often invaluable, and for this reason a play diagnostic or peer-group observation is a crucial piece of the comprehensive evaluation in complex cases, especially when there is significant variability between raters (e.g., mother, father, teacher, therapist). No single set of data (e.g., ADOS, IQ test, rating form, observation) should be viewed as conclusive and definitive in the determinism of autism spectrum disorders. All data should be integrated for conceptualization, for greatest accuracy and to reduce the risk of misdiagnosis.

The clinical acumen of the assessor is not to be underestimated. Despite the advancement of standardized batteries and comprehensive rating forms, the neuropsychologist must look beyond the quantitative to consider the qualitative and the meshing, or lack thereof, of symptoms into a specific cluster. The neuropsychologist is responsible for integrating and explaining the diagnostic impression based on the qualitative and quantitative data collected. It is crucial that this provider consider alternatives based on the neurocognitive and psycho-social-behavioral profile for accurate differentiation.

The above information about assessment refers to the determination of a medical-behavioral health diagnosis of ASD. Many school systems also have procedures in place to determine if the student fits educational criteria for autism spectrum disorder as defined by the school district, in conjunction with standards and in accordance with the Individuals with Disabilities Education Act (IDEA) (20 U.S.C. § 1400, 2004). It is important to note that medical standards for diagnosing autism spectrum disorders are not identical to educational criteria. While schools adopt the DSM-5 criteria for determination of ASD, the student must meet all diagnostic criteria and those symptoms must disrupt the student's ability to function successfully in the classroom. Students that have a medical diagnosis are not automatically eligible for special education services, according to the IDEA. Educational eligibility and subsequent services are determined by conducting assessments and testing performed by a school's multidisciplinary team and not that of medical diagnostic tests. Therefore, it is common for a child to have a medical diagnosis of ASD but not meet qualifications for the educational criteria of ASD if the symptoms do not functionally impede his/her academic performance.

Complexity of Presenting Symptoms: Overlapping Symptoms and Etiology in ASD

Autism spectrum disorder is classified as a neurodevelopmental disorder within diagnostic manuals. Neurodevelopmental disorders are defined as dysfunctions and symptom clusters that often originate in the brain and have implications for the developmental trajectory of the child. Differential diagnosis of ASD relies heavily upon ruling out other neurodevelopmental presentations. Specifically, symptoms of ASD frequently overlap with those of many other neurodevelopmental disorders. The similarities in the phenotypic presentation of symptoms (e.g., limited attention, facial tics) can make diagnosis complicated. Depending on the presenting symptoms of a particular child, misdiagnosis can also be likely. For example, a study completed by Boston Children's Hospital indicated that about 20% of the children who were later diagnosed with ASD were initially diagnosed with ADHD (Miodovnik, Harstad, Sideridis, & Huntington, 2015). These children diagnosed with ADHD and later ASD were often diagnosed three years after children who were diagnosed with ADHD at the same time or after ASD. Similarly, executive functioning deficits are common in many different diagnoses. Research has found overlap in the deficits in executive functioning in children with ADHD, ASD, and Tourette's syndrome. Children with ASD tended to have more reported deficits in their cognitive flexibility as compared to children with Tourette's (Hovik et al., 2017). The importance of early intervention supports the need for accurate diagnosis of ASD in early childhood to ensure that they get the intervention necessary to improve skills and enhance functioning.

The sections below explain a wide variety of neurodevelopmental disorders and the crossover with ASD. Neurodevelopmental disorders are classified differently in the respective manual, whether DSM-5 or ICD-10R/11. Likewise, diagnostic criteria vary between manuals, although not substantially so. The following list is derived from a combination of neurodevelopmental disorders mentioned in the widely used diagnostic manuals. This list is comprehensive, but not exhaustive or all-encompassing. This chapter is meant to inform readers to recognize the intricacy of differentiation.

Neurodevelopmental Disorders

Intellectual Disability/Cognitive Impairment

Intellectual disabilities (IDs) and ASDs share numerous characteristics. The criteria required for the diagnosis of an Intellectual Disability include: deficits in intellectual functioning, encompassing skills such as reasoning, problem solving, abstract thinking, and learning; impairment in adaptive functioning; and onset of these difficulties prior to 18 years old (Pedersen et al., 2017). Intellectual disabilities are indicated when a person's intelligence testing is two or more standard deviations below the mean, including measurement error. The DSM-5 identifies several levels of intellectual disabilities, including mild (IQ = 55–70), moderate (IQ = 40–55), severe (IQ = 25–40), and profound (IQ < 25). Based on statistical measures, approximately 1% of the general population is in range for an intellectual disability. The CDC indicated that 38% of children with ASD had a comorbid ID (Centers for Disease Control, 2014). Thus, these diagnoses are often present together. However, in many cases, people with ASDs do not have a co-occurring ID. Alternatively, there are also many people with ID that do not have ASD. There are many similarities in etiologies for ASD and ID. Genetic syndromes such as Fragile X, Rett disorder, Down syndrome, and CHARGE syndrome are some common etiologies for both ASDs and severe ID. Regardless, symptomology varies between people with ID, ASD, or ASD with ID. These diagnoses often share struggles in the development of language and communication generally. Children with ASD and/or ID are slower in language development. Conversely, they can be differentiated by other factors. Pedersen et al. (2017) indicated that DSM-5 criteria of stereotyped behaviors and social interactions were most effective in differentiation, while the delays in communication were least indicative.

Attention-Deficit Hyperactivity Disorder (ADHD)

The last several decades have seen a dramatic increase in the diagnosis of ADHD. This may be due to the increased awareness and understanding of the symptoms and the presentation in children and adults. However, the surge may also be due to the misidentification of this disorder, whose symptoms are highly associated with other syndromes. ADHD occurs in 3% to 5% of the U.S. population (Michielsen et al., 2013). The National Organization for Children and Adults with ADHD (CHADD), summarizes a recent population-based study using DSM-IV-TR criteria which reported 15.5% of schoolchildren enrolled in Grades 1 to 5 have ADHD (Rowland et al., 2015). Statistical information regarding the prevalence rates in adults is less available; however, according to a screening conducted in 2006 of adults aged 18–44 by the National Comorbidity Survey Replication, 4.4% of U.S. adults had ADHD; of these adults with ADHD, 62% were male (Kessler et al., 2006). Comorbidity rates in adults are believed to be equal to or higher than those in children, although very few studies have examined these patterns over time.

Attention in and of itself is a soft neurological symptom, meaning that this skill is highly vulnerable to the effects of biological and environmental stimuli. In this regard, ADHD may present in a number of medical/genetic conditions, psychological conditions, and a variety of environmental, traumatic, and circumstantial influences. ADHD is associated with abnormalities in the frontal lobe (Zametkin et al., 1990), so naturally any neurological disorder that originates in these regions would increase the risk for ADHD. Zhang et al. (2014) evaluated children with frontal lobe epilepsy for the prevalence of ADHD and found that 89.4% of the children with an abnormal EEG had coexisting ADHD, compared with only 25% of children with normal EEG readings.

There is a high degree of crossover in symptoms for children with diagnoses of ADHD and ASD. Previous research has indicated that about 30–50% of individuals with ASD show ADHD symptoms. This is especially common in young children. It has also been found that about two-thirds of people with ADHD show symptoms of ASD (Simonoff et al., 2008). In a broad review of research examining the overlapping traits of ADHD and ASD, Taurines et al. (2012) stated that inattention and hyperactivity were often reported in individuals with ASD, and children with ADHD often suffered from social difficulties. His investigation of existing studies found that only one epidemiological study on comorbid disorders in ASD reported a 30% prevalence of comorbid ADHD (Simonoff et al., 2008). Externalized behaviors, including poor impulse control, lack of body awareness, hyperactivity, and distractibility, diminish social capability. Diagnostic differentiation seeks to go beyond these surface symptoms to examine the individual's cognition and social competency when the externalizing behaviors are managed. Hence, when a child is diagnosed with ADHD and receives the appropriate treatment, it is expected that the social challenges would improve along with the child's increased locus of control. In the child with a comorbid presentation of ADHD and ASD, the social challenges are pervasive and are not likely to improve substantially following the appropriate treatment of their ADHD symptoms. In many cases, the symptoms of ADHD presenting in an individual with ASD are not fully responsive to traditional medications (e.g., psychostimulants), and perhaps exacerbate other presenting concerns, such as sensory adaptability, anxiety, agitation, and mood.

Researchers have postulated that attention deficits in individuals with ASD present differently in neuroimaging compared to individuals with ADHD absent of ASD. Specifically, Wolff et al. (2014) argues that inattention in ASD originates in the right brain and its deficiencies rather than primarily frontal lobe under-arousal, as found in Zametkin (1990). In another study, which examined executive functioning skills between groups of children—normal control, ADHD only, ASD only, and ASD + comorbid ADHD—results showed the ADHD-only group displayed impairment in inhibition and working memory, while the ASD-only group showed deficits in planning and flexibility (Sinzig et al., 2008).

Speech, Language, and Communication Disorders

Speech delay and developmental speech disorders are perhaps one of the most challenging presentations in the differentiation of ASDs. Given the comorbidity of speech/language disturbance in autism, researchers and clinicians have examined the intricate differences in order to provide the most accurate diagnostic clarity (Matson & Neal, 2010; Mitchell, Cardy, & Zwaigenbaum, 2011; Ventola et al., 2007). The late onset of language in toddlers is one of the screening criteria for autism and one that can prompt a referral to early intervention and speech therapy. The development or delay in speech has been a distinguishing difference between the differentiation between autism and Asperger's syndrome (Bennett et al., 2008). Prior to the exclusion of Asperger's syndrome in the DSM-5, children with language delay did not meet the criteria for Asperger's syndrome as listed in the DSM-IV-TR or ICD-10. However, this was often confused with "late talking" due to poor articulation or fluency rather than the absence of language. Fluency and articulation disorders may be associated with childhood apraxia of speech, which can have ramifications for the child's social and emotional development as well. The difficulties with social relationships can overlap with characteristics seen in ASD. Beyond speech production and fluency, children can have difficulties with language comprehension and/or communication. Similar to the challenges seen in children who have social problems and a speech fluency disorder, children with a mixed receptive/expressive language disorder have limited ability to understand and then respond accordingly in conversation. Speech and language pathologists also work to enhance children's communication by focusing on the semantics and pragmatics of language. Semantic-pragmatic language disorder was previously recognized as a speech/language disorder in the DSM-IV-TR but is now considered a social communication disorder (Brukner-Wertman, Laor, & Golan, 2016). Baird and Norbury (2016) report on the strong association of semantic and pragmatic challenges in children with ASD and make a case for differentiating criteria. They argue that, while many individuals with autism have overlapping features of language and communication struggles, the presence of idiosyncratic/repetitive behaviors and restricted interests remains a crucial delineation of ASD from social communication disorder.

Motor Disorders

Developmental Coordination Disorder

Developmental coordination disorder refers to a lack of coordination in fine and/or gross motor abilities. Children with a developmental coordination disorder can have challenges that are also defined as an apraxia or dyspraxia. Apraxia refers to a motor-planning issue that prevents the smooth and fluid transmission of signals from the brain to the coordinated effort of the body movement. Apraxia and dyspraxia can present as language and motor dysfunctions. There are children on the autism spectrum who also have a lack of coordination. Research has shown differentiation between gestural posturing in children with ASD as compared to children with a developmental coordination disorder. Dewey, Cantell, and Crawford (2007) found that children with ASD had difficulties with incorrect action and orientation errors to commands which were not solely attributable to muscle weakness or motor coordination skill level. Other researchers have shown that dyspraxia in autism could not be entirely accounted for by impairments in basic motor skills (Dziuk et al., 2007). They stipulated that dyspraxia may be a marker of the neurological abnormalities underlying autism spectrum disorders. Similarly, the results of a study conducted by MacNeil and Mostofsky (2012) yielded the following: "Whereas both children with ADHD and children with ASD show impairments in basic motor control, impairments in performance and recognition of skilled motor gestures, consistent with dyspraxia, appear to be specific to autism." Similar to children with autism, children with developmental coordination disorder such as dyspraxia may have difficulties with social integration. As a result, these children may not engage in the same activities, resulting in an inadvertent social withdrawal. In any respect, the nature of identification and discrimination between ASD and developmental coordination disorder remains to be a complex process and one that seems to be ever overlapping. Those looking to treat these children have argued that, despite dyspraxia, ADHD, and ASD being the most common neurodevelopmental disorders of childhood, the respective etiology is complex and multifactorial, with little progress made in determining predisposing factors at the biological level (Richardson & Ross, 2000).

Stereotypic Movement Disorder

Stereotypic movement disorder is also referred to as primary (non-autistic) motor stereotypies. This diagnosis consists of behaviors that are rhythmic, repetitive, fixed, predictable, but purposeless movements that occur in children who are otherwise developing normally (Johns Hopkins Pediatric Neurology, n.d.). The movements are often reminiscent of what is seen in children with ASD, such as flapping and waving of the arms, hand flapping, head nodding, and rocking back and forth. Also similar to ASD, these movements usually appear in the first three years of a child's life and often continue. Motor stereotypies can also occur in children who have developmental problems, such as a child with mental retardation, or vision or hearing impairment. In such cases where a behavioral or neurological disorder has been diagnosed, the movements are called secondary motor stereotypies. In Singer's (2011) text, it is argued that stereotypic movement disorder should be closely examined and distinguished from compulsions found in obsessive-compulsive disorder, tic disorders, trichotillomania, skin picking disorder, or the direct physiological effect of a substance. He also reports that there is increasing evidence backing an underlying neurological condition and that the individual's response to behavioral and pharmacological therapies has been variable. Children presenting with stereotypic movement should be closely monitored and evaluated. Examining the child's development in other areas is necessary to make an appropriate differential diagnosis.

Tourette's Syndrome and Other Tic Disorders

Tic disorders are commonly seen in children at varying ages of onset. The age of onset helps in determining the specific syndrome. The DSM-5 classifies tic disorders into three groups including Tourette's syndrome (TS), persistent motor or vocal tic disorder, and provisional tic disorder. In a summation of parent surveys, the CDC stated that 0.3% of U.S. children ages 6–17 were diagnosed with Tourette's (Centers for Disease Control, n.d.). The National Survey of Children's Health (Bitsko et al., 2014) found that, among children with TS, 86% had also been diagnosed with at least one comorbid mental, behavioral, or developmental condition, such as: ADHD, 63%; behavioral or conduct problems, 26%; anxiety, 49%; depression, 25%; autism spectrum disorders, 35%; learning disability, 47%; speech or language problem, 29%; intellectual disability, 12%; and developmental delay affecting his or her ability to learn, 28%.

Tics are defined as involuntary movements or vocalizations occurring with a sudden onset. They are brief, repetitive, stereotyped, but non-rhythmical. Motor tics can be simple or complex, while verbal tics can be phonic or vocal (e.g., grunts, throat clearing, or verbalizations). Tics are commonly confused with stereotypies. Stereotypies are defined as coordinated, patterned, repetitive, and rhythmic movements. These can occur involuntarily or in response to a stimulus, whether preferred or non-preferred (e.g., excitement, anxiety, overstimulation). The involuntary urges and the natural instinct to suppress those urges are a primary distinction between tics and stereotypies. While both can be triggered by internal physiological arousal, in tic disorders there is likely an unwanted urge to force a movement or vocalization to relieve the discomfort and agitation of the individual. One could argue, however, that stereotypies are brought on by an unconscious effort, often resulting in enjoyment or comfort. Tics and stereotypies also differ in duration (tics are usually variable, abrupt, and quick; stereotypies are usually fixed, identical, and prolonged). They also vary in response to medication (tics can often resolve with neuroleptics, while stereotypies are often non-responsive) (Mills & Hedderly, 2014). This distinction is important to consider in the differentiation between a tic disorder and ASD—or perhaps the less prevalent comorbid presentation.

Brain Anomalies (Including Congenital Conditions Which Cause Cerebral Palsy)

Children with structural brain differences, either congenital or acquired, may have symptoms and characteristics reminiscent of ASD. In many cases, the congenital conditions may be the biological underpinning or etiology to the subsequent presentation of autism. Specifically, ASD features are commonly associated with agenesis of the corpus callosum (also referred to as ACC). ACC is a rare birth defect that impacts the development of the white matter band connecting the right and left hemispheres of the brain. Frazier and Hardan (2009) examined 253 individuals with autism and found the majority had a substantially smaller corpus callosum when compared to healthy controls. Therefore, when considering a differential diagnosis of autism in an individual with ACC, it is statistically more likely that the individual will meet criteria for ASD. Similar brain structure abnormalities and associated ASD may be seen in conditions such as polymicrogyria (too many and tiny folds in the brain at birth), in-utero stroke, and cysts. A recent Finnish study examined the connection between the wide spectrum of ASD and associated brain anomalies. They reported the following:

> The association between childhood autism and PDD/PDD-NOS and congenital anomalies is stronger among children with intellectual disability is stronger than among those without intellectual disability. These results may have relevance in examining early risk factors in autism during fetal neurodevelopment.
>
> *(Timonen-Soivio et al., 2015)*

Cerebral palsy is also a common occurrence that may overlap with ASD. The nature of cerebral palsy, spastic or non-spastic, can assist in the determination of ASD differentiation—namely, researchers have examined the prevalence of comorbid ASD in children afflicted with cerebral palsy. It was found that the comorbid presentation was "6.9% and was higher (18.4%) among children with non-spastic cerebral palsy, particularly hypotonic cerebral palsy" (Christensen et al., 2014).

VI Genetic Disorders

Down Syndrome

Down syndrome is the result of a chromosomal abnormality defined as trisomy 21, referring to the third copy of chromosome 21. Prevalence rates of ASD in children with Down syndrome have ranged depending on the reported ASD subtype. DiGuiseppi and colleagues (2010) found that prevalence for Down syndrome with autistic disorder was 6.4%, but this number increased to 18.2% when the other ASD subtypes were considered, such as Asperger's syndrome and pervasive developmental disorder. This rate also increased with the presence of cognitive impairment. Those researchers emphasized the importance of accurate diagnostic tools and sensitive measures to determine the presence of ASD in children with Down syndrome. Primarily, it is important to make this determination, because dually diagnosed children are likely to require different forms of service to enhance development.

Fragile X Syndrome

"Fragile X Syndrome (FXS) is the most commonly known single gene cause of ASD" (https://fragilex.org). People with Fragile X syndrome often present with behaviors seen in the criteria for the diagnosis of ASD. Most males with Fragile X show significant intellectual disabilities as well as physical dysmorphologies, whereas females often present with milder intellectual disabilities. Males are more likely to have comorbid diagnoses of ADD/ADHD, autism, social anxiety, repetitive behaviors, sensory processing issues, and increased likelihood for aggression. Females often show learning disabilities and anxiety. Children with FXS and ASD display poorer outcomes, which makes early identification of the ASD symptoms important in FXS. Even at nine months old, children with FXS and ASD show the clear social deficits were present in eye contact and social reciprocity (Hogan et al., 2017).

Other Genetic Conditions

As ASD is a commonly viewed as a behavioral health diagnosis, there can be underlying genetic contributors that cause the presentation of these behaviors. Several specific genetic conditions include comorbid diagnoses of ASD. As previously mentioned, genetic syndromes such as Fragile X, Rett disorder, Down syndrome, tuberous sclerosis, and CHARGE syndrome are some common etiologies for both ASDs and severe intellectual disability. There is also research to suggest that *De novo* copy number gene mutations may also increase the risk for ASD (Sebat et al., 2007).

Exposure to Neurotoxins

Prenatal exposure to neurotoxicants including drugs and alcohol and metal exposure (i.e., lead and mercury) can lead to symptoms that appear similar in phenotype to ASD. They often affect speech and motor development, intellectual functioning, and social-emotional maturity. The difference among these diagnoses is that there is an exposure to a substance at a level that causes neurological changes presenting as symptoms similar to those seen in ASD. While some of these children with prenatal exposure may be identified as having a comorbid ASD, as they meet enough of the criteria, causality may be more easily determined.

Alcohol exposure is one of the most common neurotoxicants in utero, besides cigarette exposure, according to a national survey completed in 2012 (Center for Behavioral Health Statistics, 2012). Symptoms of fetal alcohol spectrum disorders (FASD) (fetal alcohol syndrome and fetal alcohol effects) can include: poor coordination and balance, intellectual disabilities, poor attention, executive functioning skill deficits, and emotional dysregulation. With these challenges, children with fetal alcohol syndrome often struggle academically and socially. Thus, there are similarities in the presentation of symptoms for children with ASD as compared to children with FASD.

Developmental Trauma and Reactive Attachment Disorder

Developmental Trauma

Children with histories of sustained trauma can also show deficits that appear similar to those with ASDs. Research has suggested that, especially in children with histories of neglect, that they will likely struggle to develop relationships with others and can struggle with reading nonverbal cues (van der Kolk, 2005). Similar to children with ASD, they often have underdeveloped right hemispheres due to a lack of interaction with their caregivers during a crucial time for the development of attachment (Schore, 2001). Because of the resemblance in the behaviors and symptoms, there is an increased risk for misdiagnosis. Symptoms observed in both diagnoses often affect the person's ability to develop and sustain meaningful relationships. Both groups can also show significant mood swings, attention and executive functioning deficits, and other externalizing behaviors. Differential diagnosis for children with ASD as compared to children with attachment disorders or other developmental trauma symptoms is vital in order to ensure appropriate treatment interventions.

Attachment Disorders

Reactive attachment disorder (RAD) was separated into two separate diagnoses in the DSM-5 instead of a general label of RAD with subtypes such as disinhibited and inhibited. The two diagnoses are now disinhibited social engagement disorder (DSED), previously disinhibited type, and reactive attachment disorder, previously inhibited type (American Psychiatric Association, 2013). Notably, little research has focused on the similarities between RAD, formerly inhibited type, because this presentation is so rare. Thus, much of the following information focused on DSED. Children with DSED are indiscriminately friendly and show little checking in with primary caregivers, even in novel environments with new people. The DSM has indicated that DSED cannot be diagnosed as comorbid with ASD. Nevertheless, attachment disorders often have overlap with the symptoms of ASD, because the deficits in social relationships are a primary feature of both diagnoses.

Because of this, research has been completed to help differentiate DSED from ASD. Children with DSED are often unaware of appropriate social boundaries such as being overly friendly with strangers and also less checking in with adult caregivers even in new situations. People with DSED frequently show deficits in social reciprocity, empathy, and lack of awareness to social skills. Though not part of the criteria for DSED, there are also deficits seen in executive functioning skills and behavioral challenges that can be misdiagnosed as ASD (Davidson et al., 2015).

Unlike ASD, DSED is caused by early maltreatment, trauma, and/or neglect often prior to 2 years old. ASD is more commonly associated with a genetic cause, teratogen exposure, or other developmental issues such as premature birth. ASD also may present as idiopathic, which is not the case with DSED. Notably, differential diagnosis is more challenging when early history is unknown as both groups show significant impairments in social interaction. Previous research has shown that children with DSED were less likely to show repetitive, stereotyped behaviors, though displayed similar deficits in pragmatic language to children with ASD (Sadiq et al., 2012). Davidson et al. (2015) found that ASD children showed less "indiscriminate friendliness" as compared the RAD (DSED) group. While some children with ASD also showed decreased caution when interacting with a stranger, this was usually to share a repetitive or stereotyped interest. Children with DSED also do not typically struggle to maintain a conversation, even if it is not modulated (Bennett et al., 2009). Moran (2010) also indicated a clinical difference in developing a rapport with children with ASD versus DSED.

Processing and Learning Disorders

Central Auditory Processing Disorder (CAPD)

People with autism spectrum disorders often experience deficits in processing auditory stimuli and language. While, in some cases, this can include sensory sensitivities to auditory stimuli, in other cases, children can struggle with processing intonation of speech. On the other hand, people with central auditory processing disorders are also prone to some difficulties in social interaction, which can mimic some of the symptoms of ASD such as slow response speed in social situations and trouble keeping up with conversation in group situations (O'Connor, 2012). Language development can also be delayed in people with auditory processing disorders, which can lead to slower social development. The crossover in symptoms can be problematic in making an accurate diagnosis without a thorough assessment.

Nonverbal Learning Disorder (NLD/NVLD)

Over the past three decades, great strides have been made toward the formal understanding of difficulties processing nonverbal information. Neuropsychologists have long recognized a pattern of difficulties in clusters of children who struggle with mathematics, handwriting, and social relationships. These challenges were then linked to an intellectual and learning profile consisting of a discrepancy between language-based tasks and those which require the processing of nonverbal material (Rourke & Tsatsanis, 1996). The processing of visual information is typically a function of the brain's right hemisphere. The right side of the brain is usually responsible for the understanding of spatial relationships, social skills, nonverbal cues, and problem solving. These challenges were found in individuals who have an acquired brain injury resulting in right hemispheric dysfunction (Harnadek & Rourke, 1994). Clinicians have found that these challenges were not necessarily restricted to acquired brain injury, but that this presentation may be developmental in nature, given asynchronous hemispheric development (Pennington, 2009). Several subtypes of nonverbal learning disabilities have been considered, including the nonverbal perceptual-organization-output subtype, Asperger's syndrome, developmental Gerstmann syndrome, left hemisyndrome, right hemisphere syndrome, and right parietal lobe syndrome (Semrud-Clikeman & Hynd, 1990). Nonverbal learning disorder (NLD/NVLD) is not considered a form of autism spectrum disorder, but it has been considered as a subtype or frequent presentation in individuals diagnosed with high-functioning autism spectrum disorder (HF-ASD) or Asperger's syndrome. However, there are believed to be a number of individuals who fit the proposed profile of NLD without meeting all criteria for HF-ASD/Asperger's (Klin et al., 1995). Researchers and clinicians closely monitoring the literature in this area suggest that NLD is comprised of difficulties in four areas, including visual-spatial, motor coordination, sensory integration, and socialization (Rourke, 1987). The variation of challenges, differences in etiology, and poor consensus of symptomology has prevented NLDs from formal recognition (Fine et al., 2012). While NLD is not formally recognized in diagnostic manuals, this presentation has been defined under other labels which capture the functional weaknesses within the NLD learning profile. Specifically, NLD may be considered an "other) pervasive developmental disorder in some cases when considered an atypical presentation of ASD that does not fit all other criteria. NLD may also be explained under an unspecified form of scholastic or learning disorder. The ASD diagnosis may apply to those individuals that fit the neuropsychological profile of NLD but also meet the necessary criteria befitting of the ASD or Asperger's syndrome diagnosis. In 2000, Columbia University began a large-scale research initiative, the NVLD Project, to operationalize the definition and diagnostic criteria of NLD, including neuroimaging to pinpoint neurobiological markers of this dysfunction:

> The overarching goal of The NVLD Project is to validate NVLD as a distinct diagnostic entity recognized in the Diagnostic and Statistical Manual of Mental Disorders (DSM) of the American Psychiatric Association. This will allow people who have NVLD to be covered for clinical care and it will foster more rigorous empirical research on the causes of and best treatments for NVLD. The NVLD Project also hopes to develop research-based clinical interventions that will focus on helping people with NVLD learn adaptive social skills that can be integrated into real-life situations.
>
> *(Columbia University, n.d.)*

Other Developmental Disorders

Premature Birth

Children who are premature are at a higher risk for a number of different mental health and developmental disabilities than children who have been born at full term. Researchers at Kaiser Permanente found a negative correlation between the risk for a diagnosis of an autism spectrum disorder and decreasing gestational age (Kuzniewicz et al., 2014). Each week that gestational age decreased, the probability of ASD symptoms increased. A smaller size for gestational age was another risk factor, as children who were born below the fifth percentile for weight were more likely to show ASD symptoms later in life. Children born with intracranial hemorrhage were also at a higher risk for ASD, even when the hemorrhage was grade 1–2. High frequency for ventilation was another identified risk factor for this group.

Sensory Processing Disorder

Sensory processing disorder (SPD) has been a debated diagnosis for decades, and attempts have been made to include this diagnosis in diagnostic manuals such as the DSM-5 and ICD-10. A study completed by Ben-Sasson, Carter, and Briggs-Gowan (2009) indicated that sensory issues are present in one of every six children, which negatively impacts their daily life, though the frequency is notably increased in the clinical population. Sensory issues can include one or many senses, and people can be over- or under-responsive to the sensory input. SPD is considered to be a difference in the way the nervous system processes sensory input, which can impact activities of daily living. However, it is important to recognize that certain sensory issues impact children more than others. Sensory processing disorder is often separated into three subtypes, including sensory modulation disorder, sensory-based motor disorder, and sensory discrimination disorder.

Clinical evidence of these issues has been identified and treated by occupational therapists for decades. Unfortunately, it has been a struggle to identify diagnostic criteria, understand etiology, and separate SPD from other developmental disorders like ASD and ADHD. In treatment and research, it is often identified through caregiver questionnaire, but also can be observed behaviorally. Research has shown some support for a separate diagnosis for sensory processing disorder, including differences in parasympathetic response (Schaaf et al., 2014) and increased electrodermal responses (McIntosh, Rajah, & Lobaugh, 1999). A genetic etiology is also suggested by an increased frequency in monozygotic twins (Goldsmith et al., 2006). Though evidence of SPD is increasing, with more research focused to understand and treat these symptoms, it continues to be excluded from the DSM-5 and ICD-10. Despite this diagnosis being excluded from the diagnostic manuals, research has found that children with sensory processing differences were much more likely to show social-emotional problems than children without the sensory processing deficits (Ben-Sasson et al., 2009). Given this information, children with SPD are prone to similar challenges seen in ASD. It has been suggested that, while children with ASD frequently show symptoms consistent with SPD, it is not believed that all children with SPD show symptoms of ASD. However, research on differential diagnosis between children with SPD and ASD is sparse. This is likely due to the previously mentioned lack of agreement about the criteria of SPD. Schoen et al. (2009) attempted to identify some difference between children with ASD or sensory modulation disorder (SMD). Both groups showed more sensory-related difficulties than typically developing children. However, this research also demonstrated "physiological arousal and sensory reactivity were lower in children with ASD whereas reactivity after each sensory stimulus was higher in SMD." The SMD group had increased atypical sensory responses while the ASD group showed more symptoms of sensory under-responsiveness and increased smell/taste sensitivity. However, further research needs to be completed to help differentiate between ASD and SPD to help better-informed treatment.

References

20 U.S.C. § 1400. Individuals with Disabilities Education Act (2004).

American Psychiatric Association. (2013). *Diagnostic and Statistical Manual of Mental Disorders* (5th ed.). Washington, DC: American Psychiatric Association. retrieved from https://doi.org/10.1176/appi.books.9780890425596

Ardila, A. (2002). Houston Conference: Need for More Fundamental Knowledge in Neuropsychology. *Neuropsychology Review, 12*(3), 127–130. Retrieved from https://doi.org/10.1023/A:1020370728584

Baird, G., & Norbury, C. F. (2016). Social (Pragmatic) Communication disorders and Autism Spectrum Disorder: *Archives of Disease in Childhood, 101*(8), 745–751. Retrieved from https://doi.org/10.1136/archdischild-2014-306944

Ben-Sasson, A., Carter, A. S., & Briggs-Gowan, M. J. (2009). Sensory Over-Responsivity in Elementary School: Prevalence and Social-Emotional Correlates. *Journal of Abnormal Child Psychology, 37*(5), 705–716. Retrieved from https://doi.org/10.1007/s10802-008-9295-8

Bennett, J., Espie, C., Duncan, B., & Minnis, H. (2009). A Qualitative Exploration of Children's Understanding of Indiscriminate Friendliness. *Clinical Child Psychology and Psychiatry, 14*(4), 595–618. Retrieved from https://doi.org/10.1177/1359104509339137

Bennett, T., Szatmari, P., Bryson, S., Volden, J., Zwaigenbaum, L., Vaccarella, L., . . . Boyle, M. (2008). Differentiating Autism and Asperger Syndrome on the Basis of Language Delay or Impairment. *Journal of Autism and Developmental Disorders, 38*(4), 616–625. Retrieved from https://doi.org/10.1007/s10803-007-0428-7

Bitsko, R. H., Holbrook, J. R., Visser, S. N., Mink, J. W., Zinner, S. H., Ghandour, R. M., & Blumberg, S. J. (2014). A National Profile of Tourette Syndrome, 2011–2012. *Journal of Developmental & Behavioral Pediatrics, 35*(5), 317–322. Retrieved from https://doi.org/10.1097/DBP.0000000000000065

Brukner-Wertman, Y., Laor, N., & Golan, O. (2016). Social (Pragmatic) Communication Disorder and Its Relation to the Autism Spectrum: Dilemmas Arising From the DSM-5 Classification. *Journal of Autism and Developmental Disorders, 46*(8), 2821–2829. Retrieved from https://doi.org/10.1007/s10803-016-2814-5

Center for Behavioral Health Statistics, S. (2012). *Results from the 2012 National Survey on Drug Use and Health: Summary of National Findings.* Retrieved from www.samhsa.gov/data/sites/default/files/NSDUHresults2012/NSDUHresults2012.pdf

Centers for Disease Control. (n.d.). *Prevalence of Diagnosed Tourette Syndrome in Persons Aged 6--17 Years—United States, 2007.* Retrieved December 23, 2017, from www.cdc.gov/mmwr/preview/mmwrhtml/mm5821a1.htm

Centers for Disease Control. (2014). Prevalence of Autism Spectrum Disorder Among Children Aged 8 Years—Autism and Developmental Disabilities Monitoring Network, 11 Sites, United States, 2010. *Surveillance Summaries, 63*(2). Retrieved from www.cdc.gov/mmwr/pdf/ss/ss6302.pdf

Centers for Medicare & Medicaid Services. (2015). *What is different with ICD-10?* Retrieved January 29, 2017, from www.roadto10.org/whats-different/

Christensen, D., Van Naarden Braun, K., Doernberg, N. S., Maenner, M. J., Arneson, C. L., Durkin, M. S., . . . Yeargin-Allsopp, M. (2014). Prevalence of Cerebral Palsy, Co-occurring Autism Spectrum Disorders, and Motor Functioning—Autism and Developmental Disabilities Monitoring Network, USA, 2008. *Developmental Medicine & Child Neurology, 56*(1), 59–65. Retrieved from https://doi.org/10.1111/dmcn.12268

Columbia University. (n.d.). *Non-Verbal Learning Disability—The NVLD Project—Funding Research and Education.* Retrieved January 13, 2018, from http://nvld.org/non-verbal-learning-disabilities/

Davidson, C., O'Hare, A., Mactaggart, F., Green, J., Young, D., Gillberg, C., & Minnis, H. (2015). Social Relationship Difficulties in Autism and Reactive Attachment Disorder: Improving Diagnostic Validity Through Structured Assessment. *Research in Developmental Disabilities, 40*, 63–72. Retrieved from https://doi.org/10.1016/j.ridd.2015.01.007

Dewey, D., Cantell, M., & Crawford, S. G. (2007). Motor and Gestural performance in Children with Autism Spectrum Disorders, Developmental Coordination Disorder, and/or Attention Deficit Hyperactivity Disorder. *Journal of the International Neuropsychological Society, 13*(2), 246–256. Retrieved from https://doi.org/10.1017/S1355617707070270

DiGuiseppi, C., Hepburn, S., Davis, J. M., Fidler, D. J., Hartway, S., Lee, N. R., . . . Robinson, C. (2010). Screening for Autism Spectrum Disorders in Children with Down Syndrome: Population Prevalence and Screening Test Characteristics. *Journal of Developmental and Behavioral Pediatrics: JDBP, 31*(3), 181–191. Retrieved from https://doi.org/10.1097/DBP.0b013e3181d5aa6d

Dziuk, M. A., Larson, J. C. G., Apostu, A., Mahone, E. M., Denckla, M. B., & Mostofsky, S. H. (2007). Dyspraxia in Autism: Association with Motor, Social, and Cmmunicative Deficits. *Developmental Medicine & Child Neurology, 49*(10), 734–739. Retrieved from https://doi.org/10.1111/j.1469-8749.2007.00734.x

Fine, J. G., Semrud-Clikeman, M., Bledsoe, J. C., & Musielak, K. A. (2012). *A Critical Review of the Literature on NLD as a Developmental Disorder.* Retrieved from https://doi.org/10.1080/09297049.2011.648923

Frazier, T. W., & Hardan, A. Y. (2009). A Meta-Analysis of the Corpus Callosum in Autism. *Biological Psychiatry, 66*(10), 935–941. Retrieved from https://doi.org/10.1016/J.BIOPSYCH.2009.07.022

Goldsmith, H. H., Van Hulle, C. A., Arneson, C. L., Schreiber, J. E., & Gernsbacher, M. A. (2006). A Population-Based Twin Study of Parentally Reported Tactile and Auditory Defensiveness in Young Children. *Journal of Abnormal Child Psychology, 34*(3), 393–407. Retrieved from https://doi.org/10.1007/s10802-006-9024-0

Harnadek, M. C. S., & Rourke, B. P. (1994). Principal Identifying Features of the Syndrome of Nonverbal Learning Disabilities in Children. *Journal of Learning Disabilities, 27*(3), 144–154. Retrieved from https://doi.org/10.1177/002221949402700303

Hogan, A. L., Caravella, K. E., Ezell, J., Rague, L., Hills, K., & Roberts, J. E. (2017). Autism Spectrum Disorder Symptoms in Infants with Fragile X Syndrome: A Prospective Case Series. *Journal of Autism and Developmental Disorders, 47*(6), 1628–1644. Retrieved from https://doi.org/10.1007/s10803-017-3081-9

Hovik, K. T., Egeland, J., Isquith, P. K., Gioia, G., Skogli, E. W., Andersen, P. N., & Øie, M. (2017). Distinct Patterns of Everyday Executive Function Problems Distinguish Children With Tourette Syndrome From Children With ADHD or Autism Spectrum Disorders. *Journal of Attention Disorders, 21*(10), 811–823. Retrieved from https://doi.org/10.1177/1087054714550336

Johns Hopkins Pediatric Neurology. (n.d.). *Primary (Non-Autistic) Motor Stereotypies.* Retrieved December 17, 2017, from www.hopkinsmedicine.org/neurology_neuro surgery/centers_clinics/pediatric-neurology/conditions/motor-stereotypies/index.html

Kessler, R. C., Adler, L., Barkley, R., Biederman, J., Conners, C. K., Demler, O., . . . Zaslavsky, A. M. (2006). The Prevalence and Correlates of Adult ADHD in the United States: Results from the National Comorbidity Survey Replication. *American Journal of Psychiatry, 163*(4), 716–723. Retrieved from https://doi.org/10.1176/ajp.2006.163.4.716

Klin, A., Volkmar, F. R., Sparrow, S. S., Cicchetti, D. V., & Rourke, B. P. (1995). Validity and Neuropsychological Characterization of Asperger Syndrome: Convergence with Nonverbal Learning Disabilities Syndrome. *Journal of Child Psychology and Psychiatry, 36*(7), 1127–1140. Retrieved from https://doi.org/10.1111/j.1469-7610.1995.tb01361.x

Kuzniewicz, M. W., Wi, S., Qian, Y., Walsh, E. M., Armstrong, M. A., & Croen, L. A. (2014). Prevalence and Neonatal Factors Associated with Autism Spectrum Disorders in Preterm Infants. *Journal of Pediatrics, 164*(1), 20–25. Retrieved from https://doi.org/10.1016/j.jpeds.2013.09.021

McIntosh, A. R., Rajah, M. N., & Lobaugh, N. J. (1999). Interactions of Prefrontal Cortex in Relation to Awareness in Sensory Learning. *Science, 284*(5419), 1531–1533. Retrieved from www.ncbi.nlm.nih.gov/pubmed/10348741

MacNeil, L. K., & Mostofsky, S. H. (2012). Specificity of Dyspraxia in Children With Autism. *Neuropsychology, 26*(2), 165–171. Retrieved from https://doi.org/10.1037/a0026955

Matson, J. L., & Neal, D. (2010). Differentiating Communication Disorders and Autism in Children. *Research in Autism Spectrum Disorders, 4*(4), 626–632. Retrieved from https://doi.org/10.1016/J.RASD.2009.12.006

Michielsen, M., Comijs, H. C., Semeijn, E. J., Beekman, A. T. F., Deeg, D. J. H., & Sandra Kooij, J. J. (2013). The Comorbidity of Anxiety and Depressive Symptoms in Older Adults with Attention-Deficit/hyperactivity Disorder: A Longitudinal Study. *Journal of Affective Disorders, 148*(2–3), 220–227. Retrieved from https://doi.org/10.1016/j.jad.2012.11.063

Mills, S., & Hedderly, T. (2014). A Guide to Childhood Motor Stereotypies, Tic Disorders and the Tourette Spectrum for the Primary Care Practitioner. *Ulster Medical Journal, 83*(1), 22–30. Retrieved from www.ncbi.nlm.nih.gov/pubmed/24757265

Miodovnik, A., Harstad, E., Sideridis, G., & Huntington, N. (2015). Timing of the Diagnosis of Attention-Deficit/Hyperactivity Disorder and Autism Spectrum Disorder. *Pediatrics, 136*(4), e830–e837. Retrieved from https://doi.org/10.1542/peds.2015-1502

Mitchell, S., Cardy, J. O., & Zwaigenbaum, L. (2011). Differentiating Autism Spectrum Disorder From Other Developmental Delays in the First Two Years of Life. *Developmental Disabilities Research Reviews, 17*(2), 130–140. Retrieved from https://doi.org/10.1002/ddrr.1107

Moran, H. (2010). Clinical Observations of the Differences Between Children on the Autism Spectrum and Those With attachment Problems: The Coventry Grid. *Good Autism Practice, 11*(2), 44–57. Retrieved from https://johnwhitwell.co.uk/wp-content/uploads/2014/05/TheCoventryGrid.pdf

O'Connor, K. (2012). Auditory Processing in Autism Spectrum Disorder: A Review. *Neuroscience & Biobehavioral Reviews, 36*(2), 836–854. Retrieved from https://doi.org/10.1016/j.neubiorev.2011.11.008

Pedersen, A. L., Pettygrove, S., Lu, Z., Andrews, J., Meaney, F. J., Kurzius-Spencer, M., . . . Cunniff, C. (2017). DSM Criteria That Best Differentiate Intellectual Disability From Autism Spectrum Disorder. *Child Psychiatry & Human Development, 48*(4), 537–545. Retrieved from https://doi.org/10.1007/s10578-016-0681-0

Pennington, B. F. (2009). *Diagnosing Learning Disorders: A Neuropsychological Framework.* New York, NY: Guilford Press.

Richardson, A. J., & Ross, M. A. (2000). Fatty Acid Metabolism in Neurodevelopmental Disorder: A New Perspective on Associations Between attention-Deficit/Hyperactivity Disorder, Dyslexia, Dyspraxia and the Autistic Spectrum. *Prostaglandins, Leukotrienes and Essential Fatty Acids (PLEFA), 63*(1–2), 1–9. Retrieved from https://doi.org/10.1054/PLEF.2000.0184

Rourke, B. P. (1987). Syndrome of Nonverbal Learning Disabilities: The Final Common Pathway of White-Matter Disease/Dysfunction? *Clinical Neuropsychologist, 1*(3), 209–234. Retrieved from https://doi.org/10.1080/13854048708520056

Rourke, B. P., & Tsatsanis, K. D. (1996). Syndrome of Nonverbal Learning Disabilities. *Topics in Language Disorders, 16*(2), 30–44. Retrieved from https://doi.org/10.1097/00011363-199602000-00005

Rowland, A. S., Skipper, B. J., Umbach, D. M., Rabiner, D. L., Campbell, R. A., Naftel, A. J., & Sandler, D. P. (2015). The Prevalence of ADHD in a Population-Based Sample. *Journal of Attention Disorders, 19*(9), 741–754. Retrieved from https://doi.org/10.1177/1087054713513799

Sadiq, F. A., Slator, L., Skuse, D., Law, J., Gillberg, C., & Minnis, H. (2012). Social Use of Language in Children with Reactive Attachment Disorder and Autism Spectrum Disorders. *European Child & Adolescent Psychiatry, 21*(5), 267–276. Retrieved from https://doi.org/10.1007/s00787-012-0259-8

Schaaf, R. C., Benevides, T., Mailloux, Z., Faller, P., Hunt, J., van Hooydonk, E., . . . Kelly, D. (2014). An Intervention for Sensory Difficulties in Children with Autism: A Randomized Trial. *Journal of Autism and Developmental Disorders, 44*(7), 1493–1506. Retrieved from https://doi.org/10.1007/s10803-013-1983-8

Schoen, S. A., Miller, L. J., Brett-Green, B. A., & Nielsen, D. M. (2009). Physiological and Behavioral Differences in Sensory Processing: A Comparison of Children with Autism Spectrum Disorder and ensory Modulation Disorder. *Frontiers in Integrative Neuroscience, 3*, 29. Retrieved from https://doi.org/10.3389/neuro.07.029.2009

Schore, A. N. (2001). The Effects of Early Relational Trauma on Right Brain Development, Affect Regulation, and Infant Mental Health. *Infant Mental Health Journal, 22*(1–2),

201–269. Retrieved from doi.org/10.1002/1097-0355(200101/04)22:1<201::AID-IMHJ8>3.0.CO;2–9

Sebat, J., Lakshmi, B., Malhotra, D., Troge, J., Lese-Martin, C., Walsh, T., . . . Wigler, M. (2007). Strong Association of De Novo Copy Number Mutations with Autism. *Science*, *316*(5823), 445–449. Retrieved from https://doi.org/10.1126/science.1138659

Semrud-Clikeman, M., & Hynd, G. W. (1990). Right Hemisphere Dysfunction in Nonverbal Learning Disabilities: Social, Academic, and Adaptive Functioning in Adults and Children. *Psychological Bulletin*, *107*(2), 196–209. Retrieved from https://doi.org/10.1037/0033-2909.107.2.196

Simonoff, E., Pickles, A., Charman, T., Chandler, S., Loucas, T., & Baird, G. (2008). Psychiatric Disorders in Children With Autism Spectrum Disorders: Prevalence, Comorbidity, and Associated Factors in a Population-Derived Sample. *Journal of the American Academy of Child & Adolescent Psychiatry*, *47*(8), 921–929. Retrieved from https://doi.org/10.1097/CHI.0b013e318179964f

Singer, H. S. (2011). Stereotypic Movement Disorders. *Handbook of Clinical Neurology*, *100*, 631–639. Retrieved from https://doi.org/10.1016/B978-0-444-52014-2.00045-8

Sinzig, J., Morsch, D., Bruning, N., Schmidt, M. H., & Lehmkuhl, G. (2008). Inhibition, Flexibility, Working Memory and Planning in Autism Spectrum Disorders With and Without Comorbid ADHD-Symptoms. *Child and Adolescent Psychiatry and Mental Health*, *2*(1), 4. Retrieved from https://doi.org/10.1186/1753-2000-2-4

Taurines, R., Schwenck, C., Westerwald, E., Sachse, M., Siniatchkin, M., & Freitag, C. (2012). ADHD and Autism: Differential Diagnosis or Overlapping Traits? A Selective Review. *ADHD Attention Deficit and Hyperactivity Disorders*, *4*(3), 115–139. Retrieved from https://doi.org/10.1007/s12402-012-0086-2

Timonen-Soivio, L., Vanhala, R., Malm, H., Leivonen, S., Jokiranta, E., Hinkka-Yli-Salomäki, S., . . . Sourander, A. (2015). The Association Between Congenital Anomalies and Autism Spectrum Disorders in a Finnish National Birth Cohort. *Developmental Medicine and Child Neurology*, *57*(1), 75–80. Retrieved from https://doi.org/10.1111/dmcn.12581

van der Kolk, B. A. (2005). Developmental Trauma Disorder: Toward a Rational Diagnosis for Children with Complex Trauma Histories. *Psychiatric Annals*, *35*(5), 401–408. Retrieved from https://doi.org/10.3928/00485713-20050501-06

Ventola, P., Kleinman, J., Pandey, J., Wilson, L., Esser, E., Boorstein, H., . . . Fein, D. (2007). Differentiating Between Autism Spectrum Disorders and Other Developmental Disabilities in Children Who Failed a Screening Instrument for ASD. *Journal of Autism and Developmental Disorders*, *37*(3), 425–436. Retrieved from https://doi.org/10.1007/s10803-006-0177-z

Wilson, C. E., Gillan, N., Spain, D., Robertson, D., Roberts, G., Murphy, C. M., . . . Murphy, D. G. M. (2013). Comparison of ICD-10R, DSM-IV-TR and DSM-5 in an Adult Autism Spectrum Disorder Diagnostic Clinic. *Journal of Autism and Developmental Disorders*, *43*(11), 2515–2525. Retrieved from https://doi.org/10.1007/s10803-013-1799-6

Wolff, M., Cochran, J., Warholic, C., Manor, R., Lockerd, M., & Lecyzcki, A. (2014). Cutting Edge: Autism, Asperger's and ASD: Are There Differences? *Autism Spectrum Quarterly*, *Spring*, 42–45.

World Health Organization. (n.d.). *International Classification of Diseases (ICD)*. World Health Organization. Retrieved from www.who.int/classifications/icd/en/

Zametkin, A. J., Nordahl, T. E., Gross, M., King, A. C., Semple, W. E., Rumsey, J., . . . Cohen, R. M. (1990). Cerebral Glucose Metabolism in Adults with Hyperactivity of Childhood Onset. *New England Journal of Medicine, 323*(20), 1361–1366. Retrieved from https://doi.org/10.1056/NEJM199011153232001

Zhang, D.-Q., Li, F.-H., Zhu, X.-B., & Sun, R.-P. (2014). Clinical Observations on Attention-Deficit Hyperactivity Disorder (ADHD) in Children With Frontal Lobe Epilepsy. *Journal of Child Neurology, 29*(1), 54–57. Retrieved from https://doi.org/10.1177/0883073812470004

3

KEY ASPECTS OF TESTING IN AUTISM SPECTRUM DISORDER

Cassandra E. Marschall, Jesse J. Piehl, and D. J. Bernat

Autism Spectrum Disorder and Diagnostic Impressions

With respect to professional diagnostic considerations for the identification of autism spectrum disorder, the principal objective of this chapter is to discuss the need for a comprehensive psychological/neuropsychological evaluation beyond the cosmetic nature of typical standardized assessment measures. The overarching goal of this chapter is to highlight the sophisticated nature of autism spectrum disorder through review of current literature, to provide a platform for discussion of neuropsychological underpinnings of the complexity of ASD. Furthermore, this chapter offers dialogue of the key aspects of testing in ASD. Thus, the cognitive and sensory aspects of executive functioning, social language, attention, motor skills, daily living skills, and emotional well-being will be emphasized topics of discussion.

Implications of Diagnostic Criteria: ASD

> Determination of how to communicate assessment data is a responsibility of psychologists.
>
> *(Lezak, 2002)*

For the purposes of diagnostic impressions, a comprehensive psychological or neuropsychological evaluation provides well-rounded evidence to diagnose or identify any disorder, disability, or disease with increased levels of confidence. To reiterate, for the sake of accurate identification of autism spectrum disorder, this chapter aims to support the need for a comprehensive psychological or neuropsychological evaluation.

According to the Centers for Disease Control and Prevention (CDC) (2015), diagnosing ASD requires two steps: developmental screening and a comprehensive diagnostic evaluation. It is recommended a child be seen by a specialist to complete the comprehensive evaluation, such as a licensed developmental pediatrician, child neuropsychologist, child psychologist, or child psychiatrist. A Developmental Screening might look like a professional asking parent questions about developmental milestones, talking or playing with the child, and observing how the child learns, speaks, behaves, and moves. This chapter will cover these aspects of functioning in detail. The CDC (2015) endorses the second step of diagnosis is a comprehensive evaluation, reviewing the child's behavior and development, as well as a parent interview, and may include vision and hearing screenings, genetic testing, neurological testing, or other medical testing. Interaction with the patient is paramount. We hope to impress upon readers the vital aspects a comprehensive diagnostic evaluation provides in diagnostics, beyond singular reliance on popularly marketed diagnostic measures, including: the *Autism Diagnostic Observation Schedule—Second Edition* (ADOS-2), *Autism Diagnostic Interview—Revised* (ADI-R), *Childhood Autism Rating Scale—Second Edition* (CARS-2), and *Gilliam Autism Rating Scale—Third Edition* (GARS-3) (Gilliam, 20014; Lord et al., 2012; Rutter, LeCouteur, & Lord, 2003; Schopler & Van Bourgondien, 2010). Similarly, we hope to impress to readers that these norm-referenced diagnostic measures are very helpful in identifying children on the spectrum and provide useful avenues of data collection and observation comparisons. Metaphorically, standardized diagnostic screening assessments provide utility much like the frame of a vehicle, whereas the diagnostic impressions developed by an informed practitioner are likened to the engine, working together to move forward with accurate diagnoses and treatment planning. Inevitably, communication, observations, and interactions provide diagnostic clarity (CDC, 2015).

Gardner et al. (2016) provide parallel reasoning supporting the variety of purposes the assessment process serves while addressing symptomology required for identification of children with autism spectrum disorder, including screening when concerns are raised in the surveillance process during initial evaluations, in addition to comprehensive diagnostic evaluations for ASD. Recent research supports this modern shift in effort for early identification of young children at risk for ASD, proposing a minimum of a two-tiered screening process with enhanced quality assessment, in addition to "interagency collaboration and coordination" to improve early identification and intervention (Rotholz et al., 2017).

Consider the extensive amount of research, observations, and data collection necessary to create a norm-referenced assessment. Research suggests that statistical indices of measurement precision required to develop a norm-referenced, standardized assessment are essential for understanding diagnostic reliability of diagnostic tests (O'Connor, 2017). Fascinatingly, O'Connor (2017) states, "Unlike tape measures, the precision of numbers that are provided by psychological tests can vary across trait spectrums," inferring relationships of data between test results, standard errors of measurement, reliability, and sizes are all key components of the relationship between levels of test information and diagnostic reliability. This also suggests that practitioners should be aware of the standard error of measurement and reliability coefficients when applying testing data to diagnostic impressions.

Pause, for a moment, to consider the process of inquisition in the context of a clinical or school setting, and the informed steps to complete a comprehensive psychological or psychiatric evaluation. In a realistic world, it would be quite impossible to expect every practitioner to be trained within the contexts of a specific norm-referenced standardized diagnostic measure; and, while specialists are well sought after through avenues of home-school collaboration and private practice, the breadth of examiner usage of assessment materials often goes beyond the capacity of the practitioner's workplace and budget. How, then, is it possible to evaluate an individual to meet the diagnostic criteria of autism spectrum disorder?

There may exist a myriad of individualized ways to diagnose a child with autism spectrum disorder, but it is critical for licensed practitioners to rely upon diagnostic impressions informed by the *Diagnostic and Statistical Manual of Mental Disorders—Fifth Edition* (DSM-5) in order to maintain standards for diagnostic criteria across settings (APA, 2013). With the major changes to diagnostic criteria from the DSM-IV-TR to the current DSM-5, practitioners must be aware of the impact on prevalence rates, as well as change in trends in the characteristics of individuals on the Spectrum (Burns & Matson, 2017). Licensed practitioners must offer best practice services when working with clients, parents, teachers, families, and administrators to promote appropriate and effective services. Best practice may offer measures and methods used to assess the core symptomology of autism spectrum disorder, including memory, attention, visual and spatial skills, and behavioral tendencies (Kroncke, Willard, & Huckabee, 2016a).

ASD and Executive Functioning

Executive functions (EFs) have been a particular area of focus in the autism literature in recent decades, for a variety of reasons. The most salient reason for the hypothesis that EF deficits are a feature of ASD is the difficulty with cognitive flexibility and non-literal thinking that is a hallmark symptom of this condition. As such, many have hypothesized that this presentation is reflective of executive dysfunction (Pellicano, 2012). Findings in the areas of executive dysfunction vary, based on a number of hypothesized factors, such as overall scores on measures of g (global intelligence) using norm-referenced assessments that offer related subscale scores such as Verbal Intelligence Quotient (VIQ) and Performance Intelligence Quotient (PIQ), as well as nationality, socioeconomic status, and public health factors (Wechsler, 2003).

While the debate over the utility for differential diagnosis does not yield conclusive results, the overwhelming evidence supports a degree of executive dysfunction is likely to be present, relevant diagnostic information may be extremely useful for treatment planning while working with individuals with ASD. Executive dysfunction is likely to affect an individual's mental health and performance across a number of executive functioning domains, such as academic performance and adaptive functioning (McCloskey & Perkins, 2012; Ozonoff et al., 2004). Furthermore, detailed information about the exact nature of correlated impairment may be invaluable to patients and clinicians. Assessment results may augment treatment planning. Treatment planning may look like development of an Individualized Education Plan (IEP), capacity assessment, creation of occupational recommendations, or career counseling. Results may also aid in providing a thorough explanation of the presenting problem(s) and the patient's area(s) of deficit. Other findings suggest results from executive functioning assessment may be predictive of severity of symptoms (Bramham et al., 2009).

One issue that is more widely debated is the utility of this information for clinicians. While some authors have presented evidence that profile analysis may aid in differential diagnosis between conditions such as ADHD and ASD (Geurts et al., 2004; Ozonoff & Jensen, 1999; Pennington & Ozonoff, 1996), others have presented evidence suggesting that there is no clear, consistent pattern of executive dysfunction in autism spectrum disorders (Demetriou et al., 2017). In the context of a school setting, differentiating symptoms of ADHD can be aided by using norm-referenced measures, such as the BASC-3 (Reynolds & Kamphaus, 2015) series of rating scales. Research results show that behavioral scales of executive functioning and functional communication provided incremental utility in ADHD diagnosis (Zhou et al., 2017). When pairing multiple assessment measures, such as Autism Spectrum Rating Scales with alternative behavioral rating scales, practicing psychologists can achieve a full understanding of presenting signs and symptoms.

Historically, individuals with autism spectrum disorder were presumed to demonstrate relationships between factors of social cognition, executive functions, and intelligence limited to the distinctive parameters of ASD (Ozonoff, Pennington, & Rogers, 1991). This suggests specific intervention guidelines may develop greater executive functioning skills, which may ultimately yield benefits in other skillsets, while failure to implement interventions may lead to increase in widespread deficits. Indeed, some researchers have explicitly argued that training of planning, and other skills related to executive functioning, is a key avenue for intervention (Demetriou et al., 2017).

Research has also supported the notion that improvement in either theory of mind (ToM) or executive functions will benefit the other, and social interaction with similarly aged, neurotypical peers such as siblings appears to aid in development of these abilities (McAlister & Peterson, 2013), though some research suggests that the connection between ToM and EF is not equal bidirectionally. For instance, Hughes and Ensor (2007) found that, while EF skills appear to facilitate development of theory of mind, gains in ToM were not as strongly related to gains in executive functioning. While the exact nature of this relationship between improving executive functioning skills and ToM skills remains unclear, it is evident that this is an area where intervention is feasible. Children may benefit from interventions as simple and cost-effective as increased exposure to neurotypical peers.

Researchers have argued executive function difficulties may also contribute to difficulty in developing multiple key functioning skills that are often consistently impaired in individuals with ASD, such as adaptive skills and theory of mind (Pellicano, 2012) and researchers continue to posit there likely exists a relationship between the level of executive dysfunction and these abilities (Ozonoff & McEvoy, 1994; Ozonoff et al., 2004; Pellicano, 2012. Indeed, EF difficulties appear to impair performance on theory of mind tasks for all individuals regardless of ASD diagnosis, though the degree of impairment may be greater for those with ASD.

Language exposure can greatly impact executive functioning. For example, Elsheikh et al. (2016) found that Finnish children tended to exhibit a superior performance to Egyptian peers on a number of neuropsychological measures, including those related to executive functioning; the authors hypothesized this may be due to differences in language (e.g., differences in the "transparency" of languages utilized by the participants), as this was particularly true of verbal tasks, but also cited a potential failure to intervene early in the development process in Egypt due to reduced availability of medical professionals with knowledge of ASD. Another potential mediator on assessment performance is the type of stimuli involved; the ability to shift attention is considered a key component of executive functions, and children with ASD appear to fail to develop the preference for verbal and other biological sounds that is seen in neurotypical children (discussed in greater length in the following sections). While the exact degree and type of impairment may vary, meta-analysis suggests that some degree of executive dysfunction occurs in most individuals with an ASD diagnosis (Demetriou et al., 2017).

ASD and Auditory Processing

Research suggests that individuals with ASD show different levels of response compared to controls when exposed to novel responses, as measured by event-related potentials (ERPs), indicating this may be particularly true of "biological sounds" (Lortie et al., 2017). This impairment in re-orienting attention to surroundings, chiefly other people in their environment, is a likely contributor to the social deficits seen in autism spectrum disorders. A number of potential neurological factors are implicated in this deficit, including irregularities in neurotransmitter systems, which regulate "cholinergic arousal." Cholinergic arousal allows individuals to re-orient their attention effectively (Orekhova & Stroganova, 2014, p. 1).

Impairment in brain systems involved in differentiation of vocal and non-vocal sounds has also been hypothesized as playing a role in impaired social engagement in individuals with ASD (Bidet-Caulet et al., 2017). Due to these differences, some have argued that impaired verbal auditory processing may be a hallmark feature of autism spectrum disorders (Minshew, Goldstein & Siegel, 1997). This finding correlates with research supporting impaired verbal working memory in individuals with ASD (Pennington & Ozonoff, 1996). Conversely, some current research findings contradict differences in auditory sensitivity in individuals with ASD, particularly looking at a sample of adults with comorbid ADHD/ ASD, where the authors found auditory sensitivity differences present—however, they appeared to be a manifestation of ADHD rather than autism (Bijlenga et al., 2017). This finding is consistent with historical findings, which suggest that a high rate of comorbidity between auditory processing disorders and ADHD exists (e.g., Tillery, Katz & Keller, 2000). Considering the parameters of an evaluation for individuals with ASD or an other health impairment (i.e., medical reason, ADHD, anxiety, depression, etc.), psychologists in schools must be aware of how the dual nature of comorbidity may present itself when working with a variety of student clients. Environmental factors may increase or decrease auditory sensitivity, making the quick act of hearing screenings beneficial for evaluation routines.

ASD and Language

Delays in language development were considered a primary diagnostic criterion for an autistic disorder diagnosis in the *Diagnostic and Statistical Manual of Mental Disorders—Fourth Edition* (DSM-IV-TR) (APA, 2000). However, changes in the categorization of pervasive developmental disorders, and the transition toward an umbrella term, autism spectrum disorder, modified these criteria upon release of the current DSM-5 in 2013 (APA, 2013). This update allowed for continued diagnosis of children who typically would have normal language development but classified under Asperger's syndrome or pervasive developmental disorder Not Otherwise Specified (PDD-NOS). As a result, language delays are no longer a primary requirement for diagnosis of ASD. Yet, these language delays continue to be a common symptom in children and adolescents with ASD. Language delays are especially true for children on the lower functioning levels of the spectrum. It was previously considered 50 percent of individuals with an autism diagnosis would not develop any functional verbal language (Eigsti et al., 2011). More recent research suggests a drop in this percentage, although the exact estimates are not yet available. This improvement has been primarily attributed to an increase in early diagnosis and interventions to address language concerns at an earlier age.

There has been some suggestion in the past that, for those with language delays, expressive language appeared to be less impacted than receptive language (Kwok, Brown, Smyth, & Cardy, 2015). However, the research regarding this difference has been somewhat mixed, and a meta-analysis conducted by Kwok et al., (2015) found no significant difference in receptive and expressive language in ASD populations. This meta-analysis revealed the vast majority of research analyzing differences between receptive and expressive language found less than one standard deviation difference when discovered, suggesting this difference is not clinically significant. Yet, children with ASD do perform, on average, approximately 1.5 standard deviations below their neurotypical peers on language-based tasks. This is especially true for younger children, where the statistical difference appears to be especially significant. The difference in ages may suggest children with ASD do develop oral language skills as they progress, with some suggestion that children may be able to develop from severe levels of receptive and expressive language impairment to relatively average functioning. Yet, nonverbal IQ has also been found to be lower in younger individuals, suggesting that these delays may be more globally apparent beyond just language.

One concern found in the aforementioned meta-analysis was the tendency for children with ASD to have inflated vocabulary scores when compared to other measures of language (Kwok et al., 2015). This is concerning given the frequent use of vocabulary-based tasks, such as "Vocabulary" and "Similarities" subtests on the *Wechsler Intelligence Scales for Children—Fifth Edition*, as a substitute for language reasoning (Wechsler, 2014). Higher performance on these subtests may underreport the extent of language delays in the ASD population.

Pragmatic language typically refers to the use of language as a social tool (Eigsti et al., 2011). Children with ASD consistently perform below their neurotypical peers on measures of pragmatic language, even in children with Asperger's syndrome, a diagnosis typically considered to experience intact language development. This deficit may include odd phrasing, or "little professor" speech, with use of overly formal style in communication that impacts peer interactions. Yet, these delays in pragmatic language are not confined solely to ASD. Similar delays can also be found in individuals with intellectual deficits, such as cognitive impairment or intellectual disability. As a result, differentiation between these two populations cannot necessarily be done based on assessment of pragmatic language alone. The quality of expressive language can also be attributed to prosody, impacting rhythm, stress, and intonation of speech. Further, recent examination of syntax has also found to be an area of concern within the ASD population. For example, children and adolescents with ASD may speak with more rigid grammatical structure and follow fewer syntactical rules.

While language is often considered to be highly lateralized to the left hemisphere, this lateralization may be atypical in individuals with autism spectrum disorder (Lindell & Hudry, 2013). There does appear to be a higher rate of abnormality in the left hemisphere functioning based on magnetic resonance imaging (MRI) studies. There may also be a relationship between reduced left frontal volume and language in children with ASD. Additional research has suggested that disruption in development of the superior temporal gyrus, specifically, and failure to lateralize language to the left hemisphere, may be involved (Bigler et al., 2007). Research examining letter fluency found greater activation in the right frontal and right superior temporal lobes in an ASD population compared to control groups (Kleinhans et al., 2008). However, no differences were found in the left prefrontal cortex. Furthermore, a category fluency task found no between-group differences, thus further suggesting some structural asymmetries and differences in functional organization in ASD individuals.

ASD and Visual-Spatial Deficits

As Ozonoff & Griffith (2000) explained, "Despite a dearth of empirical study, the idea that autism spectrum disorder is noten wit [sic] visuospatial impairment and higher Verbal than Performance IQ has become generally accepted by many clinicians" (pp. 81–82). One potential explanation is that individuals with autism have a unique impairment in visual-spatial processing as it relates to human figures, similar to their failure to develop comparable abilities to orient to and process auditory cues related to social interactions described in the prior section.

Research demonstrates tasks that tap into executive functions appear to be more impaired in individuals with ASD, particularly tasks that are more open-ended in nature (White, 2013), such as tasks involving use of identifying human or human-like figures (Blake et al., 2003). For example, Blake and colleagues (2003) found that children with autism performed similarly to controls on a visual-spatial task that involved lines and shapes but demonstrated impairment on a similar task that made use of human figures. Conversely, previous research by Wainright and Bryson (1996) found that individuals with autism demonstrated differences in responding to geometric visual stimuli (crosses), but posited this may have been due to perseveration when the object appeared directly in their field of vision (e.g., in the center of their field of vision, rather than to the left or right); it was determined that manifestation of impaired attention shifting was the cause of these differences, rather than a true visual-spatial deficit.

Others have argued visual-spatial deficits found in individuals with ASD may be a manifestation of a comorbid condition. For example, Piek and Dyck (2004) argued that poor visual-spatial skills are a hallmark symptom of developmental coordination disorder (DCD). When pinpointing true diagnostic attributions, fine motor movement is an important consideration for individuals with and without a diagnosis of autism. Poor performance on measures of visual-spatial skills may aid in differential diagnosis between ASD and DCD, provided that motor impairment is a shared symptom between these conditions and impaired motor skills may contribute to other developmental delays, which may mimic

ASD such as impaired development of social skills. Additionally, there are consistent findings suggesting individuals with ASD tend to perform poorly on graphomotor and processing speed subtests and activities (Miller et al., 2016). Across school psychology settings, there is a high correlation with high frustrational levels and lack of written expression skills across studies from a psychoeducational perspective. Fine motor assessment is required by law in school settings for determining if clients need OT services. When assessing students for autism spectrum disorder within a school setting, a fine motor assessment is required by law to be incorporated in a psychoeducational evaluation to determine if clients need OT services; this can be assessed through observation on fine motor subtests, as well as through a full occupational therapy examination (20 U.S.C. § 1400, 2004; Beery, Buktenica, & Beery, 2010; Weschsler, 2014).

Visual-motor research by Kroncke, Willard, and Huckabee (2016b) supports the significance of providing a comprehensive evaluation for ASD, including the need to assess visual, spatial and motor skills. Furthermore, recommended measures include, but are not limited to The *Wechsler Inteligence Scales for Children—Fourth Edition* subtests for visual spatial reasoning and/or perceptual reasoning (i.e., visual spatial tasks on WISC-V; perceptual reasoning tasks on WISC-IV), spatial tasks on the *Differential Ability Scales, Second Edition—Preschool version* (Elliot, 2007), *The Beery-Buktenica Developmental Test of Visual-Motor Integration—Sixth Edition*, the Rey Complex Figure Test, and more (Beery, Buktenica, & Beery, 2010; Elliot, 2007; Meyers & Meyers, 1995; Wechsler, 2014). For children learning academic-achievement-related skillsets, fine motor deficits may also present as a problem, as fine motor dexterity and handwriting can be adversely affected (Kroncke et al., 2016b). As with most deficit-related disorders, targeting treatment recommendations is an overarching goal for practitioners. Informed recommendations may likely help achieve improved lifestyle with treatment fidelity.

ASD and Attention

The potential comorbidity of autism spectrum disorder (ASD) and attention deficit hyperactivity disorder (ADHD) is a hot topic for researchers and caregivers alike. As previously discussed, what appear to be attention deficits in autism may actually be a manifestation of perseverative behaviors and/or a preference for non-human stimuli associated with autism rather than the traditional behavioral phenotype that would be considered "inattentiveness" (see Wainwright & Bryson, 1996, and Blake et al., 2003, respectively). With that said, there is a substantial body of evidence suggesting that ASD and ADHD are often comorbid conditions (Antshel, Zhang-James, & Faraone, 2013; Reiersen & Todd, 2008), with some research finding comorbid ADHD in as much as 59 percent of their sample ASD population. It is troubling that the existence of comorbidity is associated with a delay in diagnosis and, therefore, a delay in treatment

(Stevens, Peng, & Barnard-Brak, 2016). It is a logical assumption that many others with ASD display symptoms of ADHD without reaching the clinical threshold for diagnosis. Interestingly, current research provides supporting evidence that individuals with an ADHD diagnosis often have comorbid Autistic symptoms at a greater rate than neurotypical controls (Bijlenga et al., 2017).

Mayes et al. (2012) found that the Checklist for Autism Spectrum Disorder (CASD) (Mayes & Calhoun, 1999) was particularly useful for differentiating ASD and ADHD, though their sample looked only at ADHD-combined subtype and ADHD-inattentive subtype (the primarily hyperactive/impulsive subtype was not included in this sample). Interestingly, the authors found no substantial differences in performance on measures of attention for those with autism and ADHD with an IQ of 80 or higher. This is consistent with past findings that measures of attention are not clinically useful in distinguishing individuals with autism from healthy controls (Minshew, Goldstein & Siegel, 1996).

Research generally supports the efficacy of the use of stimulant medication in reducing ADHD-like symptoms in those with autism, with modest gains in use of non-stimulant medications such as atomoxetine and reboxetine (for a thorough review on the use of psychotropic medication to treat autism, see Antshel, Zhang-James, and Faraone, 2013). While there is a dearth of evidence evaluating behavioral treatments for comorbid ADHD and ASD, one study suggests comorbid ADHD interferes with effectiveness of an intervention, containing a comparison comorbidity of ASD and anxiety and ASD in isolation (Antshel et al., 2011).

Emotional Well-Being

The human mind has the capacity to regulate emotions, through both sympathetic and parasympathetic nervous systems or, rather, the autonomic nervous system (Shiota et al., 2011). The dual nature of the autonomic nervous system allows emotion regulation to occur simultaneously with action and reaction. Under the notion of dysregulation, the simultaneous action, reaction, consequence can present with behavioral challenges, supporting emotional well-being as worthy of diagnostic attention when evaluating for ASD.

Results from a study conducted by Samson et al. (2014) demonstrate that, when compared to typically developing individuals, children and adolescents with ASD show more emotion dysregulation and have significantly greater symptom severity on all scales assessing emotion dysregulation within this study. Furthermore, this study supports emotion dysregulation was related to all core features of ASD, with the strongest associated behavior being repetitive behaviors. Emotion dysregulation can look like signs of anxiety, depression, hyperactivity, inattention, obsessive-compulsive thoughts or behaviors, and potentially maladaptive behavior (Elliot, 2007). While emotion dysregulation is not considered a core feature symptom utilizing the DSM-5, parents and clinicians emphasize the important role associated with maladaptive emotional responses in ASD (Samson et al., 2014).

Under the premise of ASD referrals in school systems, school psychologists are required to utilize a variety of assessments to provide enough reasoning for service eligibility within the parameters of an Individualized Education Plan (20 U.S.C. § 1400, 2004). School psychologists must provide resources for parents in alignment with IDEA (20 U.S.C. § 1400, 2004) and ASD, "along with the explanation that schools do not 'diagnose' children's conditions, but only describe observable behaviors that match eligibilities for special education services" (Wagner, 2014). Rating scales are common forms of data review when assessing a student for special education services and may offer solace for many school psychologists who rely upon norm-referenced criteria to identify students, especially when school psychologists are typically the sole providers of mental health assessment procedures within school districts (Gilliam, 2014; Schopler & Van Bourgondien, 2010). However, this chapter continues to uphold using caution with relying only on rating scales for diagnostic impressions, especially considering parents and teachers who complete rating forms are often under informed of the language and definitional criteria within rating scales. If clinical practice across settings wishes to provide a thorough diagnostic assessment to conclude an individual client reaches diagnostic impressions for autism spectrum disorder, then clinicians should necessitate utilizing the DSM-5 (APA, 2013). While every state mandates varying levels of service per child, the *Diagnostic and Statistical Manual of Mental Disorders—Fifth Edition* is a nationwide, universal reference for assessment conclusions and recommendations for treatment plan purposes.

Consider the potential environmental diversity within a school setting or workplace. For a person with ASD, diverse environments can be challenging to adapt to. Circumstantial intolerance to environmental change can result in heightened autonomic responses. During a state of arousal, the result of bodily changes within individuals with ASD often appears in social contexts as a lack of control of emotional self-expression. Gross and Barrett (2011) chart out emotions systematically, which provides a way to collect and interpret emotional appraisal with a data-driven scope: "An emotion (1) is time limited, (2) is triggered by at least one appraisal, (3) is guided by at least one appraisal, (4) contains bodily changes (e.g., arousal) that are felt, and (5) involves a perceptual or intellectual episode."

Carleton (2016) proposes that IU (intolerance of uncertainty) is an individual's dispositional incapacity to endure the aversive response triggered by the perceived absence of salient, key, or sufficient information, and sustained by the associated perception of uncertainty. Furthermore, the definition of IU follows the well-known ABC model—antecedent, behavior, consequence model—rendering itself to assessing subjective reactions to environmental stimuli.

Research suggests "the definition of IU allows for distinguishing between the triggering stimuli (i.e., an unknown), the response (i.e., fear of the unknown), and the incapacity to endure that aversive (i.e., fearful) response which is sustained by the associated perception of uncertainty (i.e., IU), while recognizing the importance of distinguishing between subjectively relevant and irrelevant information (Carleton, 2016).

Research demonstrates there are several possible characteristics associated with emotion dysregulation in ASD, including any of the following associated characteristics: alexithymia, limited emotional language, cognitive rigidity, poor flexibility, lower inhibition (i.e., of behavior responses), poor problem-solving and abstract reasoning, sensitivity to change and environmental stimulation, biological predisposition (i.e., physiological arousal, neural circuitry, genetics), and difficulty reading social cues (Mazefsky & White, 2014). These characteristics of emotion dysregulation rely on a broad landscape of neuronal networks, suggesting the disorder projects as an amalgam of deficits. Mazefsky and White (2014) indicate that specific interventions for ASD clients with impaired emotion regulation are developing, and rely upon provision of positive behavioral supports, exposure to enhanced emotional language, and practice of modified cognitive behavior therapy.

What can be done for individuals with emotion–regulation deficits? Selection of interventions, therapies, and goals requires clinician discernment when interpreting relevant assessment data. Cognitive-behavioral therapy (CBT) continues to prevail in effectiveness when addressing emotion regulation deficits, which is promising for clients with ASD (Mazefsky & White, 2015). Mindfulness methods, such as meditation, distress-tolerance, and problem-solving approaches, are beneficial multi-modal methods of treatment for emotion regulation (ER) and promote overall emotional well-being (Naragon-Gainey, McMahon, & Chacko, 2017). Considering how challenging controlled emotion regulation (ER) can be for individuals with ASD, incorporation of mindfulness methods with traditional CBT strategies may enhance a client's willingness and ability to develop stronger adaptive regulatory strategies (Mazefsky & White, 2015). Research regarding ASD and emotional well-being continues to be a developing topic, especially with new diagnostic criteria.

What could diagnostic criteria possibly have to do with emotional well-being? Everything! First and foremost, living with any type of diagnosis from a mental health care provider can dramatically alter a person's view on life. For families, infants, children, and adolescents, receiving a diagnosis of autism spectrum disorder results in endless questions about daily living and functioning living skills. A key objective of cross-system, or home-school, collaboration concerns the improvement of knowledge, understanding, and communication, with the goal to enhance learning across settings (Sheridan & Kratochwill, 2008).

ASD and Testing

As this chapter previously purposed, according to the Centers for Disease Control and Prevention (2015), diagnosing ASD requires two steps: developmental screening and a comprehensive diagnostic evaluation. While there exist many benefits to utilization of published screeners, diagnostic kits and assessments, this chapter hopes to shed light on the significance of professional diagnostic procedures when evaluating children and adolescents for behaviors, developmental milestones, language, executive functioning, attention, emotional well-being, and other medically relevant neuropsychological implications associated with diagnostic criteria for ASD.

The traits of ASD are marked by the aforementioned sectors of social and behavioral functioning; thus, it is challenging to put exact specifiers on emotional functioning. Instead, measures rely upon observations and interviews. Researchers, psychologists, and examiners alike have goals to assess individual differences regarding emotional capacity, emotion regulation, self-direction, self-awareness, coping skills, and empathic understanding, all of which fall under the umbrella term of emotional well-being. For example, the *Gilliam Autism Rating Scale—Third Edition* (GARS-3) assesses for "Emotional Responses," specifically measuring extreme emotional responses to everyday situations, and clearly indicates that "The Emotional Responses subscale is not part of the diagnostic criteria for ASD, but contributed strongly to the overall diagnostic picture," concluding that its incorporation is relevant "because of its clinical importance and relevance for instruction" (Gilliam, 2014).

Another select measure for ASD is the *Autism Diagnostic Observation Schedule—Second Edition* (ADOS-2), a semi-structured, norm referenced assessment designed to provide an accurate assessment and diagnosis of autism and similar pervasive developmental disorder across ages, developmental levels, and language skills (Lord, Rutter, et al., 2012). For scenarios that require home-school collaboration, a form of standardized assessment such as the ADOS-2 may provide a psychologist, neuropsychologist, and/or school psychologist with important information regarding a child or adolescent's emotional functioning in social settings.

The *Autism Diagnostic Interview—Revised* (ADI-R) is a well-researched diagnostic interview tool that has been proven useful in formal diagnosis, treatment planning, and educational planning for ASD (Rutter et al., 2003). The ADI-R focuses on three functional domains, including: language and communication; reciprocal social interactions; and restricted, repetitive, and stereotyped behaviors and interests. Furthermore, the ADI-R provides a data-collection method to assist in analyzing the child's background information, behaviors, and developmental milestones.

A thorough evaluation has many benefits for the client involved, including determining an accurate representation of disorders or disabilities that may be present and siphoning out irrelevant factors. For example, due to the challenges that internalizing symptoms present (e.g., depression, anxiety, trauma symptoms), practitioners should consider information from multiple informants, including students, parents, and teachers. With respect to universal screenings, the student should be the primary informant (Levitt et al., 2007). However, when considering the diverse nature of externalizing problems (e.g., observable behaviors), teachers, parents, and caregivers often provide accurate and reliable information, which provides a more complete and balanced picture of the child's behaviors on a grand scale (Reynolds & Kamphaus, 2015).

ASD and Social Functioning

Emotions can be exhibited in a variety of ways, with anxiety as no exception. Adolescents with comorbid anxiety and high-functioning autism disorder may not have the capacity to identify their own symptoms, which places clinical importance on use of multiple raters within the diverse practices of assessment and diagnostic measures (White, 2012). According to White et al. (2012), anxiety may exacerbate interpersonal difficulties and contribute to behavioral problems in individuals with high-functioning autism spectrum disorder (HFASD), particularly adolescents with comorbid anxiety disorders.

Conclusions from a study conducted by Shtayermann (2007), suggest that adolesents diagnosed with (the previousy named) Asperger's syndrome are at higher risk for overt victimization and relational victimization, based on data from rating measures, corresponding with relevant symptom reports of major depressive disorder, generalized anxiety disorder, and even clinically significant levels of suicidal ideation. In high stakes cases, it is imperative for practitioners to be aware of potential comorbid symptoms, and consider informed avenues to differentiate them with data and observations. Awareness of presenting severe mental health symptomology is critical for all mental health practitioners across health service platforms. In the field of psychology, licensed practitioners, supervisors, researchers, clinicians and advocates, being presently aware of the adverse personal effects of social deficit disorders on an individual's emotional well-being and social functioning, should be held with educated regard and receive noteworthy attention (NASP, 2013). A thorough evaluation does not simply diagnose or find eligibility for the sake of labelling a child or adult with ASD—a comprehensive evaluation looks at all aspects of the individual, encompassing cognitive abilities, academic achievement, adaptive functioning, daily living skills, behaviors, physical condition, and emotional well-being. Prunty (2011) claims children's rights are a critical aspect of Individualized Education Plan implementation, especially for pupils with autism spectrum disorder.

Bougher-Mucklan et al. (2016) researched a comparison of the effects that children's emotional socialization practices have on children with ASD and a control group, revealing significant differences in child responses to anger and fear. With regard to the variability of a child or student's everyday circumstances, varied exposure to environmental stressors could play a significant factor in a child's ability to adapt to adversity in the form of fear or anger responses. Furthermore, Bougher-Mucklan et al. posit that these results have implications for early intervention practice, which gives hope to the implementation of parent-child interventions for pediatric groups.

Furthermore, this chapter emphasizes the multi-faceted traits of autism spectrum disorder, and why such a significant social-emotional emphasis exists when moving forward with accuracy in diagnostic responsibilities. In essence, the chapter surmises that the social-emotional functioning of the human mind withholds the capacity to expand into multiple dimensions of universal thought, a concept which may be applied to all individuals with spectrums of thought, beyond what an assessment or rating scale may recommend. It is up to readers to determine how to approach emotional well-being during diagnostic procedures in real time.

Theoretical Conclusions

The purpose of this chapter regarding autism spectrum disorder and testing is multi-faceted. This chapter provides readers an expansive look into the literature regarding individuals with autism spectrum disorder, emphasizing the need for comprehensive evaluation procedures to ensure accurate assessment of diagnostic criteria for all individuals.

This chapter provides readers an expansive look into the literature regarding individuals with autism spectrum disorder, emphasizing the need for comprehensive evaluation procedures to ensure accurate assessment of diagnostic criteria for all individuals. We hope to advocate the need for practitioners to maintain involvement in continuous incorporation of evidence-based findings in everyday practice.

Diagnostic impressions when assessing an individual with ASD require acute attention to observable external behaviors. This foundational concept is the basis for diagnostic hypotheses across the widespread demographics of psychology (APA, 2013). The testing hyper-correlates of diagnostic impressions involved in assessing for ASD included in this chapter encapsulate the following mental and physical processes: executive functioning, social language, reasoning and attention, motor skills, daily living skills, and emotional well-being.

Collectively, this chapter provides an interwoven collaboration of literature revealing evidence-based research, data, theory, results, and inevitably future discussions. Thus, readers and professionals are advised to interpret the findings included within this chapter with an open mind. As the depth of literature regarding autism spectrum disorder develops, efficacious precision must be applied when judging for diagnostic criteria with all clientele.

References

20 U.S.C. § 1400. Individuals with Disabilities Education Act (2004).

American Psychiatric Association. (2000). *Diagnostic and Statistical Manual of Mental Disorders: DSM-IV-TR*. Washington, DC: American Psychiatric Association.

American Psychiatric Association. (2013). *Diagnostic and Statistical Manual of Mental Disorder—Fifth Edition (DSM-5)*. Washington, DC: American Psychiatric Association.

Antshel, K. M., Polacek, C., McMahon, M., Dygert, K., Spenceley, L., Dygert, L., . . . & Faisal, F. (2011). Comorbid ADHD and Anxiety Affect Social Skills Group Intervention Treatment Efficacy in Children with Autism Spectrum Disorders. *Journal of Developmental & Behavioral Pediatrics, 32*(6), 439–446.

Antshel, K. M., Zhang-James, Y., & Faraone, S. V. (2013). The Comorbidity of ADHD and Autism Spectrum Disorder. *Expert Review of Neurotherapeutics, 13*(10), 1117–1128.

Beery, K. E., Buktenica, N. A., & Beery, N. A. (2010). *Beery-Buktenica Developmental Test of Visual Motor Integration*, 6th ed. (Beery-VMI). London, UK: Pearson Clinical.

Bidet-Caulet, A., Latinus, M., Roux, S., Malvy, J., Bonnet-Brilhault, F., & Bruneau, N. (2017). Atypical Sound Discrimination in Children with ASD as Indicated by Cortical ERPs. *Journal of Neurodevelopmental Disorders, 9*(1), 13.

Bigler, E. D., Mortensen, S., Neeley, S., Ozonoff, S., Krasny, L., Johnson, M., . . . & Lanhart, J. E. (2007). Superior Temporal Gyrus, Language Function, and Autism. *Developmental Neuropsychology, 31*(2), 217–238.

Bijlenga, D., Tjon-Ka-Jie, J. Y. M., Schuijers, F., & Kooij, J. J. S. (2017). Atypical Sensory Profiles as Core Features of Adult ADHD, Irrespective of Autistic Symptoms. *European Psychiatry, 43*, 51–57.

Blake, R., Turner, L. M., Smoski, M. J., Pozdol, S. L., & Stone, W. L. (2003). Visual Recognition of Biological Motion is Impaired in Children with Autism. *Psychological Science, 14*(2), 151–157.

Bougher-Mucklan, H. R., Root, A. E., Coogle, C. G., & Floyd, K. K. (2016). The Importance of Emotions: The Socialization of Emotion in Parents of Children with Autism Spectrum Disorder. *Early Child Development and Care, 186*, 10.

Bramham, J., Ambery, F., Young, S., Morris, R., Russell, A., Xenitidis, K., . . . & Murphy, D. (2009). Executive Functioning Differences Between Adults with Attention Deficit Hyperactivity Disorder and Autistic Spectrum Disorder in Initiation, Planning and Strategy Formation. *Autism, 13*(3), 245–264.

Burns, C. O., & Matson, J. L. (2017). An evaluation of the clinical application of the DSM-5 for the diagnosis of autism spectrum disorder. *Expert Review of Neurotherapeutics, 17*(9), 909–917.

Carleton, R. N. (2016). Into the unknown: A Review and Synthesis of Contemporary Models Involving Uncertainty. *Journal of Anxiety Disorders, 39*, 30–43.

Centers for Disease Control and Prevention (2015). *Autism Spectrum Disorder: Screening and Diagnosis*. Retrieved from www.cdc.gov/ncbddd/autism/screening.html

Demetriou, E. A., Lampit, A., Quintana, D. S., Naismith, S. L., Song, Y. J. C., Pye, J. E., . . . & Guastella, A. J. (2017). Autism Spectrum Disorders: A Meta-analysis of Executive Function. *Molecular Psychiatry, 5*, 1198–1204, doi:10.1038/mp.2017.75

Eigsti, I., de Marchena, A. B., Schuh, J. M., & Kelley, E. (2011). Language Acquisition in Autism Spectrum oDisorders: A Developmental Review. *Research in Autism Spectrum Disorders, 5*, 681–691.

Elliot, C. D. (2007). *Differential Ability Scales-II (DAS-II)*. London, UK: Pearson Clinical.

Elsheikh, S., Kuusikko-Gauffin, S., Mattila, M. L., Jussila, K., Ebeling, H., Loukusa, S., . . . & Moilanen, I. (2016). Neuropsychological Performance of Finnish and Egyptian Children With Autism Spectrum Disorder. *International Journal of Circumpolar Health*, *75*(1), 29681.

Gardner, L., Erkfritz-Gay, K., Campbell, J. M., Bradley, T., & Murphy, L. (2016). Purposes of Assessment. In J. L. Matson & J. L. Matson (Eds), *Handbook of Assessment and Diagnosis of Autism Spectrum Disorder* (pp. 27–43). Cham, Switzerland: Springer International Publishing.

Geurts, H. M., Verte, S., Oosterlaan, J., Roeyers, H., & Sergeant, J. A. (2004). How Specific Are Executive Functioning Deficits in Attention Deficit Hyperactivity Disorder and Autism. *Journal of Child Psychology and Psychiatry*, *45*(4), 836–854.

Gilliam, J. (2014). *Gilliam Autism Rating Scale—Third Edition: Examiner's Manual.* (GARS-3). Austin, TX: Pro.Ed.

Gross, J., & Barrett, L. F. (2011). Emotion Generation and Emotion Regulation: One or Two Depends on Your Point of View. *Emotion Review*, *3*, 8–16. Retrieved from http://dx.doi.org/ 10.1177/1754073910380974

Hughes, C., & Ensor, R. (2007). Executive Function and Theory of Mind: Predictive Relations from Ages 2 to 4. *Developmental Psychology*, *43*(6), 1447.

Kleinhans, N., Muller, R., Cohen, D., & Courchesne, E. (2008). Atypical Functional Lateralization of Language in Autism Spectrum Disorders. *Brain Research*, *1221*(24, July), 115–125.

Kroncke, A. P., Willard, M. & Huckabee, H. (2016a). *Assessment of Autism Spectrum Disorder: Critical Issues in Clinical, Forensic, and School Settings.* Cham, Switzerland: Springer International Publishing.

Kroncke, A. P., Willard, M., & Huckabee, H. (2016b) Visual, Spatial, and Motor Assessment. In *Assessment of Autism Spectrum Disorder. Contemporary Issues in Psychological Assessment.* Springer. Cham, Switzerland: Springer International Publishing.

Kwok, E. Y. L., Brown, H. M., Smyth, R. E., & Cardy, J. O. (2015). Meta-analysis of Receptive and Expressive Skills in Autism Spectrum Disorder. *Research in Autism Spectrum Disorders*, *9*, 202–222.

Lindell, A. K. & Hudry, K. (2013). Atypicalities in Cortical Structure, Handedness, and Functional Lateralization for Language in Autism Spectrum Disorders. *Neuropsychological Review*, *23*, 257–270. doi: 10.1007/s11065-013-9234-5

Levitt, J. M., Saka, N., Romanelli, L. H., & Hoagwood, K. (2007). Early Identification of Mental Health Problems in Schools: The Status of Instrumentation. *Journal of School Psychology*, *45*, 163–191. doi: 10.1016/j.jsp.2006.11.005

Lezak, M. D. (2002). Responsive Assessment and the Freedom to Think for Ourselves. *Rehabilitation Psychology*, *47*(3), 339–353.

Lord. C., Rutter, M., et al. (2012). *Autism Diagnostic Observation Schedule—Second Edition* (ADOS-2). London, UK: Western Psychological Services/Pearson Assessment.

Lortie, M., Proulx-Bégin, L., Saint-Amour, D., Cousineau, D., Théoret, H., & Lepage, J. F. (2017). Brief Report: Biological Sound Processing in Children with Autistic Spectrum Disorder. *Journal of Autism and Developmental Disorders*, *47*(6), 1904–1909.

McAlister, A. R., & Peterson, C. C. (2013). Siblings, Theory of Mind, and Executive Functioning in Children Aged 3–6 Years: New Longitudinal Evidence. *Child Development*, *84*(4), 1442–1458.

McCloskey, G., & Perkins, L. A. (2012). *Essentials of Executive Functions Assessment.* Hoboken, NJ: John Wiley & Sons.

Mayes, S. D., & Calhoun, S. L. (1999). Symptoms of Autism in Young Children and Correspondence with the DSM. *Infants and Young Children, 12*, 90–97.

Mayes, S. D., Calhoun, S. L., Mayes, R. D., & Molitoris, S. (2012). Autism and ADHD: Overlapping and Discriminating Symptoms. *Research in Autism Spectrum Disorders, 6*(1), 277–285.

Mazefsky, C. A. & White, S. A. (2015). Emotion Regulation: Concepts & Practice in Autism Spectrum Disorder. *Child and Adolescent Psychiatric Clinics of North America, 23*, 1–12.

Meyers, J. E. & Meyers, K. R. (1995). *Rey Complex Figure Test and Recognition Trial (RCFT)*. Lutz, FL: PAR.

Miller, J. L., Saklofske, D. H., Weiss, L. D., et al. (2016). Issues related to the WISC-V assessment of cognitive functioning in clinical and special groups. *WISC-V Assessment and Interpretation*, 287–298.

Minshew, N. J., Goldstein, G., & Siegel, D. J. (1997). Neuropsychologic Functioning in Autism: Profile of a Complex Information Processing Disorder. *Journal of the International Neuropsychological Society, 3*(4), 303–316.

Naragon-Gainey, K., McMahon, T. P., & Chacko, T. P. (2017). The Structure of Common Emotion Regulation Strategies: A Meta-analytic Examination. *Psychological Bulletin, 143*(4), 384–427. doi:10.1037/bul0000093

NASP. (2013). *PREPaRE School Crisis Prevention and Intervention Training Curriculum.* Retrieved from www.nasponline.org/prepare/index.aspx

O'Connor, B. P. (2017). An Illustration of the Effects of Fluctuations in Test Information on Measurement Error, the Attenuation of Effect Sizes, and Diagnostic Reliability. *Psychological Assessment.* doi:10.1037/pas0000471

Orekhova, E. V., & Stroganova, T. A. (2014). Arousal and Attention Re-orienting in Autism Spectrum Disorders: Evidence from Auditory Event-Related Potentials. *Frontiers in Human Neuroscience 8*, 34. doi:10.3389/fnhum.2014.00034/abstract

Ozonoff, S., Cook, I., Coon, H., Dawson, G., Joseph, R. M., Klin, A., . . . & Rogers, S. J. (2004). Performance on Cambridge Neuropsychological Test Automated Battery Subtests Sensitive to Frontal Lobe Function in People with Autistic Disorder: Evidence from the Collaborative Programs of Excellence in Autism Network. *Journal of Autism and Developmental Disorders, 34*(2), 139–150.

Ozonoff, S., & Griffith, E. M. (2000). Neuropsychological Function and the External Validity of Asperger Syndrome. In A. Klin et al. (Eds.), *Asperger Syndrome* (pp. 72–96). New York, NY: Guilford Press.

Ozonoff, S., & Jensen, J. (1999). Brief Report: Specific Executive Function Profiles in Three Neurodevelopmental Disorders. *Journal of Autism and Developmental Disorders, 29*(2), 171–177.

Ozonoff, S., & Mcevoy, R. E. (1994). A Longitudinal Study of Executive Function and Theory of Mind Development in Autism. *Development and Psychopathology, 6*(3), 415–431.

Ozonoff, S., Pennington, B. F., & Rogers, S. J. (1991). Executive Function Deficits in High-Functioning Autistic Individuals: Relationship to Theory of Mind. *Journal of child Psychology and Psychiatry, 32*(7), 1081–1105.

Pellicano, E. (2012). The Development of Executive Function in Autism. *Autism Research and Treatment, 2012.* doi:10.1155/2012/146132

Pennington, B. F., & Ozonoff, S. (1996). Executive Functions and Developmental psychopathology. *Journal of Child Psychology and Psychiatry, 37*(1), 51–87.

Piek, J. P., & Dyck, M. J. (2004). Sensory-Motor Deficits in Children with Developmental Coordination Disorder, Attention Deficit Hyperactivity Disorder and Autistic Disorder. *Human Movement Science, 23*(3), 475–488.

Prunty, A. (2011). Implementation of Children's Rights: What is in "the Best Interests of the Child' in Relation to the Individual Education Plan (IEP) Process for Pupils with Autistic Spectrum Disorders (ASD)? *Irish Educational Studies, 30*(1), 23–44.

Reiersen, A. M., & Todd, R. D. (2008). Co-occurrence of ADHD and Autism Spectrum Disorders: Phenomenology and Treatment. *Expert Review of Neurotherapeutics, 8*(4), 657–669.

Reynolds, C. R., & Kamphaus, R. W. (2015). *Behavior Assessment for Children—Third Edition (BASC-3)*. London, UK: Pearson Education.

Rotholz, D. A., Kinsman, A. M., Lacy, K. K., & Charles, J. (2017). Improving Early Identification for Children at Risk for Autism Spectrum Disorder. *Pediatrics, 139*(2, February). doi:10/1542/peds.2016-1061

Rutter, M. LeCouteur, A., & Lord, C. (2003). *Autism Diagnostic Interview—Revised (ADI-R)*. London, UK: Western Psychological Services/Pearson Education.

Samson, A. C., Phillips, J. M. et al. (2014). Emotion Dysregulation and the Core Features of Autism Spectrum Disorder. *Journal of Autism and Developmental Disorders, 44*(7), 1766–1772.

Schopler, E., & Van Bourgondien, M. E. (2010). *Childhood Autism Rating Scale—Second Edition (CARS-2)*. London, UK: Western Psychological Services/Pearson Education.

Sheridan, S. M., & Kratochwill, T. R. (2008). *Conjoint Behavioral Consultation: Promoting Family-School Connections and Interventions*, 2nd ed. New York: Springer.

Shiota, M. N., Neufeld, S. L., Yeung, W. H., Moser, S. E., & Perea, E. F. (2011). Feeling Good: Autonomic Nervous System Responding in Five Positive Emotions. *Emotion, 11*(6), 136–1378. doi:10.1037/a0024278

Shtayermann, O. (2007). Peer Victimization in Adolecents and Young Adults Diagnosed with Asperger's Syndrome: A Link to Depressive Symptomology, Anxiety Symptomology and Suicidal Ideation. *Issues in Comprehensive Pediatric Nursing, 30*(3), 87–107.

Stevens, T., Peng, L., & Barnard-Brak, L. (2016). The Comorbidity of ADHD in Children Diagnosed with Autism Spectrum Disorder. *Research in Autism Spectrum Disorders, 31*, 11–18.

Tillery, K. L., Katz, J., & Keller, W. D. (2000). Effects of Methylphenidate (Ritalin) on Auditory Performance in Children with Attention and Auditory Processing Disorders. *Journal of Speech, Language, and Hearing Research, 43*(4), 893–901.

Wagner, S. J. (2014). Continuum of Services and Individual Education Plan Process. In L. A. Wilkinson (Ed.), *Autism Spectrum Disorder in Children and Adolescents: Evidence-Based Assessment and Intervention in Schools* (pp. 173–193). Washington, DC: American Psychological Association.

Wainwright, J. A., & Bryson, S. E. (1996). Visual-Spatial Orienting in Autism. *Journal of Autism and Developmental Disorders, 26*(4), 423–438.

Wechsler, D. (2003). *Wechsler Intelligence Scale for Children—Fourth Edition* (WISC-IV). London, UK: Pearson Clinical.

Wechsler, D. (2014). *Wechsler Intelligence Scale for Children—Fifth Edition* (WISC-V). London, UK: Pearson Clinical.

White, S. J. (2013). The Triple I Hypothesis: Taking Another('s) Perspective on Executive Dysfunction in Autism. *Journal of Autism and Developmental Disorders, 43*(1), 114–121.

White, S. W., Schry, A. R., & Maddox, B. B. (2012). Brief Report: The Assessment of Anxiety in High-Functioning Adolescents with Autism Spectrum Disorder. *Journal of Autism and Developmental Disorders, 42*, 1138–1145.

Zhou, X., Reynolds, C. R., Zhu, J., Kamphaus, R. W., & Zhang, O. (2017). Evidence-Based Assessment of ADHD Diagnosis in Children and Adolescents. *Applied Neuropsychology: Child, 7*(2), 150–156. doi: 10.1080/21622965.2017.128466

4

CURRENT RESEARCH IN THE STATE OF UNDERSTANDING AUTISM SPECTRUM DISORDER THROUGH NEUROANATOMY

What Do We Know

Michael Wolff and Paige Mission

It is not deemed to be necessary to try to broach the complexity and wealth of research into the neuroanatomy of ASD for this chapter. After 15 years of reviewing the neuroanatomical literature for ASD, the conclusion is that every major brain region and countless structures has been implicated. At this point in time, there is no one region or structure that would fully account for a neurological pattern for an autistic spectrum disorder. The same holds true at this point for finding a similar genetic profile or EEG or other electrical physiological profile. Rather, autism spectrum disorders are an incredibly dynamic cluster of individuals meeting behavioral criteria to support a diagnosis by surpassing cut-off criteria. The attributes that contribute to who these individuals are vary vastly from those who are cognitively impaired, nonverbal, and struggle to meaningfully engage in activities of daily living to those who are highly capable individuals leading research in our prominent universities and organizations throughout the world. There are few classifications of disorders that run the breadth of neuro-diversity as ASD. And, it is important to recognize the development of symptoms that come together to be classified, as an ASD will be affected by other health factors, coping strategies, intervention, and their environment, which remain highly researched areas in ASD as well

Theories of Connectivity

However, there are clear patterns in some areas that will encompass a majority of individuals on the spectrum. We are also seeing research shift from a focus on unique structure variants, it is still beneficial to review unique structures that have been implicated with autism spectrum disorder. Kanner (1943) and numerous researchers have subsequently documented that individuals with autism tend to have larger head circumference and brain volume than typically developing individuals. More specifically, this would be better delineating individuals who historically had demonstrated patterns of autism. Courchesne et al. (2001) documented that 90 percent of boys between the ages of 2 and 4 who had been diagnosed with autism had increased brain volume, but this variation does not necessarily persist into older children or adults. Thereafter, the neuroanatomical attributes demonstrate significant heterogeneity (McAlonan, 2004; Sivapalan & Aitchison, 2014).

One of the primary theories that has been in prominence discusses intrinsic functional connectivity in the brain. A majority of research has documented that there is often intra-hemispheric functional under-connectivity or hypo-connectivity (Di Martino et al., 2014). The patterns of hypo-connectivity tend to be more cortical and inter-hemispheric hypo-connectivity. McFadden and Minshew (2013) suggest that this may be the result of an initial proliferation of cortical neurons, but subsequent failure of development resulting in excess apoptosis resulting in the variation in axonal abnormality. Kana et al. (2015) suggest that the under-connectivity is consistent with the theory of mind and discusses the difficulties between the frontomedial, frontoparietal, and medial under-connectivity with individuals who have ASD. Similar ideas are put forth in the work of Ghanbari et al. (2015). Yet, further exploration in the literature suggests that the under-connectivity theory is again demonstrated more in the neocortex. There can be a higher prevalence of hyper-connectivity in subcortical regions, including the margins of the thalamus, globus pallidus, and cerebellum (Chen et al., 2011; Kana et al., 2014; Maximo, Cadena, & Kana, 2014).

Furthering the discussion, Hernandez et al. (2015) presented a discussion of the functional connectivity network, otherwise known as the Default Mode Network, that has been associated with ASD. It is suggested that social cognition tends to be most influenced by challenges in the connectivity between the posterior cingulate cortex, medial prefrontal cortex, lateral temporal cortex, inferior parietal lobe, and hippocampal formation. The interhemispheric communication between the structures encompassed in the Default Mode Network will inherently contribute to challenges being able to engage others effectively. Further, David et al. (2014) suggest that the social perception difficulty results from the correlation of change in connectivity in the right temporal parietal gray matter. Yet, Hernandez goes on to talk about the salience network where connections in the anterior cingulate cortex and anterior insula may be more highly connected, resulting in potential unusual sensitivity in the identification of information in one's environment whereupon the clustering of information for nonverbal cues in one's environment may be confused. Others have suggested this salience network may not be errant by necessary over-identification of environmental and social stimuli, but could be slower processing speed of information (Speirs et al., 2014) or, more specifically, in the global efficiency of reading nonverbal cues (Roine et al., 2015), and that the discourse of a nonverbal cue in social perception also cannot be mentioned without research demonstrating variation in the functionality of the fusiform gyrus. As one example, Kleinhans et al. (2011) suggested that there is decreased activity in the fusiform gyrus, resulting in slower encoding of nonverbal cues and facial recognition in those who have been diagnosed with ASD.

A recent review by Deshpande et al. (2013) demonstrated that there are 19 pathways that appear to be unique (Figure 4.1). Considering the ASDs as an accumulated group, there was reduced functional connectivity between the temporal and frontal regions and weaker ventral premotor regions in the temporal parietal junction. Additional areas that were involved in these pathways included the middle temporal gyrus, inferior frontal gyrus, inferior parietal lobe, fusiform gyrus, and supplementary motor areas.

Further, Bakhtiari et al. (2012) describe a maturation process influencing connectivity. In adolescence, there was decreased fractional anisotropy (FA) in the inferior longitudinal fasciculus connecting the occipital cortex with the anterior temporal lobes and amygdala. These regions contributed to a negative

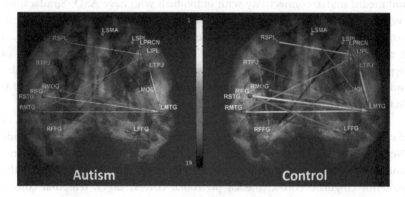

FIGURE 4.1   The 19 paths whose effective connectivity values were top-ranked features for classification of the two groups (Autism and Controls) with maximum accuracy (left: participants with autism; right: control participants).

Note: The width of the arrows represents the path strength, and the color of the path indicates its rank, obtained during classification, 1 being the most significant and 19 being the least significant (Deshpande et al., 2013).

Key: Supplementary motor area (SMA), left and right inferior frontal gyrus (LIFG, RIFG), left and right precentral cortex (LPRCN, RPRCN), left and right middle temporal gyrus (LMTG, RMTG), right superior temporal gyrus (RSTG), left and right inferior parietal lobule (LIPL, RIPL), left and right fusiform gyrus (LFFG, RFFG), left and right superior parietal lobule (LSPL, RSPL), left and right middle occipital gyrus (LMOG, RMOG), and left and right temporal parietal junction (LTPJ, RTPJ).

correlation between scores on the ADOS (Autistic Diagnostic Observation System), a psychological assessment for autism spectrum disorders. As fractional anisotropy decreases, there was an increased likelihood for symptomology suggestive of an autism spectrum disorder based on scores from the ADOS (above patterns were also discussed in Travers et al., 2012). There were also decreases in connectivity between the inferior fronto-occipital fasciculus connecting the occipital cortices through the uncinate fasciculus and the orbital frontal cortex. Additionally, the superior longitudinal fasciculus connectivity was more altered in adolescence than in adulthood, contributing to disruption between the frontotemporal and parietal regions. With maturation, however, there was a normalization in adult connective pathways, a factor that may contribute to the reductions in behavioral symptomology.

Other authors have discussed the challenges with frontal disconnectivity (Cheng, 2010 et al.; Hodge et al., 2009; Mueller et al., 2013) and frontal cortical cerebellar circuits (Hodge et al., 2009). In addition, the fusiform gyrus (FFG) and mirror neuron systems in ASD have garnered significant attention. Hadjikhani et al. (2004, 2006) brought this discussion more actively to the forefront, noting that there seemed to be a thinning of the mirror neuron systems. There is also the supposition that the FFG in ASDs activates similar to controls, but that the pathways connecting to the FFG are altered. In particular, the research suggested that there may be increased activation in the inferior occipital gyri. Functionally, this could contribute to challenges that result in overanalyzing details of the face without actually processing this information as an overall emotional expression, a finding that is consistent with Courchesne et al.'s (2001) research.

More Specific Patterns Relating to ASD Symptoms

Emotional Sensitivity

As most who work with the individuals on spectrum have recognized, there can be unusually emotional reactivity. The excitement and anticipation of an activity can result in hand flapping, jumping up and down, asking incessantly when the event might happen even if they have been told that it may be weeks away, and there can be very quick irritable reactions when limits are put in place on activities that they are seeking. This could be a limiting access to trains, dinosaurs, or more recently the addictive nature that individuals on the spectrum seem to have for technology. These emotional reactions, which are often prevalent from infancy, can result in clinicians misdiagnosing ADHD or bipolar in children who are actually on the autism spectrum continuum. This pattern of functional change in emotional vulnerability may well result from research documenting higher amygdalar volume in early development and reduced volume in adulthood (Munson, 2006; Pierce et al., 2001; Stanfield, 2008). The literature has also demonstrated that higher cortical volume in the amygdala may initially give way to diminished receptivity in the amygdala as these individuals develop. It is likely that this is resultant from glutamatergic lesions due to over-excitatory activity in the amygdala (Barnea-Goraly et al., 2004). As a result, individuals, as they progress into late childhood and adulthood, may have emotional blunting, seem to be more withdrawn, and may not be as emotionally expressive.

Language

Furthering the discussion in corroboration of symptoms consistent with ASD, expressive language is a prominent diagnostic quality. Lombardo et al. (2015) documented hypoactivity in the superior temporal cortices of toddlers as reducing the likely positive outcome of normal language development. Further, the lack of fiber coherence and other abnormal macro- and micro-structural change through the corpus callosum will also have a negative influence on the ability to pair the content of language with social attributes (Kana et al., 2014). Although the callosal influence is important in being able to help individuals understand the dynamic use of language (e.g., "cool" indicates either that an object/person is cold or neat), there is also the importance of the arcuate fasciculus in supporting the reception of language (Wan & Schlaug, 2010). Once language is received, the arcuate fasciculus aids in bringing information forward into functional communication to keep up with expressive language and further impact an individual's ability to read nonverbal cues and fully communicate effectively in the moment. More research has been completed in recent years on the maturation of the attention network, and more specifically the auditory processing system (Edgar et al., 2015; Karten & Hirsch, 2015. As a result of the difficulties encompassed in the increased activity in the pre-stimulus auditory superior temporal gyrus, there is increased auditory sensitivity. Functionally, this would result in individuals on the spectrum to have increased sensitivity to sounds in their environment. Because they are struggling to ignore someone's shoes squeaking, swallowing loudly, ruffling their papers, they become frustrated and pay more attention to the extraneous sounds, and miss what is being conveyed in language use. This will not only complicate their ability to understand directions and to follow along in group dynamics as a result of there being a higher likelihood of extraneous sounds, but can also result in irritability. Edgar et al. (2015) also documented that the executive functioning attributes of social language are also influenced in those with ASD as a result of involvement in the cerebellum, which tends to help modulate emotion and language for social language.

Repetitive Behavior/Motor Patterns

OCD and other repetitive behaviors have commonly been associated with variation in functional performance in the orbital cortex, anterior cingulate, thalamus, and caudate nucleus (Sivapan & Aitchinson, 2014). However, the involvement of the basal ganglia and associated structures has gained additional research as of late (Calderoni et al., 2014. More specifically, the involvement of the caudate nucleus was noted (Sears et al., 1999). The efforts of these individuals to pattern the structural change in restrictive and repetitive behaviors as associated with basal ganglia have resulted in demarcating the cortical basal ganglia thalamic circuit as a pathway that is functionally unique in ASD (Kim, Limb, & Kaang, 2016). Unfortunately, the implication of the basal gangliar structure will neuroanatomically involve the cerebellum, as the cerebellar basal gangliar pathways have commonly been documented as being hypoplastic. Pierce and Courchesne (2001) have begun discussing this connection; however, others have subsequently discussed models of possible cerebellar disconnection syndromes, which would be consistent with many of the ASD symptoms that are observed in those with ASD. Many are less coordinated, are not actively involved in sports, and also do not have the competitive edge, even if they are interested, as a result of not being able to perform effectively. This could easily result in emotional frustration and overreaction in response to trying to help them develop motor skills, stay physically active, and engage the physical world rather than be complacent and isolated (e.g., playing video games for hours alone). Wang, Kloth, and Badura (2014) have also advanced the cerebellar hypothesis to denote that this same pathway will also have influences in sensory performance and be able to learn affect modulation. Schumann et al.'s (2004) research on cerebellar cognitive affective disorder further recognizes the importance of the cerebellum in affect modulation.

Biscaldi et al. (2014) also provided additional discourse regarding the reduced motor speed and gross motor coordination associated with sensory motor activity. They put forth that there are deficits in white matter abnormalities decreasing the functional connectivity from the frontostriatal, cerebellar, and/or frontocerebellar circuits. Within Biscaldi et al.'s discussion, the mention of the striate circuits becomes incredibly salient, as this is also highly influenced in visual-spatial performance. Additionally Muth, Hönekopp, and Falter (2014) suggested that there are significant challenges in functional recruitment in order to navigate the complexity of a dynamic world. The challenge with recruiting broader neurological connectivity and function is demonstrated in Courchesne et al.'s (2011) fMRI study (Figure 4.2).

While normal subjects use medial frontal and parietal regions to process familiar faces, autistic individuals only show activity in medial parietal regions (posterier cingulate and precious). Autistic subjects showed no frontal activation, but rather relied on more basic perceptual "low-level" areas such as the occipital cortex and fusiform gyrus. Similarly, on a visual shift attention task, control subjects showed activation in the cerebellum and dorsolateral portion of the frontal cortex while autistic participants did not. All of these are very

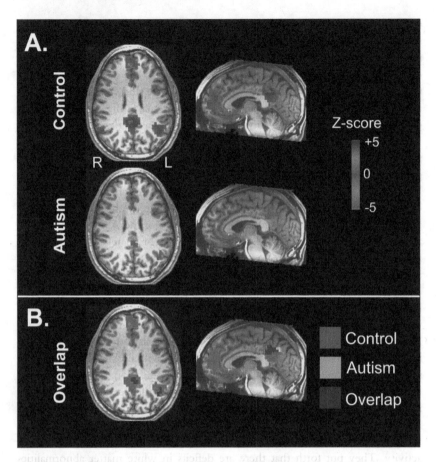

FIGURE 4.2 Significant functional activity in the familiar faces versus stranger faces comparison for both the autism (left) and normal (right) groujo. Note that the only brain region significantly active in the autism group was in the posterior cingulate and precuneus region.

Source: Pierce et al. (2004, p. 10, figure 5).

prominent pathways that will also have negative implications in motoric activity, particularly in social contact. Chen et al. (2011) also documented the under-connectivity in the region of the primary parietal and sensorimotor regions, coinciding with the pronounced sensory deficits that many individuals on the spectrum demonstrate throughout their life. Yet, early and active intervention can moderate these vulnerabilities and, with the change in healthcare coverage for autism in most U.S. states, early and active intervention is demonstrating the ability to change the expressed influence of sensory deficits.

Attention and Concentration

Finally, there cannot be discussion of ASD and neuroanatomy without also mentioning the importance of attention and concentration. Historically, the diagnosis of ADHD would be omitted from an autism spectrum disorder's diagnostic profile. As recent as the DSM-IV, it was suggested that, if you are diagnosing ASD, you would not diagnose ADHD simultaneously. This is because it has become common clinical knowledge that a majority of individuals on the spectrum have an attention problem. I will commonly comment to families that if you have an individual with an autism spectrum disorder and let them do what they want in terms of a desired activity, they will pay attention to this for hours and hours and hours on end without thinking about eating, using the restroom, or other activities that they need to complete in the day. However, if you try to get them to do something you are interested in, or want them to do, the attention span disappears. Families who have a child on the spectrum commonly recognize this as troublesome. Unfortunately, this is not ADHD, even though we are having more and more professionals misdiagnose ASD and ADHD simultaneously. Many individuals on the spectrum may in fact respond somewhat favorably to an ADHD medication, more commonly a psychostimulant, but this is not diagnostically informative. In fact, it is likely that a majority of individuals, whether they have ADHD or not, would partially respond to a psychostimulant medication favorably. The medications are meant to be cognitively enhancing. In those with ASD, there can be some positive influence to also assist with being more flexible in their thought process. Those who work with children on the spectrum all too often recognize different metabolization to medications, particularly psychostimulants. We have seen children in clinic routinely require multiple doses throughout the day or doses of the Concerta at 127 mg. It is now a weekly occurrence to have ASD individuals described by prescribing psychiatrists as hyper-metabolizers and, as such, there will be a pairing with other medications to try to slow the metabolization of the psychostimulant, ultimately ending up with poly-medication therapy, which can have other consequences for these individuals. The literature does suggest that there is, again, involvement along the basal gangliar structures in ASD. Microstructural changes in the right posterior limb of the internal capsule along the cortical spinal tract and the right cerebral peduncle and midbrain have been discussed (Cooper, Thapar, & Jones, 2014). Lim et al. (2015) also documented gray matter reductions in the cerebellum for ASD, and the middle and superior temporal gyrus. Oberman et al. (2012) and Travers et al. (2015) have also discussed how the cortical spinal track not only has implications for attention but has also contributed to challenges in social cognition and motor function as a result of attentional variation in these pathways. Some more specific work in terms of working memory activation has implicated the right hippocampus and cingulate gyrus. It was put forth by Urbain et al. (2015) that typically developing individuals had higher activity response in the left dorsolateral prefrontal cortex and insula, whereas those within the spectrum did not show the same activation, thereby suspecting resultant deficits in working memory and attention.

Sample of Literature Regarding the Distinction Between Autism and Asperger's

In spite of the regional similarities between ASD and control samples, there are patterns both structurally and functionally that distinguish autism from Asperger's. Amaral et al. (2008) presented numerous neuroanatomical features of autism, including data postmortem: the anterior cingulate was coarse and poorly laminated; there tended to be higher dorsolateral prefrontal and medial frontal cortex volume; and there were also volume increases in the ventral temporal lobe, particularly in the left hemisphere. This conclusion drawn in 2008 suggests there was significant heterogeneity in the data and there tended to be early volume enlargement, but then abnormal growth trajectory thereafter. This is consistent with much of the literature discussing excitotoxicity causing potential lesions that may contribute to decreases in volume by adolescence to adulthood (i.e., Koyama, 2005; Schumann et al, 2004). Further, McAlonan et al. (2008, 2009) noted higher cortical folding in Broca's area and less white matter in the left hemisphere and corpus callosum. In fact, there have been patterns to high-functioning autism mainly involving the left hemisphere white matter systems, whereas Asperger's predominantly influences the right white matter systems. Yu et al. (2011) completed a meta-analysis reviewing qualitative differences between autistic individuals and controls. In controls, there was variation in gray matter volume that tended to be lower in the areas of the cerebellum, the right uncus, the dorsal hippocampus, and the middle temporal gyrus, whereas autistic children tended to have greater volumes in the bilateral caudate, prefrontal lobe, and ventral temporal margin. McAlonan et al. (2008) found that autistic children, in comparison to individuals with Asperger's, had smaller gray matter volumes in primary subcortical tissue, posterior cingulate, and precuneus. There were also more challenges in the frontal palatal projections.

The neuroanatomy of Asperger's has also been researched. McAlonan et al. (2002) described that there tended to be deficits in the basal ganglia extending to the thalamus and the ventral striatum. There were decreases in volume from the medial frontal lobe, through the cingulate, cerebellum, and left frontal temporal pathway to the occipital region, and there was an excess of gray matter in the external capsule. Catani et al. (2008) also documented altered cerebral neural pathways influencing social behavior. There were shorter intracerebellar fibers and lowered right superior cerebellar peduncle output. However, there was no difference in the input projections leading to the cerebellum. Challenges in Asperger's have also been documented in projection pathways having higher FA in the right and left cingulate, inferior longitudinal fasciculus and lower streamline patterns in the right uncinate (Pugliese et al., 2009). Yu et al. (2011) and Schumann et al. (2004) documented lower bilateral amygdalar volumes by adolescents or adulthood, decreased gray matter volume in the hippocampal gyrus and prefrontal lobe, and deficits in the left occipital gyrus, right cerebellum, putamen, and precuneus in comparison to controls. However, the Asperger's individuals tended to have greater volume in the bilateral inferior parietal lobe and left fusiform gyrus. Additionally, individuals with Asperger's tend to demonstrate increased activation in neural networks for attention but decreased activity in motor areas (Mueller et al., 2013). As can be seen from the data above, there are differences in neuroanatomical structures/regions.

Duffy et al. (2013) completed an electrographic analysis of individuals who had been diagnosed with autism or Asperger's. The research documented several variations. Those diagnosed with Asperger's demonstrated reduced coherence between the left anterior and posterior frontal temporal regions and, to a lesser degree, in the right anterior temporal frontal regions. In addition, there was enhanced coherence between the left middle temporal region and left central parietal and occipital regions, with reduction in the left lateral anterior posterior coherence patterns in Asperger's versus autism. The researchers were able to accurately describe children with an ASD versus controls with 96.2 percent accuracy and autism versus Asperger's with 92.3 percent accuracy. It is understood, as Dr. Ecker argues, that studies comparing existing patient populations cannot be replicated in a completely random sample. Nonetheless, this is one of the first studies that has tried to effectively describe in vivo patterns that distinguish autism from Asperger's. Dr. Duffy does conclude that this does not necessarily mean that autism and Asperger's are, in and of themselves, separate diagnostic entities. Rather, we may be describing unique patterns of performance within an Autism Spectrum Disorder population, with Asperger's being one tail of the spectrum.

The neuroanatomical data has identified structural variations unique to autism/Asperger's, noted above. Yet, it can be argued that it would be challenging for any neuroscientist to be able to review distinct structures or variation in neuropathway patterns in isolation from the behavioral patterns of an ASD individual in order to blindly make a diagnosis by imaging alone. And, without studying the variation between all other neurodevelopmental conditions (i.e., Angleman's, Williams syndrome, FAS, Disintegrative disorders, etc.), and many of the other conditions that present symptoms of ASD (repetitive behavior, poor social awareness, restricted interests), a neuroimaging study cannot definitely diagnose autism, Asperger's, and a majority of the other conditions by imaging alone. More importantly, neuropsychology and other trained psychologists can evaluate the behavioral symptoms, how the individual functions in the world, diagnose and guide other treatment modalities and/or provide direct treatment much more cost effectively and accurately than any neuroimaging study at this time.

The following is a general synopsis demonstrating the challenge in understanding variation even in the pathways commonly associated with ASD symptoms:

- Underconnectivity across hemispheres and lobes—frontomedial/fronto parietal/medial/parietal/occipital
- Hyperconnectivity in subcortical regions and agensis of the corpus callosum (ACC) and insula
- Under-activity in fusiform gyrus
- Larger amygdalar and limbic system influence early, but diminishing through adolescence and into adulthood (shifts possibly related to overactivation and subsequent neurotoxic lesions from overexcitation)
- Underactive superior temporal cortices and overactive superior temporal gyrus
- Lack of coherence across fibers through the corpus callosum
- Overactive, but less integrated, cortical basal gangliar thalamic circuit
- Cerebellum white matter abnormalities—leading to discourse in the area of cerebellar disconnection syndromes.

Conclusion

The sum of the neuroanatomical data is undoubtedly complex. The above presents a case of some prominent pathways that have been implicated in ASD and how these, in turn, influence functional abilities. This is a more influential way to try to understand the confluence of structure abnormalities and how they influence more global functioning in those with an autism spectrum disorder. There will ultimately unlikely be one profile that will encapsulate all individuals who have an autism spectrum disorder. The uniqueness of these individuals will continue to evolve as research methods continue to explore in greater detail the micro- and macro-structural pathways. However, more importantly, there may be more excitement given to the identification of various neurotrophic brain factors or chromosomal expressions that may be altered at some point in the future that could provide the opportunity to alter the patterns of synaptogenesis and apoptosis in individuals who may be candidates for severe autism. Research methodologies in the treatment of ASD continue to evolve. ABA (applied behavior analysis) has been the most prominently researched in terms of secular knowledge, but the play project, virtual reality, neurofeedback, and many other direct interventions to assist in helping these individuals to advance in communication, social and emotional interaction, and to improve activities of daily living through speech and other occupations, all offer promising outcomes.

References

Amaral, D. G., Schumann, C. M., & Nordah, C. W. (2008). Neuroanatomy of Autism. *Trends in Neurosciences, 31*(3), 137–145.

Bakhtiari, R., Zurcher, N. R., Rogier, O., Russo, B., Hippolyte, L., Granziera, C., Araabi, B. N., Nili Ahmadabadi, M., & Hadjikhani, N. (2012). Differences in White Matter Reflect Atypical Developmental Trajectory in Autism: A Tract-Based Spatial Statistics Study. *NeuroImage: Clinical, 1*, 48–56. doi:10.1016/j.nicl.2012.09.001

Barnea-Goraly, N., Kwon, H., Menon, V., Eliez, S., Lotspeich, L., & Reiss, A. L. (2004). White Matter Structure in Autism: Preliminary Evidence From Diffusion Tensor Imaging. *Biological Psychiatry, 55*(3), 323–326.

Biscaldi, M., Rauh, R., Irion, L., Jung, N. H., Mall, V., Fleischhaker, C., & Klein, C. (2014). Deficits in Motor Abilities and Developmental Fractionation of Imitation Performance in High-Functioning Autism Spectrum Disorders. *European Child & Adolescent Psychiatry, 23*(7), 599–610.

Calderoni, S., Bellani, M., Hardan, A. Y., Muratori, F., & Brambilla, P. (2014). Basal Ganglia and Restricted and Repetitive Behaviours in Autism Spectrum Disorders: Current Status and Future Perspectives. *Epidemiology and Psychiatric Sciences, 23*(3), 235–238.

Catani, M., Jones, D. K., Daly, E., Embiricos, N., Deeley, Q., Pugliese, L., Curran, S., Robertson, D., & Murphy, D. (2008). Altered Cerebellar Feedback Projections in Asperger Syndrome. *NeuroImage, 41*(4), 1184–1191. doi.org/10.1016/j.neuroimage.2008.03.041

Chen, R., Jiao, Y., & Herskovits, E.H. (2011). Structural MRI in Autism Spectrum Disorder. *Pediatric Research, 69*(5 Pt 2), 63R–8R.

Cheng, Y., Chou, K., Chen, I., Fan, Y., Decety, J., & Lin, C. (2010). Atypical Development of White Matter Microstructure in Adolescents with Autism Spectrum Disorders. *NeuroImage*, 873–882. doi:10.1016/j.neuroimage.2010.01.011

Cooper, M., Thapar, A., & Jones, D. K. (2014). White Matter Microstructure Predicts Autistic Traits in Attention-Deficit/Hyperactivity Disorder. *Journal of Autism and Developmental Disorders, 44*(11), 2742–2754.

Courchesne, E., Karns, C. M., Davis, H. R., Ziccardi, R., Carper, R. A., Tigue, Z. D., et al. (2001). Unusual Brain Growth Patterns in Early Life in Patients with Autistic Disorder an MRI study. *Neurology, 57*(2), 245–254.

David, N., Schultz, J., Milne, E., Schunke, O., Schöttle, D., Münchau, A., et al. (2014). Right Temporoparietal Gray Matter Predicts Accuracy of Social Perception in the Autism Spectrum. *Journal of Autism and Developmental Disorders, 44*(6), 1433–1446.

Deshpande, G., Libero, L. E., Sreenivasan, K. R., Deshpande, H. D., & Kana, R. K. (2013). Identification of Neural Conectivity Signatures of Autism Using Machine Learning. *Frontiers in Human Neuroscience, 7*, 1–15. doi:10.3389/fnhum.20013.00670

Di Martino, A., Yan, C. G., Li, Q., Denio, E., Castellanos, F. X., Alaerts, K., et al. (2014). The Autism Brain Imaging Data Exchange: Towards a Large-Scale Evaluation of the Intrinsic Brain Architecture in Autism. *Molecular Psychiatry, 19*(6), 659–667.

Duffy, F. H., Shankardass, A., McAnulty, G. B., & Als, H. (2013). The Relationship of Asperger's Syndrome to Autism: A Preliminary EEG Coherence Study. *BMC Medicine, 11*. Retrieved from www.biomedcentral.com/1741-7015/11/175

Edgar, J. C., Khan, S.Y., Blaskey, L., Chow, V. Y., Rey, M., Gaetz, W., et al. (2015). Neuromagnetic Oscillations Predict Evoked-Response Latency Delays and Core lLanguage Deficits in Autism Spectrum Disorders. *Journal of Autism and Developmental Disorders, 45*(2), 395–405.

Ghanbari, Y., Bloy, L., Edgar, J. C., Blaskey, L., Verma, R., & Roberts, T. P. (2015). Joint Analysis of Band-Specific Functional Connectivity and Signal Complexity in Autism. *Journal of Autism and Developmental Disorders, 45*(2), 444–460.

Hadjikhani, N., Joseph, R. M., Snyder, J., Chabris, C. F., Clark, J., Steele, S., et al. (2004). Activation of the Fusiform Gyrus When Individuals with Autism Spectrum Disorder View Faces. *NeuroImage*, 22, 1141–1150. doi:10.1016.j.neuroimage.2004.03.025

Hadjikhani, N., Joseph, R. M., Snyder, J., & Tager-Flusberg, H. (2006). Anatomical Differences in the Mirror Neuron System and Social Cognition Network in Autism. *Cerebral Cortex, 16,* 1276–1282. doi:10.1093/cercor/bhj069

Hernandez, L. M., Rudie, J. D., Green, S. A., Bookheimer, S., & Dapretto, M. (2015). Neural Signatures of Autism Spectrum Disorders: Insights into Brain Network Dynamics. *Neuropsychopharmacology, 40*(1), 171–189.

Hodge, S. M., Makris, N., Kennedy, D. N., Caviness Jr., V. S., Howard, J., McGrath, L., Steele, S., Frazier, J. A., Tager-Flusberg, H. & Harris, G. J. (2010). Cerebellum, Language, and Cognition in Autism and Specific Language Impairment. *Journal of Autism and Developmental Disorders, 40*(3), 300–316. doi:10.1007/s10803-009-0872-7

Kana, R. K., Libero, L. E., Hu, C. P., Deshpande, H. D., & Colburn, J. S. (2012). Functional Brain Networks and White Matter Underlying Theory-of-Mind in Autism. *Social Cognitive and Affective Neuroscience, 9*(1), 98–105.

Kana, R. K., Maximo, J. O., Williams, D. L., Keller, T. A., Schipul, S. E., & Cherkassky, V. L. (2015). Aberrant Functioning of the Theory-of-Mind Network in Children and Adolescents with Autism. *Molecular Autism, 6.* doi:10.1186/s13229-015-0052-x

Kana, R. K., Uddin, L. Q., Kenet, T., Chugani, D., & Muller, R-A. (2014). Brain Connectivity in Autism. *Frontiers in Human Neuroscience*, 8, 349. doi.org/10.3389/fnhum.2014.00349

Kanner, L. (1943) Autistic Disturbances of Affective Contact.. *Nervous Child, 2,* 217–250.

Karten, A., & Hirsch, J. (2015). Brief Report: Anomalous Neural Deactivations and Functional Connectivity During Receptive Language in Autism Spectrum Disorder: A Functional MRI Study. *Journal of Autism and Developmental Disorders, 45*(6), 1905–1914.

Kim, H., Lim, C. S., & Kaang, B. K. (2016). Neuronal Mechanisms and Circuits Underlying Repetitive Behaviors in Mouse Models of Autism Spectrum Disorder. *Behavioral and Brain Functions, 12*(1), 1–12.

Kleinhans, N. M., Richards, T., Johnson, L. C., Weaver, K. E., Greenson, J., Dawson, G., & Aylward, E. (2011). fMRI Evidence of Neural Abnormalities in the Subcortical Face Processing System in ASD. *NeuroImage, 54*(1), 697–704.

Koyama, A. (2005). *A Review on the Cognitive Neuroscience of Autism.* Retrieved October 21, 2005, from http://cogprints.org/5208/1/AutismCogNeuroReview.pdf

Lim, L., Chantiluke, K., Cubillo, A. I., Smith, A. B., Simmons, A., Mehta, M. A., & Rubia, K. (2015). Disorder-Specific Gre Matter Deficits in Attention Deficit Hyperactivity Disorder Relative to Autism Spectrum Disorder. *Psychological Medicine, 45*(5), 965–976.

Lombardo, M. V., Pierce, K., Eyler, L. T., Barnes, C. C., Ahrens-Barbeau, C., Solso, S., et al. (2015). Different Functional Neural Substrates for Good and Poor Language Outcome in Autism. *Neuron, 86*(2), 567–577.

McAlonan, G. M., Cheung,. V, Cheung, C., Suckling J., Lam, G. Y., Tai, K. S., et al. (2004). Mapping the Brain in Autism. A Voxel-Based MRI Study of Volumetric Differences and Intercorrelations in Autism. *Brain, 128*(2), 268–276.

McAlonan, G. M., Cheung, C., Cheung, V., Wong, N., Suckling, J., & Chua, S. E. (2009). Differential effects on white-matter systems in high-functioning autism and Asperger's syndrome. Psychological Medicine, 39(11), 1885–1893.

McAlonan, G. M., Daly, E., Kumari, V., Critchley, H. D., van Almesvoort, T., Suckling, J., et al. (2002). Brain Anatomy and Sensorimotor Gating in Asperger's Syndrome. Brain, 125(7), 1594–1606.

McAlonan, G. M., Suckling, J., Wong, N., Cheung, V., Lienenkaemper, N., Cheung, C., & Chua, S. E. (2008). Distinct Patterns of Grey Matter Abnormality in High-Functioning Autism and Asperger's Syndrome. Journal of Child Psychology and Psychiatry, 49(12), 1287–1295.

McFadden, K., & Minshew, N.J. (2013). Evidence for Dysregulation of Axonal Growth and Guidance in the Etiology of ASD. Frontiers in Human Neuroscience, 7(671), 1–10.

Maximo, J. O., Cadena, E. J., & Kana, R. K. (2014). The Implications of Brain Connectivity in the Neuropsychology of Autism. Neuropsychology Review, 24(1), 16–31.

Mueller, S., Keeser, D., Samson, A. C., Kirsch, V., Blautzik, J., Grothe, M., et al. (2013). Convergent Findings of Altered Functional and Structural Brain Connectivity in Individuals with high Functioning Autism: A Multimodal MRI study. PLoS ONE, 8(6), 1–11. doi:10.1371/journal.pone.0067329

Munson, J., Dawson, G., Abbott, R., Faja, S., Webb, S. J., Friedman, S. D., et al. (2006). Amygdalar Volume and Behavioral Development in Autism. Archives of General Psychiatry, 63(6), 686–693.

Muth, A., Hönekopp, J., & Falter, C. M. (2014). Visuo-spatial Performance in Autism: A Meta-analysis. Journal of Autism and Developmental Disorders, 44(12), 3245–3263.

Oberman, L. M., McCleery, J. P., Hubbard, E. M., Bernier, R., Wiersema, J. R., Raymaekers, R., & Pineda, J. A. (2012). Developmental Changes in Mu Suppression to Observed and Executed Actions in Autism Spectrum Disorders. Social Cognitive and Affective Neuroscience, 8(3), 300–304.

Pierce, K., & Courchesne, E. (2001). Evidence for a Cerebellar Role in Reduced Exploration and Stereotyped Behavior in Autism. Biological Psychiatry, 49(8), 655–666.

Pierce, K., Haist, F., Sedaghat, F., & Courchesne, E. (2004). The Brain Response to Personally Familiar Faces in Autism: Findings of Fusiform Activity and Beyond. Brain, 127 (Part 12), 2703–2716. doi:10.1093/brain/awh289

Pierce, K., Müller, R. A., Ambrose, J., Allen, G., & Courchesne, E. (2001). Face Processing Occurs Outside the Fusiform "Face Area" in Autism: Evidence from Functional MRI. Brain, 124(10), 2059–2073.

Pugliese, L., Catani, M., Ameis, S., Dell'Acqua, F., Thiebaut de Schotten, M., Murphy, C., et al. (2009). The Anatomy of Extended Limbic Pathways in Asperger Syndrome: A Preliminary Diffusion Tensor Imaging Tractography Study. NeuroImage, 47(2), 427–434.

Roine, U., Roine, T., Salmi, J., Nieminen-von Wendt, T., Tani, P., Leppämäki, S., et al. (2015). Abnormal Wiring of the Connectome in Adults with High-Functioning Autism Spectrum Disorder. Molecular Autism, 6(1), 65.

Schumann, C., Hamstra, J., Goodlin-Jones, B., et al. (2004). The Amygdala is Enlarged in Children but not Adolescents with Autism: The Hippocampus is Enlarged at all Ages. Journal of Neuroscience, 24, 6392–6401.

Sears, L. L., Vest, C., Mohamed, S., Bailey, J., Ranson, B. J., & Piven, J. (1999). An MRI Study of the Basal Ganglia in Autism. Progress in Neuro-Psychopharmacology and Biological Psychiatry, 23(4), 613–624.

Sivapalan, S., & Aitchison, K. J. (2014). Neurological Structure Variations in Individuals with Autism Spectrum Disorder: A Review. *Klinik Psikofarmakoloji Bülteni-Bulletin of Clinical Psychopharmacology, 24*(3), 268–275.

Speirs, S. J., Rinehart, N. J., Robinson, S. R., Tonge, B. J., & Yelland, G. W. (2014). Efficacy of Cognitive Processes in Young People with High-Functioning Autism Spectrum Disorder Using a Novel Visual Information-Processing Task. *Journal of Autism and Developmental Disorders, 44*(11), 2809–2819.

Stanfield, A. C., McIntosh, A. M., Spencer, M. D., Philip, R., Gaur, S., & Lawrie, S. M. (2008). Towards a Neuroanatomy of Autism: A Systematic Review and Meta-analysis of Structural Magnetic Resonance Imaging Studies. *European Psychiatry, 23*(4), 289–299.

Travers, B. G., Tromp, D. P., Adluru, N., Lange, N., Destiche, D., Ennis, C., et al. (2015). Atypical Development of White Matter Microstructure of the Corpus Callosum in Males with Autism: A Longitudinal Investigation. *Molecular Autism, 6*(1), 15.

Travers, B. G., Adluru, N., Ennis, C., Tromp do, P. M., Destiche, D., Doran, S., et al. (2012). Diffusion Tensor Imaging in Autism Spectrum Disorder: A Review. *Autism Research, 5*(5), 280–313. doi:10.1002/aur.1243

Urbain, C. M., Pang, E. W., & Taylor, M. J. (2015). Atypical Spatiotemporal Signatures of Working Memory Brain Processes in Autism. *Translational Psychiatry, 5*(8), e617.

Wan, C. Y., & Schlaug, G. (2010). Neural Pathways for Language in Autism: The Potential for Music-Based Treatments. *Future Neurology, 5*(6), 797–805.

Wang, S. S. H., Kloth, A. D., & Badura, A. (2014). The Cerebellum, Sensitive Periods, and Autism. *Neuron, 83*(3), 518–532.

Yu, K. K., Cheung, C., Chua, S. E., & McAlonan, G. M. (2011). Can Asperger Syndrome be Distinguished from Autism? An Anatomic Likelihood Meta-Analysis of MRI Studies. *Journal of Psychiatry and Neuroscience, 36*(6), 412–421.

5

SEX DIFFERENCES IN AUTISM SPECTRUM DISORDER

Mira C. Krishnan

Introduction

Autism spectrum disorder (ASD) is a neurodevelopmental disorder that is currently estimated to affect 1:68 individuals and is characterized by deficits in social communication and interaction as well as restricted, repetitive patterns of behavior, interest, or activity (American Psychiatric Association, 2013; Christensen, Baio, Braun, et al., 2016). This CDC estimate of the prevalence of autism has increased substantially, from an initial estimate of 1:4000 in 1975 (Frieden, Jaffe, Cono, et al, 2014). Research has clearly and consistently shown that autism is more common in males than females[1] (Ferri, Abel, & Brodkin, 2018). However, two things are noteworthy about this. First, there is limited evidence the sex bias is reducing over time, possibly due to increased accuracy in detecting autism in females (Lai, Lombardo, Ayeung, et al., 2015). However, meta-analytic study of 54 studies including 53,712 autistic children, and more than 13 million children in total, suggested an overall ratio close to 3:1, statistically excluding the possibility of a 1:1 ratio (Loomes, Hull, & Mandy, 2017). Second, autism is highly heterogenous, and sex ratios are noted to differ substantially across intellectual levels, with the lowest ratios (the least overrepresentation of males) in autism associated with moderate to severe intellectual disability, and the highest ratios in intellectually normal individuals, so, depending on the subpopulation of autistic individuals being studied, the extent of the male:female bias may vary considerably (Ferri et al., 2018).

A sex difference resulting in more affected males than females is also common with other neurodevelopmental disorders, such as attention-deficit/hyperactivity disorder (ADHD) or schizophrenia, whereas other psychiatric conditions such as anxiety and depression have the opposite pattern (e.g., Supekar, Iyer, & Menon,

2017). This has led to very broad theoretical models. One of the broadest is the idea that the Y chromosome itself is a broad risk factor for neurodevelopmental problems, albeit ostensibly not for the other disorders biased in the opposite direction (Krausz, Quintana-Murci, & Forti, 2004). Contributing to this reasoning, individuals with 47, XYY karyotype have increased prevalence of multiple conditions that have a male bias, including ASD and ADHD, but not of female biased disorders such as anxiety or depression (Ross, Tartaglia, Merry, et al., 2015). The presence of not just one but several related chromosomal aneuploidies offers an interesting test case. Here, it is conceivable that the X chromosome is a protective factor, so karyotypes with more than one X chromosome would have lower rates of autism (Schaafsma & Pfaff, 2014). If an X-chromosome allele reduced the risk of autism, XX individuals would have two opportunities to acquire it. This would also be true in karyotypes other than XX with more than one X chromosome. Alternatively, it is conceivable that the Y chromosome is a *risk* factor (the opposite cases, X as a risk factor or Y as a protective factor, can be dismissed because they do not fit the sex bias data). Here, in the XY population, there is only one Y chromosome, but in karyotypes with more than one Y chromosome, there would be greater risk still, since the factor could be expressed from one or more of the Y chromosomes. Tartaglia, Wilson, Miller, et al. (2017) looked at this question in a sample of 98 individuals with XXY, XYY, and XXYY aneuploidies. This was a multisite recruitment study but did not necessarily yield a representative sample. However, in comparison to the 1.4% (1:68) base rate in the general population or the somewhat higher base rate in the 46, XY population (2.4% or 1:42), they verified rates using the Autism Diagnostic Observation Schedule (ADOS-2) of 10% in XXY, 38% in XYY, and 52% in XXYY, which would not seem to provide significant support for a protective X role and would rather argue for a risk related to the Y chromosome, with the XYY+XXYY sample having an odds ratio of 4.8:1 for autism diagnosis in comparison to XXY and more than 20 in comparison to XY. This would appear to provide more support for the model that the Y chromosome is a risk than that the X chromosome protects. There might also be a less direct link with the Y chromosome, mediated by the production or receptivity to testosterone (which is not regulated only by the Y chromosome and is present at some level in male and female individuals and in all karyotypes), for instance—something which will be investigated in greater detail in this chapter.

As initially noted, this sex effect is a fairly broad one, affecting not only autism but also ADHD, schizophrenia, and other disorders, although there is some degree of specificity, since a number of other disorders do have the opposite sex effect. This may argue that the effects under discussion are more general to this class of disorders (e.g., neurodevelopmental disorders), and less specific to autism. Critical reviews of this evidence have suggested that, while there may be some broad genetic effects, these may also interact in unique ways with factors associated with male sex that lead to the unique pattern seen in autism (Lai et al., 2015). This chapter will thus examine sex or gender differences associated specifically with autism, including proposed biological mechanisms for these differences. In this context, we will look at the Extreme Male Brain Theory, a theory of development attempting to explain the unique characteristics of the autistic brain, as well as associated diagnostic challenges. The possibility of an association between autism and transgender identity[2] will be examined, introducing a new dimension of a possible relationship between autism and sex or gender, and sexual/romantic relationships in autistic people will be considered, looking here also at the higher rate of non-heterosexual orientations in the autistic population. Finally, future directions for research in this area will be discussed.

Autism and Testosterone

Although the research is not completely consistent, there have been significant implications for testosterone on autism. Testosterone is an androgen, or sex hormone, that has organizational effects during gestation and infancy, and activation effects during puberty (Hines, Spencer, Kung, et al., 2016). Prior to puberty, testosterone is significantly elevated during two periods, both prior to the typical age of autism diagnosis. The first is gestational, from 8 to 24 weeks of gestation, but particularly during 8 to 16 weeks of gestation, also termed fetal or prenatal testosterone. The second surge occurs in infancy, peaking around three months of age, and is sometimes referred to as "mini puberty," or postnatal testosterone.

Research suggests that differences in fetal, or prenatal, testosterone are associated with autism and autistic traits (e.g., Baron-Cohen, Auyeung, Nørgaard-Pedersen, et al., 2015). Studies have also found that *post*natal testosterone correlates with autistic traits such as eye contact, but two of three studies found it does not correlate with autism itself (Aeyeung, Ahluwalia, Thomson, et al., 2012; Kung et al., 2016; Saenz & Alexander, 2013). One of these studies, that of Aeyeung et al., is notable in that both prenatal and postnatal testosterone were studied in the same children, with a finding that the former predicted autism and the latter did not, arguing for a critical developmental window during gestation (but not postnatally) in which testosterone impacts may result in ASD.

There is a question, to some extent, as to whether all cases of autism begin gestationally, or whether some autistic children develop autism not prenatally but in infancy. In autistic regression, children lose speech and sometimes have increased stereotyped activity, or behavioral or vegetative changes, typically between 12 and 24 months of age, and it is not completely clear whether all of these children displayed autistic signs prior to this regression or only afterwards (Al-Backer, 2015). Some percentage (but not all) of these cases are caused by epileptic encephalopathy, a class of disorders in which continuous epileptiform activity during sleep impairs development, with or without the presence of overt seizure symptoms outside of developmental issues, but the cause of the remaining cases is unclear (Srivastava & Sahin, 2017). Given that testosterone surges, not only prenatally but also postnatally, and the association between autism and prenatal testosterone is a moderately strong one, this does raise the question of whether regression is related to testosterone or not. This could mean regression causes a new onset of autism, in which case, the question becomes, if testosterone is crucial in autism that happens prenatally, is it also crucial in this "postnatal onset" of autism? It could also be that these children were already autistic prior to regression, in which case the question would be, did the worsening of symptoms at regression occur via a similar mechanism to the initial presence of symptoms? The studies above, which do not find a role for postnatal testosterone, seem to initially say "no" to both questions. However, postnatal testosterone was measured around three months of age, consistent with the typical timing of "mini-puberty," and not within 12 to 24 months of age, the time of interest for autistic regression, and so this research might have missed any relationship between autistic regression and testosterone. To the author's knowledge, there is no research published investigating the role of testosterone in autistic regression. There may certainly be no such association. A recent chart review study found that developmental regression in autism was associated with familial history of autoimmune disorders and, of note, most of the autoimmune diseases of interest were actually more common in females, not males (Scott et al., 2017). However, given that testosterone is implicated in non-regressive autism, this is a point that should be clarified.

Other factors associated with fetal testosterone are also associated with autism. The ratio of lengths of the second and fourth manual digits has a well-established association with testosterone availability and/or receptivity (Manning et al., 1998). Teatero and Netley (2013) conducted a meta-analysis on findings of this marker in autism, which included nine prior studies. They found an overall effect of $d = -0.43$, $p = 0.013$, a fairly substantial finding, with a more pronounced finding for the right hand than the left. Of note, most of these studies had largely male samples, with limited ability to make inferences about sex differences in the ratio. A more recent study did actually find associations in opposite directions in male and female autistic children, so more work may need to be done (Schieve, Tian, Dowling, et al., 2018). However, one of the prior nine studies in the Teatero and Netley analysis also found results in the opposite direction to all the other studies (that is, a digit ratio consistent with low, rather than high, testosterone). This emphasizes the need for meta-analysis, especially when studies have small, non-representative samples. Medical conditions such as hirsutism and polycystic ovary syndrome (PCOS) that are associated with testosterone are likewise more common in autistic individuals and, tellingly, the presence of these disorders in mothers is predictive of autism in offspring, so this may be a possible proxy for androgen levels during pregnancy (Ingudomnukul et al., 2007; Lee et al., 2017).

The Extreme Male Brain Theory of Autism

The argument in favor of this association culminates in the Extreme Male Brain Theory (EMBT), proposed by Baron-Cohen (2010). This theory posits a central organizing principle in autism, in which autistic people have cognitive strengths and weaknesses that can, respectively, be categorized as systemizing and empathizing skills. Empathizing skills in Baron-Cohen's model include both cognitive and affective empathy. Systemizing is "the drive to analyze or construct systems," essentially a predisposition to rule-governed processes or structures (Baron-Cohen, 2010). Baron-Cohen was not the first to propose a deficit in the former area, but he was among the first to demonstrate that understanding autism required both recognizing the *deficit* in empathizing, and also the *strength* in systemizing.

Prior to the DSM-5 autism was also thought to have three core features (not two), but Baron-Cohen argued that "difficulties in social development" and deficits "in the development of communication" were interrelated, because "communication is always social" (2010). As a result, he argued, one of the three symptoms was redundant (2010). This contributed strongly to the reduction to two major diagnostic symptoms of autism in the DSM-5 definition of autism spectrum disorder (American Psychiatric Association, 2013). Careful readers will note that the first DSM-5 criterion for autism, "Persistent deficits in social communication and social interaction across multiple contexts," is clearly a deficit in what Baron-Cohen calls empathizing, and the second, "Restricted, repetitive patterns of behavior, interests, or activities," is a predilection towards systemizing. Again, here Baron-Cohen's analysis is helpful in understanding symptoms based on their nature rather than their appearance. Problems using speech or the body *to communicate* are *empathizing* issues, but predilection to using either in non-communicative ways (such as "stimming" or stereotypies) are *systemizing* issues. Other leaders in the field also influenced the process of reducing the number of diagnostic criteria for ASD. Notably, the two DSM-5 criteria also match extremely well to the major scoring categories in both the original and second editions of the Autism Diagnostic Observation Schedule (ADOS/ADOS-2), which itself dates back to the 1980s (Lord, Rutter, Goode, et al., 1989).

Aside from distilling the three prior symptoms of autism into two symptoms that are more clearly conceptually grounded, Baron-Cohen went one step further, demonstrating that these two symptoms represent an exaggeration of subtle sex differences in the cognitive architectures of non-autistic[3] males and females (Baron-Cohen, 2010). That is, these skills differ slightly in the non-autistic population, such that male individuals have stronger systemizing and weaker empathizing than female individuals, but autistic people of all sexes/genders in turn have even stronger systemizing and even weaker empathizing. They thus have an "extreme" version of the "male" pattern—that is, with "A" representing autistic people irrespective of sex, "M" representing non-autistic males, and "F" representing non-autistic females, empathizing skills have the pattern F > M > A, but systemizing skills have the pattern A > M > F. Ferri et al. (2018) reviewed the literature vis-à-vis support for this Extreme Male Brain Theory. They noted that questionnaire instruments that measure empathizing and systemizing, the Empathizing and Systemizing Quotient Instruments, validate the F > M > A and A > M > F patterns, respectively. They noted as well the support for this argument in an androgen-based model of autism, as described in the prior section. They also found subtle neuroanatomical differences at the level of organization of functional networks, which are slightly sexually dimorphic. These followed an exaggerated male-typical organization in autism (that is, again, these differences fell into an F > M > A or A > M > F pattern), but they noted that other studies found that there might not be an *exaggerated male* cortical organization, but rather a more general dysfunction of sex differentiation of cortical development (the author is not aware of examination of this question at the level of meta-analysis, and the current primary source studies may not yet support such an analysis).

Social Camouflaging in Autistic Females

As noted previously, there is limited evidence that the male:female ratio in ASD may be converging, although the preponderance of evidence does suggest a likely bias towards males. One possible explanation put forward is an underdiagnosis of autistic females relative to autistic males (Zwaigenbaum, Bryson, Szatmari, et al., 2012); that is, diagnosis is more often missed, or a false negative occurs more often, in females than males, with an improving course for this effect in newer studies, due to improved standardization and sophistication of diagnostic practices.

Recent research has emphasized a possible explanatory factor that has come to be called "social camouflaging," and which is more common in autistic females than males. Lai et al. describe this process as "masking and/or developing compensatory strategies" that reduce the perception or impact of autism symptoms, particularly in the arena of social interaction, and include this among features that may differ in the presentation of female and male autism (2015). These may be present even at a very early age, in the form of stronger eye contact, more gestures, more basic social reciprocity, even though these same skills may still be deficient in subtler ways. Some of these features were seen in the Zwaigenbaum, Bryson, Szatmari et al. (2012), research even in infancy, suggesting a lesser role for socialization and a greater fundamental difference between autistic males and females.

Consequently, researchers have indicated that questionnaire instruments such as the Autism Spectrum Quotient (AQ-10) or the Vineland Adaptive Behavior Scale, or even specialized diagnostic interviews such as the Autism Diagnostic Inventory (ADI-R), may ask certain questions in a biased fashion that is more likely to identify autistic males than females (e.g., Murray, Booth, Auyeung, et al., 2017; Ratto, Kenworthy, Yerys, et al., 2017). Interestingly, the Ratto et al. study considered both the ADI-R and Autism Diagnostic Observation Schedule (ADOS-2) and found small effects on the ADI-R compared to other instruments and none on the ADOS-2, in comparison to the larger questionnaire instrument effects. Another study looked at a computerized version of the ADOS-2, and likewise found that, while there were differences in gestural use particularly, ADOS-2 scores themselves did not differ significantly (Rynkiewicz, Schuller, Marchi, et al., 2016).

None of these studies were intended to engage in a head-to-head comparison of these instruments or techniques, but the informal pattern seems to be that instruments that were more in-depth and reliant on clinician expertise, such as the ADOS-2 and ADI-R, were relatively buffered from misdiagnosis on the basis of social camouflaging. Discussion of these results sometimes leads to advancing the idea that autism in females is vastly underdiagnosed, and a few researchers have gone so far as to argue for a "female autism phenotype," which might mean that autism might have fundamentally different diagnostic criteria in females than males (Whyte & Scherf, 2018). A major problem with this is that central assertions are far from being uniform. For instance, Whyte and Scherf (2018) posit that deficient eye gaze following a behavior "may not be a part of the female autism phenotype," but most clinicians who have used the ADOS or ADOS-2 in clinical practice, as well as the ADOS standardization sample itself, could immediately point out that it is not always part of the male autism phenotype, either, and is at least sometimes present in autistic females.

Further, the small or absent effects with the ADOS-2 and ADI-R would seem to argue against this, since these are the instruments in dominant use in specialty settings, and the ones most commonly considered "gold standards," and neither is sex-adjusted. However, in considering the overall diagnostic practice of autism, screening instruments could still be a significant concern, since children who screen negative for autism with community providers, such as pediatricians, family physicians, or psychologists in more general practice, may not be referred for specialized assessments, and may thus never even undergo the ADOS-2 or ADI-R.

Autism and Transgender Identity

Case reports of co-occurrence of autism and transgender identity in the published literature date back as far as 1997, when researchers from Göteburg University reported the case of a 12-year-old youth, assigned female at birth (or AFAB)[4] with both conditions (Landén & Rasmussen, 1997). The youth had delayed speech but normalized intellect, and began expressing gender identity differing from that assigned at birth, at age 8. The authors noted successful treatment of selective mutism and obsessive behaviors associated with autism via clomipramine, but rather than gender dysphoria abating "an exacerbation, or more readily discernable symptoms, of the gender dysphoria occurred." Although the authors did not consider the current view—that transgender identity is not, itself, a mental illness—they otherwise considered diagnostic questions that remain essentially current. That is, they considered the possibility that transgender identity in the case being studied might be understood as an "inherent" aspect of autism, a form of obsessive/compulsive behavior but not part of the autism, or a true, independent comorbidity. Although there is now general acceptance that being transgender is not a mental illness (see American Psychiatric Association, 2013), the question remains active as to whether gender dysphoria can sometimes be an atypical symptom of autism in the absence of being transgender, and/or whether transgender identity is more common in autistic individuals, and vice versa.

A team of Dutch researchers working with transgender youth reported a case series of 204 youth seen in a gender identity clinic (de Vries, Noens, Cohen-Kettenis, et al., 2010). They found a rate of autism of 7.8% in this sample—substantially higher than the general population rate of 1.4%. A second study examined ASD symptoms via questionnaire responses in transgender children, autistic children, and children who were neither (van der Miesen et al., 2017). The transgender children showed elevated levels on all the autism symptomatology indicators but not the total instrument score, and the authors noted that the elevation in domains beyond stereotypy and resistance to change made it difficult to explain the findings on the basis of overlap between adjustment issues related to transgender identity (e.g., resistance to change in terms of expectations related to gendered behavior) alone. Strang, Kenworthy, Dominska, et al. (2014) conducted similar research in not only children with ASD but also children with ADHD, and found elevations in gender variance for both the ASD and ADHD samples. Akgül, Ayaz, Yildirim, and Fis (2018) used another autism-specific instrument, the Social Responsiveness Scale (SRS), and found this elevated in transgender youth. Heylens, Aspeslagh, Dierickx, et al. (2018) looked at a series of adults seen in a gender identity clinic, again in the Netherlands. For a subset of 75 individuals, they used autism questionnaires and they also reviewed charts for a larger sample of 532 individuals to identify prior autism diagnoses. Both suggested higher than expected rates of autism. With the subset completing questionnaires, 5% scored in a range potentially consistent with autism, and 6% of the larger sample were found to have prior certain diagnosis of autism.

Several researchers, notably Turban and van Schalkwyk (2018), have urged caution, noting that these studies are methodologically flawed on multiple fronts, including the kinds of control groups considered, as well as failing to clearly confirm that individuals were transgender and/or autistic, e.g., by over-use of questionnaire instruments that may or may not be sensitive to these conditions but are not specific to them (none of the studies found a negative effect, although publication bias against negative results might contribute to this). The above studies were primarily done by experts in the area of gender identity, as opposed to autism, and so none of these studies had involved directly validating autism, for instance, via the combination of the Autism Diagnostic Observation Schedule and Autism Diagnostic Interview, but in studies concerning youth some researchers do question whether gender-variant youth will ultimately continue to identify as transgender or not.

Autism and Sexual and Romantic Relationships

As one last consideration related to gender and sex, a topic that merits at least brief consideration is the romantic and sexual experiences of autistic people. With the broad question of adult sexual or romantic relationships, these results are quite variable. Marriage, Wolverton, and Marriage (2009) examined 80 individuals via chart review. They included both individuals diagnosed in child-hood and those diagnosed in adulthood, with average ages 19–37 years old for those diagnosed in childhood, and 19-55 for those diagnosed in adulthood. These results suggested that very few individuals were satisfactorily married, although a few were. In this study, a Likert scale rating current social relation-ships quality from 1 to 5, with only the score of 5 requiring even one "close and enduring friendship," had a mean score of 2.09 in autistic individuals with IQ≥70 and 1.08 in those with IQ<70, and no friendships during this timeframe would seem to bode poorly for the likelihood of attaining marriage, at least in the near term. Howlin and Moss (2012) reviewed 23 similar small data sets for adult outcomes, including the previously referenced study, and 12 of these stud-ies had data on individuals being in a long-term relationship or marriage history. The rates for this figure ranged from 0% to 38%, and the authors inferred an average of 14% across the sample. Gotham, Marvin, Taylor, et al. (2015) did a subsequent online surveying of a much larger sample of 255 autistic adults, over a broader age range (18–71 years of age), and considering a broad range of abilities, including a significant sample of individuals with legal guardians in adulthood. In their sample, of those who were their own guardian a much higher percentage, 47%, were living with a spouse or partner, but only 2% of those had legal guardians.

None of these prior studies were designed to be representative samples from which population inferences could be drawn. However, one final study *was* based on an epidemiological survey of all autistic children in the American state of Utah, born between 1960 and 1984 (Farley, Cottle, Bilder, et al., 2018). Diagnoses were clinically verified in the majority of cases (<10% were based on a "records-based re-evaluation process"). At follow-up, the participants ranged from 22 to 51 years old, and were 55% of the original sample. By the time of the study follow-up, 25% had some experience dating, with the majority of these having only dated in group and never 1:1 settings. With that being said, 16% (of the full follow-up sample) had some kind of past or present romantic relationship, 7% had a romantic relationship lasting at least six months, and 5% were or had previously been married. While this sample is representative only of autistic adults living in one part of the US, the totality of the evidence does suggest low rates of marriage and/or romantic relationships in this population. However, none of these studies reported in a systematic way the goals or preferences of autistic people in this regard. These studies also do not discuss in detail differences over time. In cross-sectional research, this necessarily confounds the intraindividual improvement over the lifespan with the cohort differences due to changes in society, availability of interventions, etc. However, in research considering other adult outcomes such as employment, there is actually not encouraging data in this regard. For instance, employment outcomes in some studies do not seem to improve over the lifespan, but actually worsen, particularly in women, overlying a general pattern of worse outcomes for women, which were also mirrored in much of the above research (Taylor & Mailick, 2014). Besides higher marriage rates in male autistic people, marriage rates were higher in intellectually normal autistic individuals and, probably not surprisingly, those who did not have legal guardians appointed for them.

These studies did not discuss explicitly the sexual orientation of individuals, although inclusive terminology, such as having a "partner" rather than a spouse, was used in some of the studies. It is worth noting in this regard that, in the United States, same-sex marriage was not legally recognized in any state prior to 2004, but rapidly became legal during the period in which many of these studies were being conducted, and same-sex marriage was legal throughout the United States beginning in 2015, again, by the time of publication of the most recent of the studies above (*Obergefell v. Hodges*, 2015). In the non-autistic population, lesbian, gay, and bisexual individuals make up a small subset of the population, but there is at least some evidence that this differs in the autistic population. George and Stokes (2018), in a study comparing 309 autistic adults and 310 non-autistic adults, found reported sexual attraction that was not heterosexual (this was a free response item, "I consider my sexual orientation as . . . ") to be substantially larger in the autistic group: 69.7% of that group vs. 30.3% of the non-autistic group. Notably, the non-autistic percentage in this study is substantially higher than population estimates, but the difference is striking, and endorsed not only higher rates of gay, lesbian, and bisexual identity, but also higher rates of asexuality. Rudolph, Lundin, Ahs, et al. (2018), in a large general adult population (47,356 respondents), examined association between self-reported autistic traits, again via AQ-10, and sexual orientation. The George and Stokes (2018) findings suggested higher rates of homosexuality (or gay/lesbian identity), more particularly bisexuality, and most particularly of sexualities other than hetero-, homo-, or bisexuality. Rudolph et al. (2018) did not find an elevated odds ratio for endorsing homosexuality, but found a 1.73 adjusted odds ratio for bisexuality and a 3.05 adjusted odds ratio for sexuality other than hetero-, homo-, or bisexuality.

These studies were in adults, and one additional study of note found similar findings in youth. May, Pang, and Williams (2017) reported on a comparison of 94 autistic adolescents, age 14–15, with a large sample of non-autistic peers. The autistic male respondents were less likely to describe purely heterosexual orientation and at a trend level (p = 0.06) more likely to not feel any attraction to others. The females, in contrast, had an odds ratio of reporting purely hetero-sexual attraction of 0.14, of bisexual attraction 6.05, and of being unsure of their attraction 10.44—all statistically significant. Although the sample was small, no autistic participant described a purely homosexual orientation.

Although a direct connection between the role of fetal testosterone and/ or the extreme male brain theory and sexual orientation, e.g., attraction to females would be higher in autistic individuals irrespective of the sex/gender of the autistic individuals, cannot be ruled out based on the current data, none of the data seem to argue in a straightforward way for this. Rather, the most prominent pattern aggregated across these studies is that sexual orientation is more varied in autism than it is in the general population. Apropos the prior discussion of autism and transgender identity, it is noteworthy that similar find-ings are found in the transgender population, compared to those who are not transgender—a large national U.S. sample found more than half of the respond-ents endorsed a sexuality other than purely heterosexual[5] or purely homosexual (Grant et al., 2011. Some researchers reviewing this finding in the transgender population go as far as the conclusion that the well-accepted nosology of het-erosexuality, homosexuality, and bisexuality is itself cis-centric—that is, that it is formulated on the experiences of people who are not transgender and may not be expected to be the appropriate framework for understanding sexuality in many transgender people (Johnson, 2015). Were the findings of these studies in the autistic population replicated, the question of co-occurrence of autism and transgender identity aside, the conclusion may ultimately be warranted that the traditional nosology of sexual orientations is not only cis-centric but also framed on a neurotypical, or at least non-autistic, basis, and may not be a good way of understanding the sexuality experiences of many autistic people.

Future Directions

The topics considered in this chapter are noteworthy in that, even at the most basic level of population epidemiology, much work remains to be done. With respect to epidemiology, although autism does appear to be more common in males than females (in the non-transgender population), how large this discrepancy is remains unclear. Given the existing research indicating that sex differences are attenuated in intellectually disabled autistic people, future research should continue to attend to the intersection of sex/gender and intellectual level with respect to the population epidemiology. Research in which autism is not diagnosed by expert clinicians using gold standard instruments such as the Autism Diagnostic Inventory (ADI-R) and Autism Diagnostic Observation Schedule (ADOS-2) should also be evaluated critically for the possibility of under-diagnosis of autism in females due to social camouflaging as well as clinician or instrument bias. To the extent that it is becoming increasingly clear that some level of difference in prevalence by sex is present, it becomes appropriate to shift the question from one of "if" to one of "why" or "how." Is this a very general factor, such as the Y chromosome as a risk; other sex-linked effects; an organizing effect of testosterone; or some combination of these and other factors? If very general factors prevail, why do they result in autism in some cases and other conditions that appear qualitatively very different from autism in others?

With respect to testosterone, replication and clarification on the role of postnatal testosterone is needed. Given the unclear basis for autistic regression, testosterone through 24 months of age should be considered, in samples that include children who ultimately display autistic regression, to determine whether testosterone plays a role in this poorly understood process. Research should also consider the role of testosterone receptivity as well as levels, since both vary in the population. This research should also consider multiple neurodevelopmental populations—that is, why does the Extreme Male Brain Theory apply to autism but not, apparently, to attention-deficit/hyperactivity disorder (ADHD) or schizophrenia?

With respect to gender and sexual diversity in the autistic population, more research is certainly needed to determine the basic questions of whether and/or to what extent transgender identity or non-heterosexual orientation are associated with autism. In the research assessing a relationship between transgender identity and autism, issues of autistic traits as opposed to autism, and gender variance as opposed to transgender identity, merit careful consideration, both separately and together. For instance, the unusual nature of restricted interests is important to understanding the difference between an autistic trait and a pattern of preference. A 6-year-old "obsessed with Disney princesses" (currently a reasonably common interest in young girls in the USA) might not be said to an autistic trait at all, no matter how intense the interest. A youth might spend a substantial amount of time practicing, training, watching, or attending football games, discussing football, even daydreaming about playing, but this would not usually be an autistic trait. On the other hand, the author recalls an autistic boy she evaluated who could draw any NFL helmet but did not show much interest in playing or talking about football outside of this kind of rote, statistical information, which would generally be considered an autistic trait. The gender typicality of the behavior may or may not relate to the question of transgender identity (interests atypical to birth-assigned sex are neither necessary nor sufficient as markers of transgender identity in themselves) but is completely irrelevant from an autism perspective. It would be circular to call an interest in Disney princesses an autistic trait in transgender girls but not cisgender girls, or likewise an interest in football an autistic trait in transgender boys but not cisgender boys. Yet, there is a history of doing exactly this in transgender research. A well-known example is a purported construct in transgender women, autogynephilia ("an erotic interest in the thought or image of oneself as a woman")—it only later became evident that this construct was similarly present in non-transgender women, questioning whether it has anything to do with being transgender at all (Moser, 2009). Much as research should look at ASD alongside conditions such as ADHD and schizophrenia, which also have a gender bias, research in gender identity and autism may require designs with more comparison groups and should make sure to include individuals with none of the conditions of interest.

The role of politicization cannot be avoided in consideration of these questions. In the USA, healthcare services have a history of being denied to both autistic and transgender individuals, and this has led to legislation requiring insurance coverage for care in 46 states and the District of Columbia requiring insurance-reimbursed care for autistic people, and in five states and the District of Columbia for transgender people, as well as actions at the federal level in both areas via the Affordable Care Act (Huetteman, 2014; State Initiatives, 2017). The complex politics and social changes involved are outside the scope of this chapter, but each of these, as well as inherent biases at the researcher, institutional, field, and funding mechanism levels, impact the quality of research, and understanding is likely to continue to be muddled while these identities remain so strongly politicized. On a practical level, care for both autistic and transgender individuals tends to be viewed as requiring a high degree of specialization, and there exist few scientists or practitioners who are well versed in both areas. Similarly, at the level of community engagement and activism, awareness of autism could improve the LGBTQ community and awareness of gender and sexual diversity could improve the autistic community.

Finally, relationship/marital outcomes in autistic people, even in the subgroups with most positive outcomes (e.g., cisgender, heterosexual, intellectually normal autistic males), are poor, at least by definitions applied from the outside (i.e., in comparison to the non-autistic population). As noted above, alongside the findings of poor relationship/marital outcomes, many autistic adults experience extreme social isolation, and support for achieving relational goals, however autistic people define them, should be a priority for supporting the autistic adult population. Here, there is a fairly consistent finding of worse outcomes for autistic females, and attention should be given to a male-centric understanding of autism, a limited understanding of the role of social camouflaging in female adult autistic outcomes, and the potential for different sexuality experiences in autistic females, so that both research and supports designed for the adult autistic population should explicitly include autistic people of all sexes/genders.

It is noteworthy that, in particular areas such as consideration of associations between transgender identity and autism, and the romantic/social lives of autistic people, a number of studies referenced in this chapter are very recent as of this writing. This represented not merely a desire to provide readers with the most up-to-date information available, but indeed a recognition that research is so nascent in some of these areas that a focus on very recent publications was unavoidable. This increases the likelihood that findings summarized here may not represent the future state of knowledge, but, given the often inconsistent or preliminary findings, this should be welcomed, even if the result may be that this chapter is more quickly susceptible to becoming dated than other parts of this book. Whatever the ultimate findings, and whether the relationships between sex (or gender) and autism are highly specific or more generalized, further research in all of these areas has the potential to improve our understanding of sex, gender, and autism.

Notes

1 Some argue that the term "sex" refers to the genetic, or biological substrate, and "gender" to expression, including socialization effects, but in practice what is biological and what is socialized is often less than clear. A later section of this chapter discusses possible associations between autism and transgender identity, and at that point this issue will be revisited, but for simplicity, for the sake of the rest of the chapter, "male" and "female sex" will be used to indicate males and females who are neither transgender nor intersex, and thus presumed to, respectively, have XY and XX chromosomes, to have been assigned, respectively, male and female sexes at birth, and to continue to endorse these sexes or genders at the time they were being studied, although this may occasionally have been untrue for the study participants in studies cited prior to the discussion of transgender identity.

2 This term is also clumsy, and it bears explanation in passing. The choice of the term "transgender identity" was chosen in this book because the most commonly used noun describing this entity, "transgenderism," is increasingly seen as offensive within the transgender community. The phrase "gender identity" is also used, but gender identity, referring to one's internal sense of gender, is an experience shared by both those whose gender identity differs from their sex assigned at birth (transgender individuals) and those who do not (cisgender individuals, or individuals who are not transgender), so transgender identity is a reference to the phenomenon of individuals whose gender identity differs from their sex assigned at birth.

3 The term "neurotypical" is also used, and "neurodiverse" to represent autistic people, but then it is unclear, for instance, if individuals with ADHD are neurotypical or neurodiverse.

4 Since transgender identity is a small portion of this chapter, as outlined in a prior note, the author elected to use the term "sex" with an assumption of individuals who were neither transgender nor intersex, up until this point. For this part of the discussion, however, "AFAB" refers to all individuals who were assigned a female sex at birth, some of whom may be transgender, and may have a gender identity that is male or nonbinary, and "AMAB" refers to all individuals who were assigned a male sex at birth. Again, some of these individuals may be transgender and may have female or

nonbinary gender identities. Further, in the DSM-IV to DSM-5 transition, much as the prior autism classifications were replaced with autism spectrum disorder, the prior diagnosis of gender identity disorder was replaced with gender dysphoria. The central difference between the prior and current diagnostic entities is that being transgender is viewed as a part of normal human variation and not a mental illness. However, due to lack of societal acceptance, stigmatization, discrimination, and exploitation, some transgender people experience adjustment symptoms, which are subsumed in the diagnosis of gender dysphoria. This diagnosis is often also used to allow transgender people to access medical services such as hormone replacement therapy or surgical interventions, but this is largely beyond the scope of this chapter. Readers are referred to the preface to the DSM-5 gender dysphoria section for further discussion of this change in conceptualization (American Psychiatric Association, 2013).

5 Here "heterosexual" would refer to a transgender person with a binary gender identity of male/man or female/woman who was attracted to the other binary gender identity, i.e., a transgender woman who is attracted to men or a transgender man who is attracted to women. The terms are used with respect to the gender identity of the transgender person, not the sex assigned at birth. An added complexity, however, is that the terms "heterosexual" and "homosexual" have unclear meanings when applied to transgender people whose gender identity is something other than binary male/man or woman/female.

References

Akgül, G. Y., Ayaz, A. B., Yildirim, B, et al. (2018). Autistic Traits and Executive Functions in Children and Adolescents with Gender Dysphoria. *Journal of Sex & Marital Therapy*, epub ahead of print. Retrieved from https://doi.org/10.1080/0092623X.2018.1437489

Al-Backer, N. B. (2015). Developmental Regression in Autism Spectrum Disorder. *Sudanese Journal of Pediatrics*, *15*, 21–26.

American Psychiatric Association. (2013). *Diagnostic and Statistical Manual of Mental Disorders* (5th ed.). Arlington, VA: American Psychiatric Publishing.

Auyeung, B., Ahluwalia, J., Thomson, L., et al. (2012). Prenatal Versus Postnatal Sex Steroid Hormone Effects on Autistic Traits in Children at 18 to 24 Months of Age. *Molecular Autism*, *3*, 17.

Baron-Cohen, S. (2010). Empathizing, Systemizing, and the Extreme Male Brain Theory of Autism. *Progress in Brain Research*, *186*, 167–175.

Baron-Cohen, S., Auyeung, B., Nørgaard-Pedersen, B., et al. (2015). Elevated Fetal Steroidogenic Activity in Autism. *Molecular Psychiatry*, *20*, 369–376.

Christensen D. L., Baio J., Braun K. V., et al. (2016). Prevalence and Characteristics of Autism Spectrum Disorder Among Children Aged 8 Years—Autism and Developmental Disabilities Monitoring Network. *Morbidity and Mortality Weekly Report Surveillance Summaries*, *65*, 1–23. Atlanta, GA: Centers for Disease Control and Prevention.

de Vries, A. L., Noens, I. L. J., Cohen-Kettenis, P. T., et al. (2010). Autism Spectrum Disorders in Gender Dysphoric Children and Adolescents. *Journal of Autism and Developmental Disorders*, *40*, 930–936.

Farley, M., Cottle, K. J., Bilder, D., et al. (2018). Mid-Life Social Outcomes for a Population-Based Sample of Adults with ASD. *Autism Research*, 11, 142–152.

Ferri, S. L., Abel, T., & Brodkin, E. S. (2018). Sex Differences in Autism: A Review. *Current Psychiatry Reports*, *20*, 9.

Frieden, T. R., Jaffe, H. W., Cono, J., et al. (2014). Prevalence of Autism Spectrum Disorder Among Children Aged 8 Years—Autism and Developmental Disabilities Monitoring Network, 11 Sites, United States, 2010. *Morbidity and Mortality Weekly Report Surveillance Summaries*, *63*, 1–22. Atlanta, GA: Centers for Disease Control and Prevention.

George, R., & Stokes, M. A. (2018). Sexual Orientation in Autism Spectrum Disorder. *Autism Research*, *11*, 133–141.

Gotham, K., Marvin, A. R., Taylor, J. L., et al. (2015). Characterizing the Daily Life, Needs, and Priorities of Adults with ASD from Interactive Autism Network Data. *Autism*, *19*, 794–804.

Grant, J. M., Mottet, L., Tanis, J., Harrison, J., Herman, J. L., & Keisling, M. (2011). *Injustice at Every Turn: A Report of the National Transgender Discrimination Survey*. Washington, DC: National Center for Transgender Equality and National Gay and Lesbian Task Force.

Heylens, G., Aspeslagh, L., Dierickx, J., et al. (2018). The Co-occurrence of Gender Dysphoria and Autism Spectrum Disorder in Adults: An Analysis of Cross-Sectional and Clinical Chart Data. *Journal of Autism and Developmental Disorders*, *48*, 2217–2223.

Hines, M., Spencer, D., Kung, K. T. F., et al. (2016). The Early Postnatal Period, Mini-Puberty, Provides a Window on the Role of Testosterone in Human Neuro-behavioural Development. *Current Opinion in Neurobiology*, *38*, 69–73.

Howlin, P., & Moss, P. (2012). Adults with Autism Spectrum Disorders. *Canadian Journal of Psychiatry*, *57*, 275–283.

Huetteman, E. (2014). D.C. Insurance Must Cover Treatment for Transgender Residents, Mayor Says. *New York Times*. Retrieved from www.nytimes.com/2014/02/28/us/dc-insurance-must-cover-treatment-for-transgender-residents-mayor-says.html

Ingudomnukul, E., Baron-Cohen, S., Wheelwright, S., & Knickmeyer, R. (2007). Elevated Rates of Testosterone-Related Disorders in Women with Autism Spectrum Conditions. *Hormones and Behaviour*, *51*, 597–604.

Johnson, A. H. (2015). Beyond Inclusion: Thinking Toward a Transfeminist Methodology. *Advances in Gender Research*, *20*, 21–41.

Krausz, C., Quintana-Murci, L., & Forti, G. (2004). Y Chromosome Polymorphisms in Medicine. *Annals of Medicine*, *36*, 573–583.

Kung, K. T., Constantinescu, M., Browne, W. V., Noorderhaven, R. M., & Hines, M. (2016). No Relationship Between Early Postnatal Testosterone Concentrations and Autistic Traits in 18 to 30-Month-Old Children. *Molecular Autism*, *7*, 15.

Lai, M.-C., Lombardo, M. V., Auyeung, B., et al. (2015). Sex/Gender Differences and Autism: Setting the Scene for Future Research. *Journal of the American Academy of Child and Adolescent Psychiatry*, *54*, 11–24.

Landén, M. & Rasmussen, P. (1997). Gender Identity Disorder in a girl with Autism—A Case Report. *European Child & Adolescent Psychiatry*, *6*, 170–173.

Lee, B. K., Arver, S., Widman, L., Gardner, R. M., Magnusson, C., Dalman, C., & Kosidou, K. (2017). Maternal Hirsutism and Autism Spectrum Disorders in Offspring. *Autism Research*, *10*, 1544–1546.

Loomes, R., Hull, L., & Mandy, W. P. L. (2017). What Is the Male-to-Female Ratio in Autism Spectrum Disorder? A Systematic Review and Meta-Analysis. *Journal of the American Academy of Child and Adolescent Psychiatry*, *56*, 466–474.

Lord, C., Rutter, M., Goode, S., et al. (1989). Autism Diagnostic Observation Schedule: A Standardized Observation of Communicative and Social Behavior. *Journal Autism and Developmental Disorders*, *19*, 185–212.

Manning, J. T., Scutt, D., Wilson, J., & Lewis-Jones, D. I. (1998). The Ratio of 2nd to 4th Digit Length: A Predictor of Sperm Numbers and Concentrations of Testosterone, Luteinizing Hormone and Estrogen. *Human Reproduction, 13*, 3000–3004.

Marriage, S., Wolverton, A., & Marriage, K. (2009). Autism Spectrum Disorder Grown Up: A Chart Review of Adult Functioning. *Journal of the Canadian Academy of Child and Adolescent Psychiatry, 18*, 322–328.

May, T., Pang, K. C., & Williams, K. (2017). Brief Report: Sexual Attraction and Relationships in Adolescents with Autism. *Journal of Autism and Developmental Disorders, 47*, 1910–1916.

Moser, C. (2009). Autogynephilia in Women. *Journal of Homosexuality, 56*, 539–547.

Murray, A. L., Booth, T., Auyeung, B., McKenzie, K., & Kuenssberg, R. (2017). Investigating Sex Bias in the AQ-10: A Replication Study. *Assessment*. Retrieved from: https://doi-org.proxy1.cl.msu.edu/10.1177/1073191117733548

Obergefell v. Hodges, 135 U.S. 2071 (2015).

Ratto, A. B., Kenworthy, L., Yerys, B. E., et al. (2017). What About the Girls? Se-Based Differences in Autistic Traits and Adaptive Skills. *Journal of Autism and Developmental Disorders, 48*, 1698–1711.

Ross, J. L., Tartaglia, N., Merry, D. E., et al. (2015). Behavioral Phenotypes in Males with XYY and Possible Role of Increased NLGN4Y Expressin in Autism Features. *Genes, Brain, and Behavior, 14*, 137–144.

Rudolph, C. E. S., Lundin, A., Ahs, J. W., Dalman, C., & Kosidou, K. (2018). Brief Report: Sexual Orientation in Individuals with Autistic Traits: Population Based Study of 47,000 Adults in Stockholm County. *Journal of Autism and Developmental Disorders, 48*, 619–624.

Rynkiewicz, A., Schuller, B., Marchi, E., et al. (2016). An Investigation of the "Female Camouflage Effect" in Autism Using a Computerized ADOS-2 and a Test of Sex/Gender Differences. *Molecular Autism, 7*, 1–8.

Saenz, J., & Alexander, G. M. (2013). Digit Ratios (2D:4D), Postnatal Testosterone and Eye Contact in Toddlers. *Biological Psychiatry, 94*, 106–108.

Schaafsma, S. M., & Pfaff, D. W. (2014). Etiologies Underlying Sex Differences in Autism Spectrum Disorders. *Frontiers in Neuroendocrinology, 35*, 205–271.

Schieve, L. A., Tian, L., Dowling, N., et al. (2018). Associations Between the 2nd to 4th Digit Ratio and Autism Spectrum Disorder in Population-Based Samples of Boys and Girls: Findings from the Study to Explore Early Development. *Journal of Autism and Developmental Disorders*. Retrieved from https://doi.org/10.1007/s10803-018-3495-z.

Scott, O., Shi, D., Andriashek, D., Clark, B., & Goez, H. R. (2017). Clinical Clues for Autoimmunity and Neuroinflammation in Patients with Autistic Regression. *Developmental Medicine & Child Neurology, 59*, 947–951.

Srivastava, S., & Sahin, M. (2017). Autism Spectrum Disorder and Epileptic Encephaloathy: Common Causes, Many Questions. *Journal of Neurodevelopment Disorders, 9*, epub ahead of print. doi:10.1186/s11689-017-9202-0

State Initiatives. (2017, March 28). Retrieved from www.autismspeaks.org/state-initiatives

Strang, J. F., Kenworthy, L., Dominska, A., et al. (2014). Increased Gender Variance in Autism Spectrum Disorders and Attention Deficit Hyperactivity Disorder. *Archives of Sexual Behavior, 43*, 1525–1533.

Supekar, K., Iyer, T., & Menon, V. (2017). The Influence of Sex and Age on Prevalence Rates of Comorbid Conditions in Autism. *Autism Research, 10*, 778–789

Tartaglia, N. R., Wilson, R., Miller, J. S., et al. (2017). Autism Spectrum Disorder in Males with Sex Chromosome Aneuploidy: XXY/Klinefelter Syndrome, XYY, and XXYY. *Journal of Developmental & Behavioral Pediatrics, 38*, 197–207.

Taylor, J. L., & Mailick, M. R. (2014). A Longitudinal Examination of 10-Year Change in Vocational and Educational Activities for Adults with Autism Spectrum Disorders. *Developmental Psychology*, *50*, 699–708.

Teatero, M. L., & Netley, C. (2013). A Critical Review of the Research on the Extreme Male Brain Theory and Digit Ratio (2D:4D). *Journal of Autism and Developmental Disorders*, *43*, 2664–2676.

Turban, J. L., & van Schalkwyk, G. I. (2018). "Gender Dysphoria" and Autism Spectrum Disorder: Is the Link Real? *Journal of the American Academy of Child & Adolescent Psychiatry*, *57*, 8–9.

van der Miesen, A. I. R., de Vries, A. L., Steensma, T. D., & Hartman, C. A. (2017). Autistic Symptoms in Children and Adolescents with Gender Dysphoria. *Journal of Autism and Developmental Disorders*, epub ahead of print. doi:10.1007/s10803-017-3417-5

Whyte, E. M., & Scherf, K. S. (2018). Gaze Following is Related to the Broader Autism Phenotype in a Sex-Specific Way: Building the Case for Distinct Male and Female Autism Phenotypes. *Clinical Psychological Science*, *6*, 280–287.

Zwaigenbaum, L., Bryson, S. E., Szatmari, P., et al. (2012). Sex Differences in Children with Autism Spectrum Disorder Identified Within a High-Risk Infant Cohort. *Journal of Autism and Developmental Disorders*, *42*, 2585–2596.

6

TREATMENT OF AUTISM SPECTRUM DISORDERS

Erin Matlosz, Stefany Tucker, Richard Solomon, Thomas J. Overly, and Janine D. Mator

Foreword by Thomas Denczek

Foreword

First and foremost, autism is a neurodevelopmental disorder which impacts the lens through which one takes in and processes information, and so interacts with the world. The focus of this lens is shaped by the countless interactions, both observable and non-observable, that occur from infancy throughout development. This lens affects all of the information which is taken in, which impacts one's ability to understand what to do next, and impacts both choices and opportunities for the person (Lord, 2017). Individuals with autism have difficulty with expressive and receptive language, which form the fundamental building block through which they learn to communicate and connect to others. This is significant because how well we talk impacts all of social behavioral interaction, including nonverbal behavior and flexible thinking (Lord, 2017). Because we do not possess an "instruction manual" detailing how to develop the skills needed to effectively communicate and interact with one another, we must learn these skills through experience. We have constructed a world dominated by a "neurotypical operating system," which makes sense. For this reason, individuals whose operating system is constructed differently are at a fundamental disadvantage. Oftentimes, the biggest problem for individuals with ASD is us.

Throughout adolescence, the development of our executive functioning system enables us to do a variety of tasks. We can see ourselves outside of the moment we are in and through the eyes of others. We have the ability to process a situation incorporating past experiences and forethought, to achieve an outcome. This process requires the active recognition and appreciation of others, their expectations, the "basic" social expectations of the situation we are in, emotional regulation, and the outcome we desire. This process requires simultaneous integration of a number of factors, which incorporate all of the skills which have been developed to that point. The negative impact of a developmental system which has been tuned to a different set of expectations each day processes thousands of events, different from what might be common sense to most. This difference from that point of view vs. the neurotypical expectation increases the risk for social, emotional, and behavioral challenges.

Emotions are impacted by the perception of one's experiences throughout development. Rita Carter, author of *Mapping the Mind*, writes, "Emotions are not feelings at all, but a set of body rooted survival mechanisms that have evolved to turn us away from danger and propel us forward to things that may be of benefit." For individuals diagnosed with autism spectrum disorders, the mechanism for evaluating "danger" is based on different set of variables. Again, it has been observed that persons with autism are more internally driven, and so less affected by the expectations of situations and others around them. Additionally, the ability to act with a plan requires smooth integration of past experiences, the current situation, and anticipated future goal. For persons with ASD, this process is impaired, leaving them to react in the moment based on the discomfort and dysregulation they are feeling in that moment. This often results in a well-practiced effort to avoid discomfort based on their internal definition, often lacking an awareness of the impact their decision has on others or their future. Consider also how this process of acting prepares one for the larger world once they must make the transition to independent functioning.

Struggling to decipher the ever-complicated social expectations for how to respond to the situations, individuals with ASD have trouble identifying and practicing appropriate social patterns of interaction, and become even more dependent on others for the management of their daily functioning.

Diagnostic Criteria of ASD and Definition of Intensive Intervention for ASD

Autism is a neuro-genetic condition affecting 1 in 68 individuals. According to the DSM-5 (the official psychiatric *Diagnostic and Statistical Manual*, fifth edition) ASD is characterized by two primary features and an age-related criterion:

1. Persistent difficulties in the social use of verbal and nonverbal communication
2. Restricted, repetitive patterns of behavior, interests, or activities
3. Symptoms must be present in the early developmental period.

In common usage, we say the individual has an *autistic spectrum disorder* because the impairments vary across individuals from severe to very mild. Neuroscientists who study the autopsied brains of children with ASD have discovered disordered neuronal development and under-connectivity between brain structures leading to functional abnormalities in the most complex activities, namely social skills and higher order thinking. The brain of the individual with autism is like a net that cannot catch the complexity of the world in its web. Environmental factors are also thought to contribute to autism's growing prevalence.

There is one saving grace for children diagnosed with ASD—brain plasticity. Brain plasticity is the ability of the brain to reshape itself from the outside in. In others words, experience changes brain structures (viz. neurons) and can profoundly affect developmental trajectories. In recognition of this, the National Research Council (NRC) convened a group of experts to recommend guidelines for the education of young children with ASD (Lord et al., 2001). Here, in a nutshell, is what they recommended: start intervention early (*18 months–5 years of age*); provide *15–25 hours/week* of direct intervention that is *engaging, individualized* (1:1 or 1:2 teacher to student ratio), and has a *strategic direction* (language, social skills, academic skills, etc.); and to address the comprehensive needs of the child with ASD.

Early intensive intervention has been shown to help children with ASD make dramatic gains in IQ and functional social development; a recent article on "optimal outcomes" for children who received early intensive intervention showed children can "demonstrate on overall level of functioning within the normal range" (Fein et al., 2013). Many children with ASD can achieve the goals of personal independence and social responsibility. Early intensive interventions are usually implemented over two to four years until the child is 6 years old.

Applied Behavior Analysis and the Treatment of Autism Spectrum Disorders

Defining Applied Behavior Analysis

Applied behavior analysis (ABA) is the science of understanding and improving socially significant human behaviors. ABA strives to make a meaningful difference in the lives of individuals. It is a scientifically valid, mainstream method of teaching functional skills and decreasing problem behaviors, and it is considered an effective teaching method for individuals diagnosed with autism spectrum disorders. In fact, as many as 40–50% of children diagnosed with autism spectrum disorders who receive high-quality, early intensive behavioral intervention can benefit from the intervention enough to return to mainstream classrooms (Lovaas, 1987; McEachin, Smith, & Lovaas, 1993; Rogers & Vismara, 2008). ABA is effective at developing a variety of functional skills, including but not limited to language and communication skills, academic skills, social interactions, positive peer relationships, daily living skills, cognitive and executive functioning skills, and decreasing and/or eliminating harmful behaviors.

ABA is based on the principles of behaviorism. The cornerstone of ABA is systematically applying intervention to teach and increase adaptive and socially significant behaviors. Baer, Wolf, and Risley (1968) outlined seven defining characteristics of ABA:

1. *Applied*: Behaviors that are targeted in treatment must be socially significant and improve the day-to-day lives of the individual and/or their significant others (parents, caregivers, teachers, peers, etc.).
2. *Behavioral*: The targeted behavior must be measurable.
3. *Analytic*: There must be a functional relationship between the environmental manipulation and the change in the targeted behavior.
4. *Technological*: All procedures involved in the intervention must be clearly outlined and able to be replicated and taught to others.
5. *Conceptually Systematic*: Procedures used in all interventions must be able to be related to and described in terms of the basic principles of behavior.
6. *Effective*: The targeted behavior must improve to a socially significant degree as a result of the intervention.
7. *Generality*: Changes in targeted behaviors must persist over time, generalize to novel environments, and/or generalize across different but related behaviors.

Basic Concepts of Applied Behavior Analysis

ABA is based on the principles of operant conditioning. Learning occurs as the result of consequences that follow a behavior, and these consequences determine the likelihood that the behavior will occur again in the future. The operant model of behavior involves the three-term contingency—antecedent, behavior, and consequence. "Antecedent" refers to what is occurring in the environment immediately before a particular behavior occurs. "Behavior" refers to the exact nature and topography of the response, and "consequence" refers to anything that occurs immediately following the behavior. Consequences fall into the categories of "reinforcement" or "punishment." Reinforcement is any consequence that strengthens behavior in the future; that is, the behavior might occur more frequently, more intensely, or for a longer period of time. Conversely, punishment refers to any consequence that weakens behavior in the future. As a result of a punisher being delivered, the behavior might occur less frequently, less intensely, or for a shorter period of time.

Applied Behavior Analysis Assessment

No two people have an identical set of life experiences. Each individual presents with a unique set of skills, deficits, and confounding variables. Therefore, applied behavior analysis programs are tailored to meet the individual needs of each client rather than taking on a "one size fits all" approach. Prior to beginning an intervention program, a thorough assessment is completed. Assessments can take anywhere from two to over 20 hours to complete. The assessment typically involves both indirect and direct methods of assessment.

Indirect methods of assessment include interviews with caregivers, teachers, previous therapists, and any other pertinent person in the client's day-to-day life. Interviews can take place in an office setting or in the natural environment, and involve gathering information regarding developmental history, a summary of previous therapies and outcomes, and current variables impacting the client's life. A detailed description of all problem behaviors (behaviors targeted for decrease) and skill deficits (behaviors targeted for increase) is also gathered during the interview portion of the assessment, as well as information regarding the individual's ability to perform age-appropriate daily living skills. Caregivers will also sometimes be asked to complete questionnaires to aid in the functional assessment or functional analysis, including the Motivation Assessment Scale (MAS) (Durand & Crimmins, 1992) or the Functional Analysis Screening Tool (FAST) (Iwata & DeLeon, 2005). Conducting a reinforcer preference assessment is also a critical element of the initial assessment, in order to identify potential items, activities, and people that might function as reinforcers for the client.

If problem behaviors are present, a functional behavior assessment (FBA) will be conducted to determine when and where the challenging behavior is most and least likely to occur, and to aid in developing hypotheses regarding why the behavior is occurring. The FBA seeks to identify relationships between the behavior and the environment. Behavior plans that are based on the results of an FBA have been shown to be more effective and efficient, and produce more significant change in the lifestyle of the individual (O'Neill et al., 1997). The goal of the FBA is to identify observable and measurable behaviors of concern, identify events and situations that predict when the target behavior will and will not occur, and identify the function(s) of the target behaviors as well as any necessary replacement behaviors that should be targeted as part of the intervention process.

Criterion-referenced tests, although not required as part of the assessment process, are another common method of ABA assessment. The Assessment of Basic Learning and Language Skills, Revised (ABLLS-R) (Partington, 2010) is an assessment tool used to measure an individual's performance on 544 skills across 25 domains. These skills are basic language and critical learning skills considered essential for being able to learn from everyday experiences, including communication skills, social skills, daily living skills, and leisure skills. Typically developing children are expected to acquire the majority of these skills prior to entering kindergarten. The ABLLS-R can be used as a guide to develop curriculum, as well as to monitor progress and skill acquisition throughout treatment.

The Verbal Behavior Milestones and Placement Program, second edition (VB-MAPP) (Sundberg, 2014), is a similar tool to the ABLLS-R in that it can be used not only for assessment but also to guide curriculum development and monitor progress. It is designed for individuals with language delays and is based on B. F. Skinner's (1957) analysis of verbal behavior, established developmental milestones, and other research in the field of ABA. The VB-MAPP examines 170 learning and language milestones that are sequenced and balanced across three developmental levels (0–18 months, 18–30 months, and 30-48 months). Domains assessed include, but are not limited to, imitation skills, play skills, social skills, visual perceptual skills, matching skills, verbal skills (requesting, labeling, and conversational skills), group and classroom skills, and early academic skills in the areas of math, reading, and writing. The VB-MAPP also contains an additional barriers assessment, which examines areas identified in the American Psychiatric Association's *Diagnostic and Statistical Manual*, fifth edition (DSM-5) diagnostic criteria for autism spectrum disorder as well as additional common learning and language acquisition barriers. Barriers assessed include issues such as defective social skills, imitation skills, requesting skills, behavior problems, self-stimulation, prompt and reinforcer dependency, and failure to generalize.

Another common assessment tool utilized in the field of ABA, often with older or more advanced clients, is the Assessment of Functional Living Skills (AFLS) (Partington & Mueller, 2012). The AFLS expands upon many of the skills from the ABLLS-R to maximize independence and includes six skills areas (Basic Living Skills, Home Skills, School Skills, Vocational Skills, Community Participation Skills, and Independent Living Skills). Essential for Living (EFL) (McGreevy, Fry, & Cornwall, 2012) is another useful assessment and curriculum guide for individuals who need a program with more of a focus on functional living skills.

After all other portions of the assessment are complete, the behavior analyst considers all information gathered and works with the client and caregivers to define goals and objectives for treatment. Goals must be specific and measurable, and include a target date for completion. The behavior analyst must also develop detailed treatment protocols to allow the behavior technicians implementing the intervention to maintain treatment fidelity, and a method of data collection for each goal must be identified prior to beginning treatment.

Types of Applied Behavior Analysis Interventions

ABA therapy is, by nature, a more intensive intervention than other methods of treatment. Individuals receiving ABA therapy typically receive anywhere from eight to forty hours of therapy per week. Sessions generally range in length from two to eight hours, a minimum of two to three times per week. Interventions may be conducted in a clinic, at the individual's home, school, or in the community, or a combination of any of these environments. Treatment protocols are developed by a Board Certified Behavior Analyst (BCBA), while the intervention is delivered by highly trained behavioral technicians who are closely supervised by the BCBA.

ABA interventions can be developed to teach a wide range of functional skills across several domains, including social, communication, academic, and behavioral. The "social" domain includes skills such as interaction skills, social skills, joint attention, friendship skills, age-appropriate play skills, independent play skills, social engagement, problem solving, and participation in social activities. The "communication" domain includes both verbal and nonverbal communicative behaviors, including but not limited to requesting, labeling, conversation skills, pragmatics, reading nonverbal cues in others, and pointing. The "academic" domain includes skills required in the school setting, and the "behavioral" domain includes adaptive behaviors and independent living skills, and appropriate alternative/replacement behaviors that are functionally equivalent to problem behaviors targeted for decrease. ABA interventions range from highly structured programs conducted in sterile, well-controlled environments to more naturalistic settings involving typically developing peers as models. Regardless of instruction method, all ABA interventions are conducted within a scientific framework and rely on the basic principles of behaviorism.

One of the most commonly known interventions in ABA is Discrete Trial Teaching (DTT). DTT is often thought of as "table work," although it can be implemented in almost any setting and does not have to occur exclusively at a table. DTT is a highly structured method of providing ABA instruction to teach discrete, basic behaviors. It involves four components: the instructor's presentation of the stimulus, the client's response (independent or prompted), the consequence, and a short pause between the consequence and the next trial (Anderson, Taras, & Cannon, 1996). The "stimulus" is the instruction (e.g., "Copy me,") and the consequence is generally either delivery of reinforcement (following a correct response) or implementation of an error correction procedure following an incorrect response. The ultimate goal of DTT is to generalize the skill to the natural environment.

Incidental teaching is another common ABA method and involves using naturally occurring or contrived situations in the natural environment to teach functional skills. Incidental teaching uses an individual's unique interests and natural motivation to facilitate skill acquisition. Incidental teaching was developed to increase language and social skills by maximizing the power of natural reinforcement and encouraging generalization to the natural environment (Hart & Risley, 1968, 1975).

Video modeling has been shown to be an effective intervention for teaching social skills to individuals diagnosed with autism spectrum disorders (Nikopoulos & Keenan, 2004), and can be used to teach a variety of other skills as well. When using video modeling as an intervention to teach social skills or other behaviors, the client is shown a video of a typically developing peer engaging in the target behavior, and then given the opportunity to engage in the skill independently immediately after viewing the video. Effects of video modeling show not only an initial increase in the target behavior, but effects tend to be maintained for months following the intervention (Nikopoulos & Keenan, 2004).

Larger, more complex behaviors such as tooth brushing, dressing, bathing, and toileting are often taught using a task analysis and a procedure called chaining. A task analysis requires breaking larger skills and routines into smaller, more manageable steps, and each step is taught individually, until each step of the chain is able to be completed independently and in combination with all other steps.

Evaluating the Effectiveness of ABA Interventions

Accurate and reliable data collection is a key component of all ABA intervention programs. To ensure programs are effective and producing the desired behavior change, data should be recorded during each treatment session. The type of data recorded is dependent on the goals targeted during the session, and can include duration, frequency, rate, inter-response time, latency, and percent of occurrence. Data is generally recorded into tables and visual representations of the data (graphs) are generated to allow trends in the data to be more easily observed. Data should be reviewed by the supervising BCBA no less than once every two weeks, depending on the frequency and intensity of treatment. For clients receiving more hours of therapy, data should be reviewed more often. If an intervention is not producing the desired result, the intervention should be modified accordingly.

The PLAY Project Autism Intervention Model

Introduction and Overview

The PLAY Project Autism Intervention (PLAY) model is an innovative, evidence-based, parent-implemented (Wong et al., 2013) early intervention program for young children (18 months through 6 years) with autism spectrum disorders (ASD) that focuses on helping families joyfully connect with their child. PLAY Consultants partner with families to build trust, promote family confidence and competence, and strengthen family–child relationships through playful engagement. Families gain knowledge and skills that enrich their child's play abilities and, research suggests, can change the child's developmental trajectory.

This section will (1) explain why parent-implemented models are needed in the field of autism intervention policy, (2) describe the 7 *Circles of PLAY*—the key elements of the PLAY model—using an illustrative case study, (3) summarize the research findings on PLAY, and (4) describe how PLAY is being implemented statewide in the Ohio Early Intervention System.

Why Are Parent-Implemented Models Needed for Young Children with ASD?

An increasing number of young children are being identified with ASD nationally and there is clear evidence that the benefits of early intensive intervention are great. Yet, there are tens of thousands of young children who do not have access to services. A recent report from the *Journal of the American Medical Association* (*JAMA*) described evidence that, despite the passage of autism insurance laws, there are still thousands of children with ASD who are not getting needed services (Mandell et al., 2016). There is an urgent national need for effective early intervention models for young children with autistic spectrum disorders. Parent-implemented models (PIM) are a practical and empowering solution to this problem.

Training parents to be the child's best interventionists has been recognized as an effective way to deliver early intervention services on a large scale, especially to the youngest children (Diggle et al., 2002). Parent-implemented autism intervention models are evidence (Wong et al., 2013). PIM are complementary and supplementary to traditional, professionally delivered autism and preschool-based services. One size of intervention does not fit all children with ASD. Families need choices among evidence-based options. To have the greatest impact on child outcomes, the active participation of families in early intervention is essential.

The 7 Circles of PLAY: Key Elements of The PLAY Project Autism Intervention (PLAY) Program

The PLAY Project Autism Intervention (PLAY) program is a parent-implemented, play-based, developmental model that was piloted from 2000 to 2005 (Solomon et al., 2007), implemented clinically in over 30 states from 2005 to 2016. PLAY was rigorously researched through a National Institutes of Health (NIH) funded study from 2009 to 2012 (Solomon et al., 2014), and disseminated statewide in Ohio's Early Intervention system (2010 to the present). PLAY is one of the most widely used, evidence-based, parent-implemented models in the US.

PLAY is the primary service program of The PLAY Project Organization. The organization's mission is "To support families in having a joyous and playful relationship with their children with autism spectrum disorders so each child can reach his or her full potential." Its vision is "To train a global network of pediatric professionals to deliver The PLAY Project's Autism Intervention program to serve as many families as needed." PLAY Consultants (PC) are master's-level pediatric professionals and child development experts (speech/language pathologists, occupational therapists, social workers, early intervention providers, psychologists, and physicians) who complete a rigorous, systematic 12- to 18-month training course to become certified in the model. In short,

The PLAY Project trains pediatric professionals and child development experts to coach parents to help their children with autism through play. The following case study will describe PLAY's key elements.

When Julian's parents noticed that, at age 16 months, he was "in his own world" and not interacting with them, they sought help from their pediatrician, who referred the family for a diagnostic evaluation at the nearby university. She also referred them to the county's early intervention (EI) program. While Julian was waiting for his diagnostic evaluation (in four months!), the family was evaluated by EI and found to have "red flags" for autism. Kirsten, the early intervention worker, a Certified PLAY Consultant and Occupational Therapist, described The PLAY Project Autism Intervention program to the family.

Julian's family embraced PLAY services. PLAY is a family-centered practice, typically delivered in the home one to four times per month, based on the family's needs and preferences. Julian's mom, Julie, stayed home with her son and was pregnant with a second child. Julian's dad, Jim, was a busy IT manager. Kirsten arranged monthly PLAY visits when both parents could be home. She built a trusting, respectful partnership through interactions that nurtured and supported the family so the family could nurture and support Julian.

During the visits, Kirsten coached Jim and Julie while they played with Julian and she modeled/demonstrated playful interactions. She videotaped herself and both parents engaging Julian, a cornerstone of the PLAY model. After the visit, Kirsten sent a detailed, written video review and PLAY Plan. A key principle of PLAY is "putting in the time" to make it intensive. Kirsten encouraged the family to PLAY for two hours per day in 15- to 20-minute sessions and during daily activities. The family followed The 7 Circles of PLAY, the key elements of the intervention:

- *Circle 1: Principles and Methods* Families learn the *core concepts* of PLAY.
  - The four principles are: (1) Having fun with people, (2) Putting in the time (two hours/day), (3) Playing at the right developmental level, and (4) Profiling the child accurately (which the PC does for the family through her video review and PLAY Plan to help them PLAY at the right level).
  - The five methods are: (1) Reading the child's cues to understand the child's intentions/ideas, (2) Following the child's lead/responding to the child's intentions and ideas, (3) Promoting "circles of interaction" (contingent reciprocal, serve and return, of social exchanges), (4) Adjusting the pace of interaction or waiting for the child's responses, and (5) Expanding on the child's ideas to make interactions fun.

- *Circle 2: Child Profile* Each child is individually profiled in terms of their Comfort Zone Activities (what they love to do), their Sensory Profile (preferred sensory modalities, like deep pressure or proprioceptive input [jumping]; and non-preferred modalities [loud, sudden noises]), and their Functional Developmental Levels (Greenspan & Wieder, 1997).

- *Circle 3: PLAY Plan* Guided by the child's unique profile, the PC collaborates with the family to determine appropriate *activities and techniques.* The PLAY Plan empowers parents to build their skills as players while supporting their child through the stages of development. Activities can be tailored by families to fit into their daily routines as well as play time. It is the flexibility of PLAY that allows parent to put in the time required for the interventions to be intensive. The PLAY Plan is updated and changed as the child makes progress.

- *Circle 4: Family Guidance* During each visit, the PC supports the family in their role of play partner with their child. The PC coaches the parents as they PLAY, models the recommended activities and techniques, and provides written feedback. Video footage is taken to be used as part of the visit review, which allows the PC to track and measure progress.

- *Circle 5: Engagement* Between visits, the family interacts with their child during daily routines and short play sessions throughout the day. The goal is to make every interaction a good interaction, providing the intensity needed to improve the child's social and emotional development.

- *Circle 6: Visit and Video Review* The PC sends *written and video feedback* so parents can refine their approach and a *PLAY Plan* that summarizes the child's profile and provides suggested techniques and activities. Written feedback is parent-friendly and clear.

- *Circle 7: Change and Growth* The program is adjusted as the child moves up Functional Developmental Levels (see below for a brief description of the FDLs).

Jim and Julie had a hard time with PLAY methods initially, as they were too ambitious and were trying to move too fast! It was hard for them to truly understand and follow what Julian wanted, but Kirsten showed them how to observe Julian's subtle cues and see that he liked deep pressure on his body and loved to be bounced up and down. Over time, the family learned to "following his lead" and find what brought him joy. Once they got the idea of PLAYing at his level, Julian took off! By meeting him right where he was in that moment, they found the fastest way to help him make developmental gains. The PLAY Project motto is "When you do what the child loves, the child will love being with you!" This desire of the child with autism to interact more and initiate toward caregivers was a key finding in the PLAY research.

Over the next several months, Julian moved up in his Functional Developmental Levels (FDLs). PLAY uses Greenspan and Wieder's Developmental, Individual-differences and Relationship-based (DIR) framework (Greenspan

& Wieder, 1997), which describes six increasingly complex FDLs whereby children gain the ability to fully relate to others.

- *Self-Regulation and Shared Attention* (FDL 1) (Birth–3 months)
- *Engagement* (FDL 2) (4–8 months)
- *Two-Way Communication* (FDL 3) (9–14 months)
- *Complex Two-Way Communication* (FDL 4) (15–24 months)
- *Shared Meanings and Symbolic Play* (FDL 5) (2–3 years)
- *Emotional Thinking* (FDL 6) (3–5 years).

As PLAY progressed, Julian was more "with us": he was sharing attention (FDL 1), staying engaged for longer periods of time (FDL 2), initiating more and having longer back-and-forth interactions (FDL 3). Within a year, he was talking in one- to two-word phrases! He was pulling his parents by the hand to get what he wanted and using more gestures (FDL 4). He was imitating and playing little song games. By the time Julian was done with PLAY two years later, he was playing pretend (FDL 5) and talking in longer sentences (FDL 6). Perhaps most importantly, he was so social and engaged that his diagnosis was coming under question by his pediatrician.

Julian's case shows what we see when PLAY is successful: joyful relating, simple and complex nonverbal gestures, long interactive sequences, spontaneous verbal communication, shared social attention (FDLs 1–3), symbolic language related to feelings (FDLs 4–6), and the ability to be "with us" continuously, rather than stuck in repetitive or stereotyped behaviors. Ultimately, children who are successful in PLAY become more socially functional and interested in others. This is what we found in our research.

PLAY Project Research

In 2005 The PLAY Project Organization was awarded a $1.85 million grant through the National Institutes of Health (NIH). In this randomized controlled trial (RCT), children were randomly assigned to either a community standard (CS) group (where they received preschool services for 12 hours per week) or CS plus PLAY. Five Easter Seals (a nonprofit service organization) sites in four states recruited 64 children per year in two cohorts (i.e., 64 children one year and 64 children the next year). PLAY Consultants made monthly home visits and provided monthly written feedback. The study was completely "blind": evaluators did not know which families/children were in the treatment or control study, nor did they know which data was pre-intervention, and which was post-intervention. Michigan State University conducted the independent evaluation. Altogether, 128 children were recruited for the study, making it the largest study on autism intervention in the country. Results of the study were published in the peer-reviewed *Journal of Developmental and Behavioral Pediatrics* (Solomon et al., 2014).

Here are the key study findings:

1. The certified PLAY Consultants at each of the Easter Seals sites showed high fidelity to the model (i.e., they delivered services as described in the fidelity manual).
2. Intervention parents (PLAY + CS) improved significantly when compared to the CS group in their ability to learn PLAY methods: they became more sensitive (reading the child's cues) and responsive (followed the child's lead) to their child and more effective (able to get more back and forth interactions) with their child.
3. PLAY parents showed a significant reduction in depression compared to control parents.
4. Children with ASD who received PLAY improved statistically and clinically in their interactional abilities (i.e., showed marked improvement in initiation), their functional development, and in their autism symptoms.

These research findings suggest that PLAY offers a replicable method that uses an efficient training and certification model that is cost effective to parents and society and can be broadly and quickly disseminated to serve the growing need and get children with ASD off of waiting list and into services. In fact, PLAY was implemented statewide in Ohio's Early Intervention system.

Statewide Implementation and Evaluation of PLAY in the Ohio Early Intervention System

From 2011 to 2013 the Ohio Department of Developmental Disabilities under the direction of John Martin funded the training of 150 Early interventionists and implemented PLAY in over 75% of Ohio's counties through Part C Early Intervention services. Hundreds of young children (< 3 years old) with red flags for, or a diagnosis of, ASD are served each year using the PLAY model as described above. In 2015, the implementation of the model was independently and rigorously evaluated by Marilyn Espe Sherwindt and team at Akron Children's Hospital, and the findings revealed that PLAY Consultants were very satisfied with training and parents were very satisfied with PLAY services. The overall implementation of PLAY was successful and has the ongoing support of the state.

Summary

The PLAY Project Autism Intervention (PLAY) is an intensive, evidence-based, parent-implemented model with successful real-world applications. PLAY is a structured, play-based approach that empowers parents to engage their hard-to-engage children with ASD. PLAY is typically provided in the home by certified master's-level child developmental specialist called PLAY Consultants. These consultants help families gain knowledge and skills by coaching and modeling the principles, methods, techniques, and activities based on the child's unique profile. Research and clinical experience have shown that parents can learn the model, can put in the time, by strengthening the parent–child relationship through play, can help their child improve in their functional development.

The PLAY Project has been implemented on a statewide basis in Ohio and disseminated in a variety of community-based organizations. Many children are not receiving desperately needed early intervention autism services, and The PLAY Project Autism Intervention model has been shown to be a practical, effective solution for practitioners to reach under-served families.

Virtual-Reality-Based Behavioral Interventions for Individuals With Autism

Developmental delays in communication and socialization are particularly common among individuals with autism spectrum disorder (ASD). As a result, behavioral interventions strive to facilitate neurotypical, or typically developing, social responses. However, anxiety and fear of rejection are frequently reported among individuals with ASD as a result of communicative incompetency (van Steensel, Bögels, & Wood, 2013). Repetitive behaviors such as motor stereotypy and echolalia (i.e., repeated words or phrases) may be engaged as a means of coping with this anxiety, particularly in situations that are unfamiliar or unpredictable. These behaviors, largely unique to ASD, often result in further isolation of the individual from neurotypical peers (Gillott, Furniss, & Walter, 2001). Similarly, research has demonstrated that behavioral interventions for individuals with ASD are most effective when implemented at a young age. Perhaps as a result of this time sensitivity, behavioral interventions commonly rely on the rapidity of techniques such as discrete-trial training, whose learning opportunities are often highly contrived and repetitive. As a result, clients with ASD occasionally struggle to exercise their learning during novel situations, and fatigue and resultant inconsistency from instructors may cause unintentional barriers to treatment (Cromby, Standen, & Brown, 1996). While generally effective in shaping specific behaviors, repetition as a learning technique is most beneficial "when embedded in more naturalistic and meaningful contexts" (Parsons & Mitchell, 2002). Similarly, behavioral interventions commonly utilize reinforcement, a principle of operant conditioning, in order to motivate the learner. However, reinforcers are immediate and tend to be tangible rather than intrinsic, especially for young children; therefore, learned behaviors are dependent on a highly unnatural contingency learned during a critical period in development (Frankel, Leary, & Kilman, 1987).

For individuals with ASD—particularly children with HFA (high-functioning autism)—computer technology is a common source of reinforcement. More specifically, persons with ASD

> have been found to have a natural interest in and affinity with computers due to the predictable, consistent, and repeatable nature of technology (Parsons & Mitchell, 2002; Parsons et al., 2006; Putnam & Chong, 2008). This, in turn, could heighten their compliance and investment in the treatment [Krämer, 2008].
>
> *(Georgescu et al., 2014)*

Neurotypical populations are commonly reinforced by computer technology as well; consequentially, there has been much research on virtual reality technology (VRT), a highly immersive form of computer technology, and its potential social and cognitive benefits. For individuals with ASD, therapy through VRT may present the opportunity to "make social mistakes without the intense anxiety or fear of rejection that is commonly associated with face-to-face social interactions" (Didehbani et al., 2016).

While there have been hundreds of studies in the last decade alone that examine the use of VRT in the treatment of anxiety spectrum disorders, such as PTSD and specific phobias, a similar effort to research its potential clinical applications in the treatment of ASD has only recently emerged. Many of the positive results achieved with anxiety disorders were possible because of VRT's inherent strength in simulating real-world environments and objects, where treatment often involves facilitating habituation to environmental stimuli. This differs significantly from the type of clinical work commonly found with ASD, where interpersonal and communication difficulties are often the treatment focus. Until recently, VRT was limited in features that facilitated interaction and communication in virtual reality (VR). However, now that these capabilities are present, accessible, and continually refined, VRT's treatment potential with ASD is being fully explored in multiple domains across populations.

With the growing variability of VR hardware and software, it is critical to consider the specialized needs of the ASD population as interventions are formulated, tested, and implemented. Considering the sensory and cognitive differences that are commonly present in those with ASD, understanding how the VRT format itself will be received is an important first step in this consideration. In order to determine how adults with ASD would respond to VRT, Newbutt et al. (2016) conducted an exploratory study that examined factors of willingness and acceptance to wear a VR head-mounted display; sense of presence and engagement in the virtual environment (VE); and reported enjoyment of the experience. Across these factors, they found that the majority of participants were actively engaged, immersed, and pleased with the experience. The importance in determining the level of immersion experienced by those with

ASD within a VE resides in the fact that it determines an individual's true sense of presence while carrying out tasks within the VE. When Miller and Bugnariu (2016) measured five aspects of immersion across multiple studies to determine how specific VRT configurations affect immersion, they found that those that had limited signals indicating the presence of devices in the physical world accommodated more than two sensory modalities; utilized head-mounted displays; utilized high-fidelity, accurate environments; and used full-body motion capture to produce the highest level of immersion currently possible. In addition to these sensory considerations, Ramachandiran et al. (2015) studied the specific environmental needs of children with ASD. While their findings yielded significant general data about the participants' environmental preferences (e.g., a bathroom/toilet scenario was the most desirable VE), they also discovered that specific cultural needs were often requested by the parents of the participating children (e.g., Muslim parents requested a small hand towel to cover their child's head in the bathroom VE). Lastly, to evaluate the validity of using virtual characters (VCs) with individuals with high-functioning autism (HFA), a review of recent studies indicates positive results have been clearly demonstrated in behavioral work involving nonverbal decoding and social learning (Georgescu et al., 2014). Taken together, these studies indicate that VRT is capable of providing an immersive and engaging platform to conduct behavioral interventions with both adults and children with ASD. Thus, the potential of VRT-based therapy for individuals with ASD endures across the lifespan (Clancy, 1996; Trepagnier, 1999).

First, it is necessary to gain an understanding of the therapeutic aspects of VRT and VEs as they appeal specifically to autistic populations. VEs are especially effective components of VRT in cases where an in vivo alternative is inaccessible or impractical (e.g., a social gathering where the clinician may not be present for guidance or feedback). For persons with ASD, "VEs may be even better suited for learning than real environments, as they allow clinicians to remove competing and confusing stimuli . . . and to add them again as learning progresses" (Lorenzo et al., 2016). Thus, VRT offers a comfortable and effective means of graduated exposure to everyday scenarios that are otherwise beyond clinical reach. Elements of graduated exposure are also common among behavioral intervention strategies—for example, script-fading prompts. VRT therapy expands upon this learning method by simultaneously permitting generalization across a variety of social settings, as well as audiences. If a client's peers are all male, for example, while facilitators are all female, then the client's skill set may face obstacles in generalizing to a female peer or vice versa. Role play is a therapeutic tool often used to overcome such obstacles among adults with ASD and children with high-functioning autism (HFA); however, in cases where the client–patient relationship is well-defined, the client may experience difficulty projecting a novel persona onto one that is already assimilated in some way. This is especially true when the facilitator possesses significantly different characteristics than the role-play "target" (e.g., of age, race, sex, or ethnicity). Additionally, autism spectrum disorder is traditionally defined by an impairment of imagination in addition to communication and socialization (Wing & Gould, 1979). This inhibiting effect may be greatly reduced through a VRT-generated avatar, whose appearance, voice, and other traits could be customized to suit the client's individual needs. Undoubtedly, there are multiple applications of VRT therapy in meeting the specific needs of autistic education.

Early diagnosis and intervention strategies for ASD are widely asserted to produce the most positive outcomes, as mentioned. Most commonly, successful outcomes are defined by the capacity for independent living as an adult (Woolf, Woolf, & Oakland, 2010). Signs of autism may present in infants as young as two months old, who may lack neurotypical instincts for eye contact, name response, or simple imitation, among other instincts (Lucas & Cutler, 2015). For ethical reasons, there is little research on the efficacy of VR headsets among infants and preschool-aged children. By the age of 7, however, children diagnosed with HFA may demonstrate improved affect recognition, analogical reasoning, and executive function after a total of 10 hours spent in Virtual Reality Social Cognition Training. This suggests that similar programs may offer the relatively fast acquisition of communication skills—for example, "confronting a bully" or "consoling a friend" (Didehbani et al., 2016). Other applications of VTR therapy for children include the aided learning of pretend play skills (Herrera et al., 2008), attention orienting (Kylliäinen & Hietanen, 2004), and personal safety practices such as street-crossing and evacuation drills (Josman et al., 2008; Self et al., 2007). As these skills are generalized to real-life situations, children with ASD may gain the ability to perform certain tasks unsupervised, such as walking to school independently like their typically developing peers. Increased self-sufficiency may, in turn, promote stronger self-esteem for developing children with ASD; those with HFA in particular are at risk for depression and other secondary psychiatric disorders (Tantam, 1988).

The benefits of VRT for individuals with ASD are perhaps best documented for adolescents between the ages of 13 and 18. Unsurprisingly, this transitional stage of development heralds new challenges and, for adolescents with HFA, increased self-awareness of the inability to meet them. For typically developing adolescents, the ability to develop intimate peer relationships may manifest in concerns of popularity and reputation; for adolescents with ASD, however, the skill "foreshadows successful transition into adult social roles and levels of adaptive functioning" (Didehbani at al., 2016). One such study suggests that the responses of participants aged 13 to 14 improved in their social understanding of a café setting, as demonstrated by actions such as "choosing appropriate seats" and "knowing how to initiate a conversation" (Didehbani et al, 2016), skills that may be considered precursory to forming lasting relationships. During later stages of adolescence, employment also becomes a primary concern for the individual, as well as any adults that may otherwise be held responsible as primary caretakers.

While there is still much to be learned about the use of VRT with children and adults with ASD, these findings from the last few years indicate that VRT will likely become an important tool in a wide range of therapeutic work. With regard to its potential role in mental health treatment outcomes in general, Oxford University researchers recently went so far as to proclaim in their exhaustive meta-analysis that "VR may merit the level of attention given neuroimaging" (Freeman et al., 2017, p. 2393. Further research must be conducted to determine behavioral outcomes for the inclusion of VRT during therapy for individuals with ASD. Moreover, the aims of this research must consider interventions for adults as well as preventative treatments for young children. While the emphasis on early interventions is undoubtedly deserved, considering the brain plasticity among this population, there remain numerous adults with ASD whose quality of life also stand to benefit from VRT research.

Other Common Interventions

Cognitive Behavioral Therapy

This is often used with ASD populations with higher levels of functional skills (Asperger's teenagers, adults); self-management (coping skills, managing emotions, etc.); daily living skills (hygiene, etc.); independent living skills (cooking, money management, transportation, etc.); vocational skills; social skills/relationship skills; anxiety.

Social Stories

Social stories were developed by Carol Gray (in 1991) and consist of short descriptions (stories) of particular situations, events, and activities. The goal of utilizing social stories is to provide the individual with specific information about what to expect in a particular situation and why.

Group Therapy

Peer-to-peer support most common (Circle of Friends, Links, etc.). But, groups also address social and communication skills, executive functioning, life skills, and may other skills that can be practiced with others.

Speech Therapy

Often used in schools and/or on an outpatient basis; maybe talk about autism and apraxia or other speech disorders that might be commonly diagnosed with autism.

Occupational Therapy

Often used in schools and/or on an outpatient basis; work on daily living skills, sensory issues that commonly go along with an ASD diagnosis, etc.

Medication Interventions

There is no one medication protocol for ASD. Treatment depends on comorbid medical or mental health concerns and symptom intensity. Medication response, metabolization, and dosing vary greatly, including many off-label use medications not anticipated for behavioral health concerns, can demonstrate effectiveness.

References

Anderson, S. R., Taras, M., & Cannon, B. O. (1996). *The Effectiveness of Early Intervention.* Baltimore, MD: Paul H. Brookes Publishing Co.

Baer, D. M., Wolf, M. M., & Risley, T. R. (1968). Some Current Dimensions of Applied Behavior Analysis. *Journal of Applied Behavior Analysis, 1*, 91–97.

Carter, R., & Frith, C. D. (1998). *Mapping the Mind.* Berkeley, CA: University of California Press.

Clancy, H. (1996). Medical Field Prescribes Virtual Reality for Rehabilitation Therapy. *Computer Reseller News, 698*, 76.

Cromby, J., Standen, P. J., & Brown, D. J. (1996). The Potentials of Virtual Environments in the Education and Training of People with Learning Disabilities. *Journal of Intellectual Disability Research, 40*(6), 489–501.

Didehbani, N., Allen, T., Kandalaft, M., Krawczyk, D., & Chapman, S. (2016). Virtual Reality Social Cognition Training for Children with High Functioning Autism. *Computers in Human Behavior, 62*, 703–711.

Diggle, T. T. J., McConachie, H. R., & Randle, V. R. L. (2002). Parent-Mediated Early Intervention for Young Children with Autism Spectrum Disorder. *The Cochrane Database of Systematic Reviews*, issue 2.

Durand, V. M., & Crimmins, D. B. (1992). *The Motivation Assessment Scale (MAS) Administration Guide.* Topeka, KS: Monaco & Associates.

Fein, D., Barton, M., Eigsti, I., Kelley, E., et al. (2013) Optimal Outcome in Individuals with a History of Autism. *Journal of Child Psychology and Psychiatry, 54*(2), 195–205.

Frankel, R., Leary, M., & Kilman, B. (1987). Building Social Skills Through Pragmatic Analysis: Assessment and Treatment Implications for Children with Autism. In A. Donnellan & R. Paul (Eds.), *Handbook of Autism and Pervasive Developmental Disorders* (pp. 333–359). New York, NY: Wiley.

Freeman, D., Reeve, S., Robinson, A., Ehlers, A., Clark, D., Spanlang, B., et al. (2017). Virtual Reality in the Assessment, Understanding, and Treatment of Mental Health. *Psychological Medicine, 47*(14), 2393–2400. doi:10.1017/S003329171700040X

Georgescu, A. L., Kuzmanovic, B., Roth, D., Bente, G., & Vogeley, K. (2014). The Use of Virtual Characters to Assess and Train Non-verbal Communication in high-Functioning Autism. *Frontiers in Human Neuroscience, 8*, 807.

Gillott, A., Furniss, F., & Walter, A. (2001). Anxiety in High-Functioning Children with Autism. *Autism, 5*(3), 277–286.

Greenspan, S., & Wieder, S. (1997). An Integrated Developmental Approach to Interventions for Young Children with Severe Difficulties in Relating and Communicating. *Zero to Three, 17*(5), 5–18.

Hart, B. M., & Risley, T. R. (1968). Establishing Use of Descriptive Adjectives in the Spontaneous Speech of Disadvantaged Preschool Children. *Journal of Applied Behavior Analysis, 1*(2), 109–120.

Hart, B. M. & Risley, T.R. (1975). Incidental Teaching of Language in the Preschool. *Journal of Applied Behavior Analysis, 8*(4), 411–420.

Herrera, G., Alcantud, F., Jordan, R., Blanquer, A., Labajo, G., & De Pablo, C. (2008). Development of Symbolic Play Through the Use of Virtual Reality Tools in Children with Autistic Spectrum Disorders: Two Case Studies. *Autism, 12*(2), 143–157.

Iwata, B., & DeLeon, I. (2005). *The Functional Analysis Screening Tool.* Gainesville, FL: Florida Center on Self-Injury, University of Florida.

Josman, N., Ben-Chaim, H. M., Friedrich, S., & Weiss, P. L. (2008). Effectiveness of Virtual Reality for Teaching Street-Crossing Skills to Children and Adolescents with Autism. *International Journal on Disability and Human Development, 7*(1), 49–56.

Kramer, N.C. (2008). Nonverbal Communication. In J. Blascovich and C. R. Hartel (eds.), *Human Behaviour in Military Contexts* (pp. 150–188). Washington, DC: The National Academies Press.

Kylliäinen, A., & Hietanen, J. K. (2004). Attention Orienting by Another's Gaze Direction in Children with Autism. *Journal of Child Psychology and Psychiatry, 45*(3), 435–444.

Lord, C., (2017, October 24). *UC Davis Mind Institute Catherine Lord.* Lecture presented at UC Davis Mind Institute 2012–2013 distinguished lecturer series in UC Davis Mind Institute 2825 50th St, Sacramento, CA 95817.

Lord, C., Bristol-Power, M., & Cafierol, J. (2001) *Educating Young Children with Autism.* Washington DC: National Academy Press.

Lorenzo, G., Lledó, A., Pomares, J., & Roig, R. (2016). Design and application of an Immersive virtual reality system to enhance emotional skills for children with autism spectrum disorders. *Computers & Education, 98*, 192–205.

Lovaas, O. I. (1987). Behavioral treatment and normal education and intellectual functioning in young autistic children. *Journal of Consulting and Clinical Psychology, 55*(1), 3–9.

Lucas, R. F., & Cutler, A. (2015). Dysregulated Breastfeeding Behaviors in Children Later Diagnosed with Autism. *Journal of Perinatal Education, 24*(3), 171–180.

McEachin, J. J., Smith, T., & Lovaas, O. I. (1993). Long-Term Outcome for Children with Autism who Received Early Intensive Behavioral Treatment. *American Journal on Mental Retardation, 97*(4), 359–372.

McGreevy, P., Fry, T., & Cornwall, C. (2012). *Essential for living: A communication, behavior, and functional skills assessment, curriculum and teaching manual for children and adults with moderate-to-severe disabilities.* Orlando, FL: Patrick McGreevy, Ph.D., P.A. and Associates.

Mandell, D., Barry, C., et al. (2016). Effects of Autism Spectrum Disorder Insurance Mandates on the Treated Prevalence of Autism Spectrum Disorder MPP; *JAMA Pediatrics, 170*(9), 887–893. doi:10.1001/jamapediatrics 1049, published online July 11, 2016.

Miller, H. L., & Bugnariu, N. L. (2016). Level of Immersion in Virtual environments mpacts the abAility to Assess and Teach Social Skills in Autism Spectrum Disorder. *Cyberpsychology, Behavior, and Social Networking, 19*(4), 246–256.

Newbutt, N., Sung, C., Kuo, H., Leahy, M. J., Lin, C., & Tong, B. (2016). Brief eport: A Pilot Study of the Use of a Virtual Reality Headset in Autism Populations. *Journal of Autism and Developmental Disorders, 46*(9), 3166–3176.

Nikopoulos, C. K., & Keenan, M. (2004). Effects of Video Modeling on Social Initiations by Children with Autism. *Journal of Applied Behavior Analysis, 37*(1), 93–96.

O'Neill, R. E., Horner, R. H., Albin, R. W., Sprague, J. R., Storey, K., & Newton, J. S. (1997). *Functional Assessment and Program Development for Problem Behavior: A Practical Handbook*, 2nd ed. Pacific Grove, CA: Brooks.

Parsons, S., & Mitchell, P. (2002). The Potential of Virtual Reality in Social Skills Training for People with Autistic Spectrum Disorders. *Journal of Intellectual Disability Research, 46*(5), 430–443.

Parsons, S., Leonard, A., & Mitchell, P. (2006). Virtual Environments for Social Skills Training: Comments from Two Adolescents with Autistic Spectrum Disorder. *Computer Education, 47*, 186–206.

Partington, J. W. (2010). *The Assessment of Basic Language and Learning Skills—Revised.* Pleasant Hill, CA: Behavior Analysts.

Partington, J. W. & Mueller, M. M. (2012). *The Assessment of Functional Living Skills.* Marietta, GA: Stimulus Publications.

Ramachandiran, C. R., Jomhari, N., Thiyagaraja, S., & Mahmud, M. M. (2015). Virtual Reality Based Behavioural Learning for Autistic Children. *Electronic Journal of e-Learning, 13*(5), 357–365.

Rogers, S. J., & Vismara, L. A. (2008). Evidence-Based Comprehensive Treatments for Early Autism. *Journal of Clinical Child and Adolescent Psychology, 37*(1), 8–38.

Self, T., Scudder, R. R., Weheba, G., & Crumrine, D. (2007). A Virtual Approach to Teaching Safety Skills to Children with Autism Spectrum Disorder. *Topics in Language Disorders, 27*(3), 242–253.

Solomon, R., Necheles, J., Ferch, C., & Bruckman, D. (2007). Pilot Study of a Parent-Training Program for Young Children with Autism: The Play Project Home Consultation Program. *Autism, 11*(3), 205–224.

Solomon, R., Van Egeren, L., Mahoney, G., Quon-Huber, M., & Zimmerman, P. (2014). PLAY Project Home Consultation Intervention Program for Young Children with Autism Spectrum Disorders: A Randomized Controlled Trial. *Journal of Developmental and Behavioral Pediatrics, 35*(8), 475–485.

Sundberg, M. L. (2014). *The Verbal Behavior Milestones Assessment and Placement Program: The VB-MAPP*, 2nd ed. Concord, CA: AVB Press.

Tantam, D. (1988). Lifelong Eccentricity and Social Isolation. II: Asperger's Syndrome or Schizoid Personality Disorder? *British Journal of Psychiatry, 153*, 783–791.

Trepagnier, C. G. (1999). Virtual Environments for the Investigation and Rehabilitation of Cognitive and Perceptual Impairments. *Neurorehabilitation, 12*(1), 63–72.

van Steensel, F. J., Bögels, S. M., & Wood, J. J. (2013). Autism Spectrum Traits in Children with Anxiety Disorders. *Journal of Autism and Developmental Disorders, 43*(2), 361–370.

Wing, L., & Gould, J. (1979). Severe Impairments of Social Interaction and Associated Abnormalities in Children: Epidemiology and Classification. *Journal of Autism and Developmental Disorders, 9*(1), 11–29.

Wong, C., Odom, S. L. et al. (2013). *Evidence-Based Practices for Children, Youth, and Young Adults with Autism Spectrum Disorder.* Chapel Hill: University of North Carolina, Frank Porter Graham Child Development Institute. Retrieved from http://autismpdc.fpg.unc.edu/sites/autismpdc.fpg.unc.edu/files/2014-EBP-Report.pdf

Woolf, S., Woolf, C. M., & Oakland, T. (2010). Adaptive Behavior Among Adults with Intellectual Disabilities and its Relationship to Community Independence. *Intellectual and Developmental Disabilities, 48*(3), 209–215.

7

AUTISM SPECTRUM DISORDER TRANSITION TO ADULTHOOD

Thomas Denczek

Barriers to Independence

Whether referring to Asperger's or high functioning autism, transitioning through late adolescence and into adulthood is difficult. Additionally, the severity of one's impairments, level of cognitive functioning, and/or the presence of a co-occurring disorder(s) can further complicate challenges. Each of these can impact what is ultimately the goal of functioning as an independent individual, which can be formidable regardless of the diagnosis that is given (Asperger's, pervasive developmental disorder not otherwise specified, or high functioning autism). Obstacles to independence include difficulty finding and sustaining employment, social connectedness, mental wellbeing, and even life expectancy. Some findings are as follows:

- The mean percentage of individuals reported with autism reported as having a good or very good outcome, and living independently or semi-independently, remains below 20% (Howlin & Moss, 2012).
- Persons with ASD are substantially less likely to attend college: roughly 34% of individuals with ASD attend, and far fewer earn a degree (Shattuck et al., 2012).
- 25% to 50% of adults with ASD report competitive employment 6 years post high school graduation. These numbers are lower for individuals with ASD with an accompanying intellectual disability, with employment rates between 12% and 24% (Shattuck et al., 2012).
- Those of all groups who report employment are often employed below their level of education and have difficulty maintaining stable employment (Howlin & Moss, 2012; Lake, Perry, & Lunsky, 2014; Taylor & Seltzer, 2010).

- Outcome studies report fewer than 14% of individuals with ASD report being married or having long-term relationships, and one-quarter report having at least one friend (Howlin & Moss, 2012; Lake et al., 2014).

Additional findings to note: there were trends within the various groups studied suggesting a strong link between early language development, functional use of sentence speech, and average to above average IQ contributing to improved overall social functioning. Though, even among those groups who reported better outcomes, their overall level of functioning was below those of their cohorts (Hofvander et al., 2009; Howlin & Moss, 2012; Lake et al., 2014).

There has been less research on co-occurring psychiatric disorders among persons with autism. Of the research that has been completed, findings suggest that a very high proportion of adults with autism present with comorbid psychiatric disorders, particularly depression and anxiety. Despite these findings, studies suggest that comorbid psychiatric disorders or even the diagnoses of ASD itself is often unrecognized among adolescents and adults, particularly if they are higher functioning (Hofvander et al., 2009; Lake et al., 2014).

There is evidence to suggest that mortality rates among persons with ASD are above that of the general population. One recent study in the *British Journal of Psychology* found the early mortality rate of persons with autism as being 2.5 times higher than that of the general population (Hirvikoski et al., 2016). Recent research on the impacts of perceived loneliness (loneliness is defined as a distressing feeling that accompanies the perception that one's social needs are not being met by the quantity or especially the quality of one's social relationships) and lack of connection with others as a contributing factor in diminished lifespan. In brief, individuals reporting prolonged loneliness are less healthy, less financially successful, will have poorer patterns of sleep, will more likely suffer from mental illness, and have a higher early mortality rate (Beadle et al., 2012; Cacioppo, Fowler, & Christakis, 2008; Luo et al., 2012).

Individuals with lower IQ struggled more in all the areas described above. However, impaired intellectual functioning does make one eligible for services through local community mental health agencies as services are often based upon need as gauged by one's intellectual functioning. These services, when applied, can help with employment, housing, and education and training. Yet, the lack of understanding as to how autism impacts one's functioning can negatively impact the efficacy of these services. Individuals with autism and average to above average IQ and strong verbal abilities will rarely be seen as meeting criteria for services through community mental health agencies despite the persistent challenges these individuals face as they attempt to transition to adult functioning (Lake et al., 2014). This may explain in part why there is less of a divide than might be expected in outcomes reported between individuals with average to above average intelligence and those with below average intelligence. This being said, the impacts of an intellectual disability have a measurably negative impact on the long-term success of an individual with autism. The mental health system as a whole struggles to identify and provide for individuals with autism, particularly those who appear as seemingly intelligent and verbal, leading to persons with autism going underserved as a whole. A final component that has emerged as an impediment to the diagnosis of autism and receiving subsequent services is the socioeconomic status of the individual's family. Families who are economically challenged struggle to access services for their adolescent, subsequently increasing one's struggle into adulthood (Thomas et al., 2011).

Adjusting to Societal Norms

Autism is largely an impairment in understanding and responding to the rules, norms, and expectations of the social system in which persons with autism live in order to function independently. Subsequent effects of this impairment are struggles with persistent patterns of low self-esteem, self-doubt, and persistent feelings of anxiety and depression. Those diagnosed with autism have a higher prevalence of both anxiety and depression. It is difficult to know how much of one's subsequent challenges with anxiety, depression, self-esteem, and confidence are impacted by routinely being seen as different, in conjunction with not feeling success in daily interactions and endeavors.

Analogy of the Computer Operating System

Computer operating systems make a useful analogy regarding the distinctions between individuals who are neurotypical and those who are diagnosed with autism. While neither operating system is perfect nor infallible, there are far more of one system than another. When one considers the distinction between a neurotypical and an autistic operating system, regardless of severity, some common threads appear. First and foremost, autism is a neurodevelopmental disorder that impacts the lens through which one takes in and processes information, and so interacts with the world. The focus of this lens is shaped by the countless interactions, subtle and overt, that occur from infancy throughout one's development. This lens that is formed "affects all of the information that is taken in, and which impacts one's ability to understand what to do next, and fundamentally impacts the choices one makes and the opportunities one has" (Lord, 2017). Individuals with autism have difficulty, perhaps from infancy, processing and utilizing expressive and receptive language abilities which form the fundamental building blocks through which we learn to communicate with, and connect to, others. This is significant, because "how well we talk with others impacts all of social behavioral interactions throughout one's development, including nonverbal behavior and flexible thinking" (Lord, 2017).

Because we have no "instruction manual" for how to develop the skills to effectively communicate and interact with one another, there is no map for how to navigate the myriad and increasingly complicated social situations in which people find themselves. You must learn the skills as you go. If, however, one's system for developing those skills is attuned differently, then all of the information that is taken in and prioritized will be done so differently. What is most significant about being neurotypical from the perspective of an individual with autism is that they are so outnumbered. Society has constructed a model for the world uniquely attuned to a particular operating system. It is this attunement that allows people to communicate effectively with one another despite the differences they might have as individuals. For this reason, individuals whose operating system is constructed differently are at a fundamental and functional disadvantage that grows as the sophistication of what is expected intensifies.

Impact of Language and Executive Functioning

As people utilize language to develop a framework for how to act in the world, they begin to develop the capacity to think and react in an ever more flexible manner. As the executive functioning system begins to come online, they use the information they have been gathering and processing throughout development to become ever more conscious and intentional with regard to actions and interactions. Consider Michio Kaku's "Theory Space-Time Consciousness," where one's conscious actions are viewed as:

> a process of creating a model of the world using multiple feedback loops (feedback loops consist of one's ability to process the myriad dynamics of a situation in which they are in) in various parameters (space, time, relation to others, etc.) to accomplish a goal. Humans create a model of the world in relation to time, both forward and backward, which includes the perspective of the individual as well as an awareness of others.
>
> *(Kaku, 2014)*

Throughout adolescence the development of the executive functioning system enables people to see themselves outside of the moment they are in, as well as through the eyes of others. This allows incorporating past experiences, and forethought, to achieve an outcome. This process requires the active recognition and appreciation of others, their expectations, and the "basic" social expectations of the situation they are in (referred to as Theory of Mind), in conjunction with productive emotional regulation, plus a picture they create of the desired outcome. Finally, the experience results in consequences of our efforts, subtly pushing us in one direction or another. This process requires a smooth and simultaneous integration of a number of factors that incorporate a great many skills. For the neurotypical person, this process occurs largely automatically, thousands of times per day, and imperceptibly fast.

Impact of Emotions

Occurring alongside, and impacting, the development of social awareness, is the manner in which one learns to manage one's emotions. A way to consider emotions is that they are "rapid decisions which are made independently of our conscious awareness" (Kaku, 2014, and which have been impacted by the perception of one's experiences throughout their development. Rita Carter, author of *Mapping the Mind*, wrote, emotions are not feelings at all but a set of body rooted survival mechanisms that have evolved to turn us away from danger and propel us forward to things that may have benefit (in Kaku, 2014). How and what neurotypical and autistic individuals perceive as threatening over time is in some ways as varied as would be expected from individual to individual.

For persons with autism, there can be a tendency towards a mild to increasingly intense fear response to social situations. Resistance to small requests can begin, when the person with autism is young, regarding the completion of daily activities, responsibilities, interactions, etc. These tasks or requests would be viewed through a neurotypical lens as benign. Resistance may be mild at first (though is sometimes quite intense) and often explained away as typical for development. If these behaviors are not considered too far outside what is expected for a child of that age, there can be an assumption that the child will "grow out of it." Over time, however, the frequency and intensity of the resistance increases, fueled by repetition, and can have a measurable impact on the responses of others. Adults begin to shape their responses in anticipation of the resistance.

People consistently rely on what has been conditioned throughout their development to perceive and evaluate "danger" as well as a greater sense of the world around in order to propel them in any direction. As we develop we subtly and consistently condition ourselves to perceive and evaluate dange. We then shape our responses to match our experiences, and the perceptions that we create shapes our choices and those situations we will expose ourselves too, and those we will aviod. This process is to a large degree impacted for neurotypical persons by the shared perception of what is expected and unexpected for us. From this process a baseline of sorts is developed to enable us to, more or less, comfortably transition in and out of a variety of situations, with a variety of individuals. For people with autism, however, the mechanism for evaluating "danger" is based upon a different set of variables. It can be that, while waiting for children with autism to "grow out of it," they are instead developing patterns (growing into) their responses. These responses will increasingly begin to appear maladaptive. The resistance is both emotional and behavioral, and begins to be supported by a narrative which is internally driven and supported by repeated and practiced explanations that form the individual's self-image.

Impact of Childhood Patterns on Adulthood

Previous research findings tell us that there are differences within amygdalas in people with autism as compared to their neurotypical peers (Morgan, Nordahl, & Schumann, 2013). Given the importance of the amygdala in supporting skills such as recognizing facial expressions, and registering fear, the implications for how this would impact upon an individual throughout their development is potentially quite meaningful. If an autistic person reacts fearfully to situations which others would frame as typical, it would impact the individual's exposure to these situations throughout their development. Combined with this previous research, recent findings suggest that individuals who have, for lack of a better term, an overzealous amygdala, are even more susceptible to experiencing what would be traditionally viewed as mildly stressful situations with greater intensity (Kwon et al., 2015). If you combine these factors, it is not a significant leap to consider that persons with autism could be more vulnerable to responding fearfully to the progressive and daily impact of perceived negative social interactions combined with perceived failures in meeting the daily expectations. Then combine this with a neurological system prone to reacting in the moment, that is more internally driven (thus keeping their feelings in and not expressing them through traditional outlets) and less likely to seek help from others or to appreciate the significance of this help. If one considers this happening for an individual on a moment-to-moment and day-to-day basis, combined with increased isolation and increased feelings of both anxiety and depression, and it would not seem so unusual that a heightened sense of resistance would develop into what might be termed "typical daily expectations." Nor would it seem unusual that a heightened defensive response could develop when one's perceptions, choices, or ideas are challenged, even a little.

The process of making decisions is consistently being made by persons with autism using a different set of variables in which cost and benefit are evaluated. Decisions are frequently based upon the avoidance of fear, uncertainty, and unfamiliarity, though the reasoning for this avoidance is often accompanied by seemingly rational explanations. The common denominator is that daily expectations go unfulfilled from the perspective of the neurotypical individual. Additionally, the potential of the person with autism is difficult to realize when milestones are progressively missed. The ultimate goal for the person with autism often becomes doing only what the individual perceives they "must" do in the moment, as defined by others, despite often bristling at the perceived encroachment of others in their lives. Once a task has been completed based upon the autistic person's perspective, the progressive pattern becomes to retreat to zones of perceived comfort and safety in that moment rather than working toward longer-term goals.

For people with autism, decisions are also impaired by feelings of anxiety, worry, and self-doubt, leaving them to react based on the discomfort and dysregulation they are feeling in that moment. This process often results in a well-practiced, though unconscious, effort to avoid discomfort or dysregulation based upon one's internal definition of what that means in the moment. Actions tend to occur absent the awareness of the impact these decisions have on others or the longer-term consequences. These incremental challenges accumulate over time to reinforce and exacerbate the underlying challenges with autism. Eventually, there can be significant challenges functioning independently when viewing the world with a lens that has not been "adjusted" to the rules of that larger world.

Transition to Adulthood

The various challenges of autism commonly coalesce throughout one's development and impair the smooth transition to adult functioning. Many late teens and young adults rely more on those around them to resolve challenges that they face day to day. Many will find that they have often not been successful in some ways in achieving their desired results. The person with autism does not perceive the discouragement they receive in response to their efforts as a means to communicate the need to act differently. The unproductive responses are often repeated by the individual, resulting in more intense responses of more active resistance, defended by "logic" based exclusively on the point of view of the person with autism. The responses they will receive will often feel antagonistic to the neurotypical person, which fuels frustration, annoyance, or anger on the part of those around the individual. The person with autism will often begin to perceive their responses as being attacked and frequently being told they are wrong. In reality, the response of the person with autism is simply different (as judged by the larger society) and ineffective, based on the established rules and norms already in place. Self-doubt and poor self-image begin to grow, resulting in increased feelings of anxiety and/or depression based on a sense of powerlessness and persecution from the perspective of the person with autism. The individual with autism attempts to resolve their discomfort internally, not seeking assistance through traditional expressions or outlets, resulting in increased isolation. The person with autism will pull more deeply into their place of comfort and begin to protect this space more intensely.

Family members and others often recognize the progressive nature of the challenges for persons with autism and seek to help through school and other providers. This help is generally provided through traditional channels that would likely be effective with a neurotypical individual, but which often misses the underlying difficulties being experienced by the individual with autism. Frustrations and tensions rise as the interventions are unsuccessful, coupled with confusion as to how an individual who is both intelligent and can communicate well cannot be more successful. Due to repeated experiences in which a response is ineffective, coupled with the progressively more complicated nature of the problems one encounters through development, a sense of insecurity and self-doubt results. The person with autism then retreats and defers to those around them to resolve challenges as they arise.

This process has the impact of causing those who care for and support these individuals to do more for the person with autism than would traditionally be expected (which the parents and caregivers will sometimes recognize and sometimes not). A byproduct of others taking on the responsibilities of individuals with autism is that this response can often lead to an impaired or even absent sense of resiliency and self-confidence for the autistic individual. Diminished self-confidence coupled with less resiliency and limited perspective on what is not working can manifest in heightened responses to anxiety, anger, and isolation as the pressure to respond more independently intensifies. The progressive nature of this pattern over time can cause people with autism to appear inflexible in their responses to most expectations that activate fear and which would result in change. This often presents as an individual seeming to implicitly trust their own perspective absent an awareness of the perspective of others or the unique dynamics of the situations in which they find themselves. They can be prone to relying heavily on others without trusting their insight and feedback. The person with autism also loses the benefits, both emotionally and functionally, that come from learning from challenging experiences. Further, struggling to decipher the ever-complicated social expectations for how to respond to the situations in which one finds oneself, individuals further impair their ability to identify and practice appropriate social patterns of interaction and become ever more dependent on others for the management of their daily functioning.

Therapeutic Treatment Approaches

A primary goal of intervention is to promote independent functioning. A diverse approach to therapy can be useful to address the multitude of obstacles to this goal. Visual cues and mobile applications can also help the individual to be more conscious of those strategies and to implement strategies outside of session.

During the initial meeting, it can be valuable to discuss how the individual, family, and therapist see autism impacting the functioning of the individual. It is important to recognize that the nature of autism commonly results in not recognizing the presence or severity of problems seen by others. Thus, those attending therapy are often in a pre-contemplation stage of change and might be attending because of external pressure. This is a primary barrier to treatment, as therapeutic interventions are innately based on both the clinician and the client having a shared vision of what must change and what is the desired outcome. An early focus of treatment is typically centered on this notion, providing education and exploring the nature of different ways of experiencing the world. In doing so, it is hoped that one can move away from a problem-focused mindset of blame and judgment for problems and toward understanding and adaptation.

Many individuals have poor self-esteem and self-confidence due to frequent "run-ins" with an uncooperative neurotypical structure. Oftentimes individuals with autism are highly sensitive to any form of critique, which is often interpreted as criticism. It can be useful to describe the individual as the identified client, while emphasizing that intervention is focused on the family as a whole. Families typically adjust their responses to match the needs of the children or family member and have themselves spent a considerable amount of time advocating and defending their loved one. Providing this understanding and involvement of all family members can be an invaluable tool in promoting investment in change.

Communication With Clients

It is typically useful to be direct when working with clients with autism. This should be discussed early in treatment with the client, as a part of treatment and not an effort to be judgmental. Autism makes it much more difficult for the individual to recognize subtlety and to interpret nonverbal cues and inferences accurately. Being more literal and direct in therapy helps to circumvent these obstacles and improve communication and mutual understanding. Society provides a lot of subtle cues and indirect feedback, which contributes to misunderstandings and escalating conflicts in relationships. Although the benefits won't necessarily be recognized immediately, it is hoped that through a more direct approach the client will gradually gain a sense of trust and comfort in a situation that is more concrete.

Direct feedback can include pointing out deviations in behavior from what could be expected given the age of the individual and agreed-upon social norms. This can mean beginning to address behavioral responses in the first session. Deviations from social norms can be immediately obvious, as many individuals with autism can display atypical hygiene, dress, hair, etc. With very little effort or intervention on the part of the clinician, the initial session can become intense quite quickly. Clinicians must be prepared for this and recognize that the response from the client, regardless of how intense, is not personal, and is at times to be expected given their experiences to that point. Regardless of the clinician's intent, they represent what has likely been an unhelpful, and at times harmful, system. The clinician should model calm in the face of responses that can sometimes be intense, and help the families to remain calm as well and so begin to develop trust in the clinician.

It is common for people with autism to state quite specifically why the need exists for others to change to adjust to their expectations. These expectations are often seen as quite reasonable given the perspective of the person with autism. This can be an opportunity to begin to distinguish the expectations of persons with autism from those around them and encourage them to begin to consider why this difference exists. It is helpful to keep in mind that families have likely rarely been supported in understanding their loved one's diagnosis or how to effectively respond. Families have likely been blamed along the way in some manner for the lack of success or progress in their child or loved one, particularly when the person with autism is seen as being intelligent.

Steve Silberman, in his book *NeuroTribes* (2015), details a long history of parents being held responsible for their child's challenges, dating back to the first attempts to classify the behaviors which outline what we see as the modern-day diagnosis of autism. In many ways, this perception from the larger systems—that the client, and the family, are "to blame"—has not changed. Parents often "blame" themselves: for not seeing the diagnosis sooner, for not doing more, etc. It is important to validate the efforts families have made while helping them to understand the changes that will be necessary for themselves and their loved in order to make change. Left unchecked, persons with autism can use the therapeutic process for weeks, months, or even years, to talk about how they are feeling, what is not working, or what they would like to see different, without ever understanding how to change a single behavior or appreciating the power that they have to make change for themselves. Families often feel resigned and will openly state that they "do not know what to do." It is imperative for clinicians to step into this void and actively take charge so that control can be transferred back to the family and eventually to the client.

Areas to consider when first meeting a client and family is whether it is realistic for the individual to develop the requisite skills to find and maintain employment, seek training or attend college if that is their preference, provide for their own transportation (which could mean obtaining a driver's license or productively using public transportation), and develop the skills to maintain themselves in an apartment or home, individually or with roommates. For some individuals, those with intellectual disabilities or pervasive challenges managing their mood, it may be necessary to seek social security income, and connect with community supports to assist with employment, housing, and transportation.

A central component of the initial meetings is to set the frame for the family and the individual as to what the process of therapy or intervention will look like. In addition to the education, it is important to support the family in changing the dynamics of their interaction with their loved one. Very rarely is it someone other than parents bringing an individual in for treatment, though, whoever that individual is, it is important to develop an alliance with them. Therapy is less often successful when individuals attend on their own, as the gap between what the individual believes is necessary and what is generally required is too large from the perspective of the person seeking treatment. On some occasions, the spouse or partner might request services. In these instances, the individual is often motivated to make change due to the awareness of what will occur within their relationship. In other instances, it is too difficult for the identified client to relax their anxiety, and instead they will strongly defend their perspective, looking for the partner to change, as opposed to themselves.

There is often a clear distinction that exists between younger individuals and older individuals newly diagnosed with autism. This experience is expressed nicely by David Finch in his book *The Journal of Best Practices* (2012). Younger individuals often see their diagnosis as evidence that they are damaged, as the diagnosis will challenge what is almost always an already fragile self-image. Finding a collaborative middle ground can be difficult. When the initial sessions are particularly contentious, it is important to work with the families to ensure they understand that such tensions are not uncommon, nor long-lived. In a few instances, the approach will be too overwhelming for the client and family to manage and this will result in therapy being terminated. It is important that the clinician identify as quickly as possible if the discord is too intense. If so, the clinician should work first with the family, and then the client, to resolve this tension and establish a baseline that allows for freedom to challenge the boundaries the client has established for themselves, while still moving forward.

A pattern which should be set early in the therapeutic process is to actively address disconnect between what the individual wants, feels, or perceives in the moment and the expectations of the larger social structure around them. It is helpful to work with the client to appreciate how their patterns have developed to defend the "comfort zone" they have constructed around them, and how this impairs their functioning. A conflict of sorts which often develops early in the process, and can present at times throughout the therapeutic process, is that the person with autism will feel that they will lose their identity if they change. At times this will be expressed as not capitulating to the larger social structure, while at others it can present as a genuine fear of losing one's identity. The truth is there is, in fact, a need to recognize and adjust to social norms and expectations in order to move forward and develop independence, and so to change. Therapy can help explore how this can be done without compromising one's identity. The fear of losing one's identity is a response to the cognitive dissonance that is created as individuals begin to appreciate their lack of movement forward, unsuccessful efforts to achieve desired outcomes, and a growing recognition of a difference between them and those around them.

An analogy for this evolution of mindset is learning to transition from thinking two-dimensionally to thinking three-dimensionally. This is a process described in part by Michio Kaku in his book *The Future of the Mind* (2014). Two-dimensional thinkers respond to a situation based upon the emotions, feelings, and wants of the moment in a manner that best suits them absent an awareness of the impacts on others, and the longer-term ramifications for their choice on themselves and others. Three-dimensional thinkers also include past experiences, future goals, impact on other people, the expectations of the situation, and what is reasonable to accomplish based upon a (more or less) shared vision of social rules, norms, and expectations. Three-dimensional thinking is a skill that people with autism are often capable of, but for which they have oftentimes not been cued to consider in their calculations throughout their development. Subsequently, individuals with autism practice and fine-tune a set of responses which will make sense to them, but not to those around them. The impacts of routinely being perceived as different are viewed by the persons with autism as bad, and so there is an emphasis to maintain consistent patterns and routines despite the ineffectiveness of these patterns and routines to that point.

People with autism will often present their "reasoning" as to why they acted as they did in a given situation, regardless of the result, and will see this explanation as sufficient to address the situation regardless of the outcome. Change is almost never a component of the individual's reasoning for why they acted as they did. Two-dimensional responses in a three-dimensional world often seem disconnected and appear more reactive to the person's perceived wants or needs in the moment. The presentation over time is that each problem an individual with autism faces is too large an obstacle to overcome. The reasoning tends to focus on what others must do or why the person with autism was not "at fault," rather than how the individual can change. This is often not an attempt to avoid responsibility, but a sincere though unconscious response to a pattern of not seeing one's self as capable of making change, as well as not understanding how to make change.

Over time there becomes less and less a sense that an expectation for change exists from the perspective of the individual, and often unintentionally supported by the family as well. The reasoning for this is often explained in a seemingly logical or rational manner. The common thread in the explanations is that the person's actions will have made sense, and any lack of progress or solution was not attributed to their efforts. The problem, however, remains unsolved. Families and other service providers appear to fear that if *they* do not step in and resolve the problem, the person with autism will not resolve the problem themselves. Over time this becomes the approach of the individual and their support system, compromising resilience to trust themselves and to manage obstacles. This, of course, becomes more problematic as the expectations for independent functioning increase. Anxiety fuels resistance and at times anger, and the individual with autism seeks to retreat to a place of comfort.

This process of seeming to resist change is not because the person with autism cannot solve the problems they face. It is often because they were unable to find a solution, or became discouraged quickly and moved on. Anxiety, stemming from the perception of past "failures" and an uncertainty as to how to move forward, is quickly activated when a solution is not immediately apparent. This, combined with impaired development of hindsight, foresight, and insight, will result in the person with autism pivoting away from the challenge and seeking refuge in a more comfortable space due to the discomfort they experience. Recognizing this pattern, families and outside service providers begin to step in more and more, and so unknowingly impair the person with autism from developing the self-confidence and expertise to resolve their challenges. Over time a sense of incompetence develops from and about the person with autism. This is a very gradual process in which each participant unintentionally plays their part. There is often an unconscious sense on the part of the individuals with autism that the world will adjust to their perspective, and that they will genuinely (from the point of view of others) not see their responsibility in making change.

A reflection of this "learned incompetence," and subsequent support from families and outside service providers, presents itself when a problem arises, and will be framed by the persons with autism as others being responsible. This often means the person with autism was asked or expected to do something they were unsure of, or uncomfortable with, or did not want to do. The individual with autism will struggle to see their accountability and contribution to the problems that have arisen between others, or for strategies that are unsuccessful. Therapists will often be framed as incompetent, though it will rarely be spoken as such. Rather, it will state that the strategy which had been suggested did not work. This might mean that the individual never tried the strategy. It might mean that the strategy was tried once or twice. It might mean that the strategy had been tried in part, or that the response the individual received was not in line with their expectations. It could also mean that the strategy was not a great strategy. It is hard to know, due to persistent inflexibility on the part of the person with autism.

Cognitive Flexibility

Autism is often associated with difficulties smoothly integrating cognitive flexibility (the ability to adapt the cognitive processing strategies to face new and unexpected conditions in the environment), cognitive dissonance (the state of having inconsistent thoughts, beliefs, or attitudes, especially as relating to behavioral decisions and attitude change), and emotional flexibility (the capacity to produce context-dependent emotional responses to these positive and negative life events that arise when expected or requested). It can seem to neurotypical people that the individual is looking for a solution which is quick, easy, works the first time, and does not require change on their part. However, an individual with autism would likely disagree vehemently. The person with autism would likely state vociferously their understanding of the need and willingness to make change. The result, however, when there is no outside pressure for prompting, is that the strategy or intervention will not be followed through on, and a reasoning as to why this was the case will be presented instead. The individual will quite likely take offense, or become self-deprecating, when it is pointed out that they had not followed through. Without a more concerted system for maintaining accountability and follow-through, this pattern will repeat itself again and again.

Considerations for Therapy

For many persons with autism, when they first enter therapy there are several underlying factors which manifest themselves throughout the developmental process. These are just a few examples of what might be experienced by clinicians or service providers. What is important to recognize is that, from the point of view of the person with autism, their perspective is both genuine and sincere. While all people are capable of manipulation, the challenges that neurotypical people encounter is often appreciating that persons with autism genuinely see and interpret the world through a unique point of view which can seem disingenuous when viewed through the perspective of someone who is neurotypical. When an intelligent and verbal person expresses a belief or point of view which seems to "miss" key points that seem blatantly obvious, it is important to recognize that "obvious" is a matter of one's perspective. A perspective that is the result of an entirely different developmental trajectory. The behaviors we identify as problematic frequently involve the individual acting in the moment based upon their reading of the situation, which is likely impacted by what they believed to be relevant, and fueled by their wants and needs in the moment. Interwoven into these behaviors and responses will also be a degree of inflexibility, perseverations, and a strong internal drive that lacks the same functional awareness and appreciation of others' wants and needs. The clinician must constantly be sifting through how these factors, which vary in both intensity and degree, might impact the response of the person in front of them.

The therapeutic process itself will take time. As the individual begins to take more ownership for their daily responsibilities and moving forward, and as the family develops a consistent system through which to support their child and loved one, the therapist can begin to assume a more traditional therapeutic stance. Progress tends to move in fits and spurts, and frequency of sessions with families and individuals with autism can fluctuate. There can sometimes be resistance on the part of the individual presented for therapy, though as the process continues many individuals eventually present on their own and of their own volition. The intent again is for these individuals to function productively and independently, to develop the skills to respond proactively to factors which trigger mood, and to develop productive relationships with family and others.

The directive nature of initial contacts is designed to validate long-held beliefs on the part of the families, and to challenge the negative self-perceptions of the persons with autism. Additionally, it can be beneficial for the therapist to take a more active role in helping them to appreciate how the differences in their perceptions impact upon their sincere and genuine desires to function in a productive and independent manner. Once the person with autism has a more complete frame from which to base their understanding as to what has contributed to their challenges, and the therapist and client are on the same page, the therapeutic process can proceed in a more traditional manner.

Conclusion

This is a cursory look at the challenges that often face individuals with autism as they transition into the adult world, and a brief description of a therapeutic approach to address these challenges. No one approach is all-inclusive, nor does it begin to meet the needs of all individuals with autism. I believe a greater awareness and better structure needs to be developed to support these individuals throughout their adolescence and into adulthood. The sooner individuals with autism are identified, the sooner they can begin to receive services to improve the functionality in those areas in which they struggle as they age. Additional areas of support can include services to assist with employment, transportation (including more specialized assistance learning to drive), assistance from colleges in targeting the unique needs of persons with autism to increase the likelihood of success (this is already occurring on a number of college campuses), assistance with developing the skills to live independently and then provide assistance to find housing, and assistance for families throughout the process to support them in supporting their loved ones. With enough education and support both for the individual and the family, many with autism demonstrate the capacity to develop and function independently in a more healthy and productive way.

Addendum: Patterns and Symptoms for Therapy Assessment

The challenge for the service provider is to evaluate the client's competence with regard to social interaction, understanding, and reasoning, functional competence, and executive functioning. The following is a summary of these areas for consideration during a clinical assessment when an autistic spectrum disorder diagnosis is being considered.

- *Social Interaction, Understanding, and Reasoning*: Impairments in the development of skills to advance social connection and interactions. Challenges are reflected by an inability to "make sense" and respond to social nuances in an age-appropriate "expected" manner in real time. Note that a subgroup of individuals will present as highly verbal, though will monopolize conversations as opposed to contributing to a balance in conversation.
  - o Nonverbal communication:
    - o Inconsistent eye contact expressed as difficulty maintaining eye contact for sustained period of time.
    - o Frequent looking away or talking without looking at listener.

- o Persistently flat affect.
- o Difficulty understanding things which are implied or not stated directly.
- o Limited to absent use of body language in communication.
- o Inability to maintain relationships in both structured and unstructured environments in an age-appropriate manner.

- o These challenges can become more problematic as one ages due to the necessity of increased social expectations. Challenges are often expressed through lack of follow-through with academics, responsibilities at home, etc. (parenthetically described as "lazy," "unmotivated," or "does not care"). Often relationships are virtually absent outside of structured setting or not initiated by the individual. Interest in others centers on personal interests. There can be a persistent inability to engage with others to solve problems. The person will often focus on a problem without seeking help to personal detriment; i.e., assignments are not turned in; projects not completed, or when older does not apply for employment, etc. These deficits can create functional impairments in productivity at home, school, and in the community.

- o Functional skill impairments intensify and become more evident with the increased sophistication required throughout one's development, resulting in a presentation that might be defined as odd or quirky.

- o Restricted, repetitive, or stereotyped behavior, interests, and activities. These patterns may appear severe, though as one ages are more likely expressed in more subtle forms. Emphasis is not an observable severity as much as the degree to which one is impaired in meeting age-appropriate expectations in daily functioning and social connections and interactions.

  - o A preoccupation with one or more stereotyped and restricted patterns of interest that are intense in content or focus; or one or more interests that are abnormal in their intensity and circumscribed nature though not in their content or focus.
  - o The preoccupation is not solely distinguished by the direct degree of intensity (which may be abnormal) so much as by the consistency and impairment this preoccupation presents to the development of age-appropriate skills of functioning and interaction.
  - o Stereotyped and repetitive motor mannerisms.

- *Functional Competence*: Delays or impairments in the areas of communication and interactions may appear along a continuum of subtle to overt. Impairments can be identified early in development, prior to age 3, though it is not uncommon for the diagnosis to be "missed" until the increased functional and social expectations of middle school are present. Overall productivity will likely be impacted by how aware the individual is of their diagnosis and subsequent challenges, and for how long. Additionally, the degree of impairment will likely appear more or less intense depending upon the structure of the environment, the individual's familiarity and comfort in that environment, degree of sensory impairments, and the individual's cognitive functioning.

o   Challenges with emotional regulation:

  o   Evidence of clinically significant feelings of anxiety oftentimes reflective of a diagnosis of generalized anxiety disorder. The intensity of feelings will likely intensify or reduce depending on the situation and expectations of the individual and outside forces. Anxiety is often activated by:

   ▪   Social requirements.
   ▪   Situations which are new or novel.
   ▪   Undesired activities, or changes in routine.
   ▪   Sensory sensitivities.
   ▪   Depression: An evaluation is important, as general presentation of the individual (flat affect, increased periods of isolation, and sullen appearance) may be confused as symptomatic of clinical depression. Depressive symptoms can flare up when a challenge is present, and then recede when the challenge has been resolved. Feelings can present as quite intense in the moment, even resulting in threats of self-harm, and then recede quickly. It is important to have a safety plan centered around the particular patterns of the individual.

• *Executive Functioning Impairment*: level or existence of impairment will fluctuate depending upon the environment and persons comfort in an environment.

  o   Response inhibition: Difficulty inhibiting responses
  o   Cognitive flexibility: perseverations on thoughts, concepts, or tasks; difficulty shifting takes, difficulty multitasking
  o   Setting and achieving goals: Difficulty setting goals and maintaining course; difficulty generating individual strategies for problem-solving.
  o   Task initiation: Reduction in self-generated behaviors, procrastination.
  o   Planning, organization, time management: Poor planning, organizational skills, insufficient use of time
  o   Abstract reasoning/concept formation: Use of concrete thinking, difficulty understanding consequences, and cause and effect relationships.
  o   Working memory: Difficulty assessing knowledge, forgetfulness.

- o   Attentional control: Poor attention, distractibility.
- o   Controlling emotions, and social behaviors: Emotional liability, poor frustration tolerance; a tendency to blame others.
- o   Emotional recognition and expression beyond basic emotions (e.g., happy, sad, angry): Moderate to severely impaired.
- o   Self-monitoring and regulation/metacognition: Poor self-control, reduced insight, and difficulty learning from past experiences (often presents as the person living in the moment and reacting based upon what is wanted in that moment absent a recognition of the wants and needs of others or the social/environmental expectations).

References

Beadle, J. N., Keady, B., Brown, V., Tranel, D., & Paradiso, S. (2012). Trait Empathy as a Predictor of Individual Differences in Perceived Loneliness. *Psychological Reports, 110*(1), 3–15. doi:10.2466/07.09.20.pr0.110.1.3-15

Cacioppo, J. T., Fowler, J. H., & Christakis, N. A. (2008). Alone in the Crowd: The Structure and Spread of Loneliness in a Large Social Network. *SSRN Electronic Journal.* doi:10.2139/ssrn.1319108

Finch, D. (2012). *The Journal of Best Practices: A Memoir of Marriage, Asperger Syndrome, and One Man's Quest to Be a Better Husband.* New York: Scribner.

Hirvikoski, T., Mittendorfer-Rutz, E., Boman, M., Larsson, H., Lichtenstein, P., & Bölte, S. (2016). Premature Mortality in Autism Spectrum Disorder. *British Journal of Psychiatry, 208*(3), 232–238. doi:10.1192/bjp.bp.114.160192

Hofvander, B., Delorme, R., Chaste, P., Nydén, A., Wentz, E., Ståhlberg, O., Leboyer, M. (2009). Psychiatric and Psychosocial Problems in Adults with Normal-Intelligence Autism Spectrum Disorders. *BMC Psychiatry, 9*(1). doi:10.1186/1471-244x-9-35

Howlin, P., & Moss, P. (2012) Adults with Autism Spectrum Disorders. *Canadian Journal of Psychiatry, 57*(5), 275–283.

Kaku, M. (2014). *The Future of the Mind: The Scientific Quest to Understand, Enhance, and Empower the Mind.* New York, NY: Doubleday.

Kwon, O., Lee, J., Kim, H., Lee, S., Lee, S., Jeong, M., & Kim, J. (2015). Dopamine Regulation of Amygdala Inhibitory Circuits for Expression of Learned Fear. *Neuron, 88*(2), 378–389. doi:10.1016/j.neuron.2015.09.001

Lake, J. K., Perry, A., & Lunsky, Y. (2014). Mental Health Services for Individuals with High Functioning Autism Spectrum Disorder. *Autism Research and Treatment, 2014,* 1–9. doi:10.1155/2014/502420

Lord, C., Dr. (2017, October 24). *UC Davis Mind Institute Catherine Lord.* Lecture presented at UC Davis Mind Institute 2012–2013 distinguished lecturer series in UC Davis Mind Institute, 2825 50th St, Sacramento, CA 95817.

Luo, Y., Hawkley, L. C., Waite, L. J., & Cacioppo, J. T. (2012). Loneliness, Health, and Mortality in Old Age: A National Longitudinal Study. *Social Science & Medicine, 74*(6), 907–914. doi:10.1016/j.socscimed.2011.11.028

Morgan, J. T., Nordahl, C. W., & Schumann, C. M. (2013). The Amygdala in Autism Spectrum Disorders. *The Neuroscience of Autism Spectrum Disorders,* chapter 3.5, 297–312. doi:10.1016/B978-0-12-391924-3.00021-1

Shattuck, P. T., Carter Narendorf, S., Cooper, B., Sterzing, P. R., Wagner, M., & Lounds Taylor, J. (2012). Postsecondary Education and Employment Among Youth With an Autism Spectrum Disorder. *Pediatrics, 129*(6). doi:10.1542/peds.2011-2864d

Silberman, S. (2015). *NeuroTribes: The Legacy of Autism and the Future of Neurodiversity.* New York, NY: Penguin Random House.

Taylor, J. L., & Seltzer, M. M. (2010). Employment and Post-Secondary Educational Activities for Young Adults with Autism Spectrum Disorders During the Transition to Adulthood. *Journal of Autism and Developmental Disorders, 41*(5), 566–574. doi:10. 1007/s10803-010-1070-3

Thomas, P., Zahorodny, W., Peng, B., Kim, S., Jani, N., Halperin, W., & Brimacombe, M. (2011). The Association of Autism Diagnosis With Socioeconomic Status. *Autism, 16*(2), 201–213. doi:10.1177/1362361311413397

8

THE RELATIONSHIP BETWEEN AUTISM SPECTRUM DISORDER AND CRIMINALITY

A Call to Arms

Amy Caffero-Tolemy

In 2012, Adam Lanza, an individual diagnosed with autism spectrum disorder (ASD), shot and killed his mother, 20 children and 6 adults, and then himself, in the Sandy Hook Elementary Shooting (Adam Lanza, 2016). This incident brought a surge of attention to whether individuals with ASD have a propensity towards violence. Although the controversy may have receded from mainstream conversation, the relationship between ASD and criminality remains an important question for psychological researchers.

While there have been many shootings in the US in recent years, the Sandy Hook massacre was the first to involve someone known to have been diagnosed with ASD. While horrific, the event fostered a great deal of research and controversy on the relationship between ASD and criminal behavior. Given the complex nature of research of this type, made even more complex by the recent change in diagnostic criteria of ASD with the release of the *Diagnostic and Statistical Manual of Mental Disorders, Fifth Edition* (DSM-5), the relationship between ASD and criminality remains somewhat cloudy. However, one thing has become clear: the criminal justice system as a whole is ill-prepared to handle individuals with ASD who commit crimes.

This chapter will present a basic overview of risk and protective factors for individuals who do not have ASD and then compare these findings with what is known about risk and protective factors for those with ASD. Following this, an overview of the two major opinions regarding ASD and criminality will be presented. Finally, we will explore the challenges facing ASD individuals in the criminal justice system as well as what needs to be done to improve their situations.

Risk and Protective Factors

While a comprehensive overview of research on the reasons for criminal behavior is beyond the scope of this chapter, a basic understanding of the topic is necessary to understand ASD's role, or lack thereof, in criminality. To that end, we will begin by examining the statistical data for juvenile and adult offenders. Once we know what a typical offender looks like, we will explore the various risk and protective factors related to both population sets.

Typical Offenders

Juvenile General

In 1991, one in seven violent crimes were charged to juveniles (Snyder & Sickmund, 1995). By 2008, one in eight violent crimes were charged to juveniles (Puzzanchera, 2009). In 2008, the crimes leading to the arrests of juveniles varied from truancy and possession of illegal substances to rape and murder. Specifically, in 2008, juveniles accounted for 16% of all violent crime arrests and 26% of all property crime arrests (Puzzanchera, 2009). Crimes such as property destruction, motor vehicle theft, arson, forcible rape, and murder were all more likely to have been committed by a child under 18 than by an adult. The most common crime for which a youth was arrested in 2008 was property destruction (Puzzanchera, 2009).

According to Garabedian and Gibbons (1970), engaging in some delinquent behavior may be considered a rite of passage in American society. Although there may be many adolescents who engage in delinquent actions, only 3% of all adolescents ever enter the juvenile courtroom. Generally, the youth who have been caught and charged with crimes have engaged in previous delinquent actions. According to Garabedian and Gibbons, many juvenile delinquents begin committing crimes as young as 6 or 7 years old. "Predelinquents," as they are referred, may feel pressure from their peers to prove that they are tough and may want to fit in with older peers (Garabedian & Gibbons, 1970, p. 9). These situations can take all sorts of forms including, but not limited to, stealing, joyriding, breaking and entering, fighting, "hustling" strangers for money, bullying peers, having sex, vandalism, drinking, and doing drugs (Garabedian & Gibbons, 1970, p. 14).

Many juvenile offenders experience challenges due to complex psychological issues (Heilbrun, Sevin Goldstein, & Redding, 2005). They generally present with multi-layered issues that may be the result of genetic, neurological, or temperamental problems, such as ADHD, frontal lobe dysfunction, impulsivity, and low intelligence. Additionally, many juvenile offenders have multiple mental health problems that are untreated. These adolescents often suffer from a combination of mood disorders, substance abuse, anxiety disorders, and learning disabilities (Heilbrun et al., 2005). In a study involving 50 adolescents in a juvenile detention center, only 24% did not meet criteria for any DSM-IV diagnosis (Pliszka et al., 2000).

A number of studies have found results consistent with Heilbrun et al.'s (2005) claims that juvenile offenders often have more than one mental health issue. Pliszka et al. (2000) found a higher incidence of substance abuse among juveniles with mental illness than those without. Furthermore, Teplin et al. (2002) found that two-thirds of males and nearly three-quarters of females in a juvenile detention center met diagnostic criteria for one or more mental health diagnosis. Huizinga et al. (2000) also found a relationship between persistent substance abuse and persistent juvenile delinquency. They found that 38% of serious male delinquents were also drug users.

Anxiety disorders, specifically post-traumatic stress disorder (PTSD), have been found to be more common in female juvenile offenders (Cauffman et al., n.d.).

Protective Factors

In order to have a thorough understanding of what contributes to offending, it is important to explore risk and protective factors. Protective factors are those that may reduce the negative effects of risk factors by moderating the risk factors (Heilbrun et al., 2005). In other words, protective factors are features of a juvenile's life that are considered to aid in preventing them from engaging in criminal acts. Protective factors fall under one of four categories: individual, family, school, peer, and environmental protective factors. Individual protective factors include high intelligence, education, sociability, positive temperament, the ability to seek social support, and utilizing effective coping strategies. Davies (2004) added that resilience, an inherent "invulnerability" that some children have to succeed despite risks, is an individual protective factor as well (p. 62).

Family protective factors include the absence of significant family disturbance, warmth of family relationships, having non-aggressive role models, strong attachment between parents and child, parental monitoring of child's behavior, and the provision of clear and consistent norms for behavior (Heilbrun et al., 2005). Parents who model appropriate coping skills, a house with rules and structure, and a supportive relationship with grandparents are additional protective factors (Davies, 2004). School-related protective factors include educational achievements, a commitment to school, and participation in school-related extracurricular activities (Heilbrun et al., 2005). A classroom that is structured around clear rules and praise, and one in which a solid relationship between teachers and parents exists, is also a school-related protective factor (Davies, 2004).

Hoge, Andrews, and Leschied (1996) conducted a study involving 338 juvenile offenders. The authors used participants' files to complete measures of risk and protective factors. The protective factors that were evaluated in this study were positive peer relationships, good academic achievement, effective use of leisure time, and positive response to authority (Hoge et al., 1996).

Intelligence as a Protective Factor

Mulder et al. (2010) also found that intelligence was one of the nine factors important in determining whether juvenile offenders would commit severe crimes in the future. There is an inverse relationship between intelligence and offending. Mulder et al. also found that antisocial behavior during treatment, family problems, and Axis I psychopathology were more highly associated with recidivism than intelligence. Stahlberg, Anckarsäter, and Nilsson (2010) reviewed the neuropsychological assessments of 100 juvenile criminals or juveniles with behaviors that were too difficult for caregivers to manage. They found that the mean Full Scale Intelligence Quotient (FSIQ) for the participants was almost one standard deviation below the mean of peers who did not engage in criminal behavior. Hays, Solway, and Schreiner (1978) assessed the intellectual abilities of 64 juvenile offenders. Hays et al. (1978) found that the offenders' verbal scores were lower than the performance scores. Nearly 30 years later, Chitsabesan et al. (2007) and Hayes (2005) supported Hays et al.'s (1978) findings.

Risk Factors

Risk factors for juvenile offending are broadly defined as external or internal influences or conditions that are associated with a negative outcome (Heilbrun et al., 2005). Risk factors can be either static or dynamic (Andrews & Bonta, 1998). Static risk factors are unchangeable, such as demographic data and historic information. Dynamic risk factors can be changed. These include access to drugs, availability of weapons, and level of education.

Risk factors at the family level include child abuse, child neglect, low level of parental involvement, high level of hostility, conflict, aggression within the family, parental criminality, inadequate parental supervision, early parental loss, parental mental illness, parental substance abuse, divorce, and emotional deprivation (Davies, 2004; Heilbrun et al., 2005). In 2009, there were an estimated 763,000 victims of child maltreatment (U.S. Department of Health and Human Services, 2010). English, Widom, and Brandford (2002) evaluated adult offenders and found that those who experienced abuse and neglect as children were at a 55% increased risk of engaging in criminal activity leading to arrest as a juvenile. Further, English et al. (2002) found offenders who were abused or neglected as children had higher rates of arrest as adolescents.

School-related risk factors include low academic achievements, poor academic performance, low commitment to school, and failing to complete school (Heilbrun et al., 2005). Peer-related risk factors include negative peer relationships and associating with delinquent youths. Environmental factors that are considered to be risk factors are low socioeconomic status and repeated exposure to violence (Heilbrun et al., 2005). Davies (2004) considered poor childcare and racism both to be environmental risk factors.

Hoge et al. (1996) found three risk factors that were all related to family functioning: family relationship problems, family structuring problems, and parent problems. Of these familial risk factors, family relationship problems and family structure problems were associated with high rates of reoffending and low compliance behaviors, similar to the findings of Heilbrun et al. (2005).

In an experiment designed to determine the most effective way to classify serious juvenile offenders, Mulder et al. (2010) conducted a factor analysis of 70 risk factors. They found nine factors that were the most meaningful when examining recidivists. The nine factors were: Axis II psychopathology, history of offending, limited conscience and empathy, family problems, antisocial behavior during treatment, and four types of sexual problems (which were unclearly defined). Many of the nine factors that were found to be critical in juvenile offenders who reoffend and have committed a serious crime were the same as those discussed by Heilbrun et al. (2005).

Adult Offenders

Adult General

There are some important differences between adult and juvenile offenders. Primarily, given the age differences, adult offenders typically have a lengthier history with the criminal justice system. Another difference is that adults are involved in the adult correction system, which is, theoretically, less focused on rehabilitation and subsequently plagued with recidivism rates of about 75% within five years post release (Durose, Cooper & Snyder, 2014). In 2010, over 11 million arrests of adults were made (Snyder, 2012), of which 13% were violent crimes, 15% were property crimes, 25% were drug-related offenses, and 45% were other crimes, including weapons charges, driving under the influence, disorderly conduct, etc. Of crimes committed by adults, 24% were committed by women. Similar to juvenile offenders, African American males are over-represented (Snyder, 2012).

Protective Factors

When an adult is brought up in a family, environment, and school that contained the protective factors listed above, they are typically considered to have continued protection. This is because a factor like education, which does not expire, instead aids in the ability to obtain further positive protective factors, including things like a job or continued education. Effectively, protective factors that are established early in life can have long-lasting positive effects.

Not surprisingly, one of the most important long-term protective factors—and one which has received a lot of academic attention—is intelligence. This may be partly due to the fact that it is relatively easy to assess and is generally considered to be stable over time. Kandel et al. (1988) found that men who were at high risk for, but avoided, antisocial behavior had higher FSIQ scores than men who engaged in antisocial behavior regardless of the risk level. This was similar to the findings of Walsh, Swogger, and Kosson (2004), who found low FSIQ scores to be a valuable predictive measure of violent crimes in European American adult males, but not in African American adult males. Further, Sampson and Laub (2003 found an inverse relationship between most adult male offenders and FSIQ score, as well as an inverse relationship between age and committed crime. Specifically, the age group that contains the largest number of adults is 20–25 years old.

Risk Factors

According to Bushway and Reuter (2002), risk factors for criminal behavior of adults is heavily dependent on employment. Specifically, adults are more likely to engage in criminal behavior when they are unemployed or under-employed, somewhat due to necessity. However, Bushway and Reuter (2002) point out that having a job can grant additional access to criminal activities, such as embezzlement and theft of inventory. Further, they note an additional risk factor for criminal behavior is living in a community with high crime.

Similar to juvenile offenders, poverty, poor education, being male, substance abuse, and mental illness (specifically personality disorders), are also known risk factors (Tanner-Smith, Wilson, & Lipsey, 2013). Satterfield and Schell (1997), found that conduct problems in childhood and severe antisocial behavior in adolescence are risk factors for adult criminal involvement. They also found that hyperactivity in childhood is a predictor for adult criminal involvement.

ASD Offenders

Due to the limited amount of information on criminality and ASD, there is not enough data to differentiate between the juvenile offender with ASD and the adult offender with ASD. Therefore, this section will discuss both age groups as one. Despite a great deal of attention being paid to ASD in the general population specifically related to detection, early intervention services, and vaccinations, minimal solid research has been conducted on the relationship between ASD and the criminal justice system. Further, the research that has been conducted has been plagued with somewhat unavoidable methodological errors (King & Murphy, 2014). According to their meta-review of the relevant research on the topic, the research is hindered by the different inclusion criteria used by various researchers. There is a significant difference between the presentation of autism, Asperger's disorder (AD), and pervasive developmental disorder not otherwise specified (PDD-NOS), making it nearly impossible to compare one research finding to another when different inclusionary criteria have been used. This situation was made more complicated by the 2013 release of the DSM-5, because diagnoses such as Asperger's disorder and PDD-NOS were removed and replaced with a more spectrum-based approach to diagnostics.

Protective Factors

Individuals with ASD make up a very diverse population—a point supported by the fact that it is a spectrum disorder. Consequently, the range of functioning varies a great deal as well. While there are many individuals with ASD who go on to live independent lives, there are many who require significant support. These individuals may reside in group homes or other residential facilities where their behavior is monitored by staff, or they may continue to live with their parents and have limited engagement in the outside world. Individuals with ASD may not be able to go on an outing without a caregiver. The limited interactions with peers and the monitoring of behavior can serve as a protective factor, if simply because it limits access. Additionally, individuals who are diagnosed at an early age and are able to receive services are at an advantage to those who do not receive services (Lerner et al., 2012).

Risk Factors Related to ASD

The fact is, most individuals with ASD will not engage in criminal acts (Krisiansson & Sorman, 2008). However, the disorder does have inherent features that may increase ASD individuals' chances of breaking the law. Howlin (2004) found that there are four factors which seem to increase someone with ASD's likelihood of committing a crime. First, they are more socially naïve, which places them at an increased risk of being manipulated by others. Second, they may become aggressive when there is a disruption of their routine due to their rigid adherence to schedule and rules. Third, they may become aggressive due to frustration because of a lack of social skills and poor frustration tolerance. Finally, they may unintentionally engage in criminal offending in an attempt to obtain their obsessional interest.

Some of the symptoms and consequences of AD and PDD-NOS are risk factors of criminal behavior (Krisiansson & Sorman, 2008). One such risk factor is social isolation. Due to deficits in social skills and awareness, individuals with AD and PDD-NOS often spend a great deal of time alone. Also, individuals with AD and PDD-NOS are often bullied as children and generally have few friends (Haskins & Silva, 2006). Social isolation may lead to sexual frustration, intrusive thoughts, and sensual fantasies (Krisiansson & Sorman, 2008). Finally, displaying repetitive, abnormal, and narrow interests can lead to perseveration and fixation. This can lead to criminal acts such as stalking. Further, Murrie et al. (2002) also found that sexual misconduct was higher in the high functioning autism spectrum disorder (HFASD) sample compared to typical offenders.

Theory of Mind as a Risk Factor

An additional risk factor that is inherent with individuals with ASD is related to their limited theory of mind, which is the ability to make inferences about what another person is thinking, feeling, or will do (Premack & Woodruff, 1978). Wing and Gould (1979) noted that children with ASD are likely to treat other people in a similar manner as they would treat objects, which is likely based on their limited theory of mind. More recently, Lerner et al. (2012) suggested that the impairment of theory of mind, along with poor emotional regulation discussed previously, may raise the risk of engaging in criminal activities. In summary, it is easy to see how one could engage in a criminal act against another person if they struggle to control their emotions and are not able to understand how the person would feel about the crime.

Risk Factors in Addition to ASD

Kawakami et al. (2012) looked to determine what risk factors were present in individuals with HFASD, which included high functioning autism and Asperger's syndrome, who engaged in criminal behavior. However, they took the research further than previous studies, as they did not focus only on those traits related to HFASD but looked at how the already identified risk factors for offending (listed in the discussion of typical juvenile offender section of this chapter) impacted those with HFASD. Similar to those without HFASD or ASD, Kawakami et al. (2012) found that a history of neglect and physical abuse significantly predicted criminal behavior, as did a later age of diagnosis with HFASD. Baron-Cohen (1988) found that engaging in a previous criminal act was likewise found as a risk factor.

Patterson, DeBaryshe, and Ramsey (1989) also found that adolescents who engage in criminal behaviors experience risk factors that are similar to those seen in adolescents with ASD. Such risk factors include poor relationships with parents, poor relationships with peers, and poor academic performance. Hartup and Moore (1990) also found that poor relationships with peers in children without ASD resulted in higher rates of social deviance than in those who had good relationships with peers.

In a meta-analysis of the research to date, Långström et al. (2009) identified risk factors in the ASD population that can lead to a greater risk for violent offending. These risk factors include being male, being of older age (M = 26.19, SD = 9.53), experiencing comorbid psychosis, experiencing substance use disorder, and/or having a personality disorder. They also noted that these match the risk factors typically noted in the non-ASD population of offenders as well.

Unfortunately, individuals with HFASD may fall through the cracks and not be diagnosed until later in life. In fact, the diagnosis may only occur once they have offended and become involved with the criminal justice system (Schwartz-Watts, 2005). Going without a diagnosis means that they do not have access to services that can provide them with emotional regulation skills, which may prevent outbursts. Also, given the fact that children and adolescents with HFASD present with social skills deficits, they are at a higher risk for being bullied by peers, which can lead to a host of other problems.

Although there may be some correlation between AD and PDD-NOS and criminal activity, it is also possible that there are other comorbid disorders, such as psychotic disorders, which contribute to criminal activities (Newman & Ghaziuddin, 2008). Kawakami et al. (2012) also found that a comorbid mental health diagnosis served as a risk factor. Green et al. (2000) compared adolescents with ASD to those with conduct disorder (CD) in regard to their social functioning and mental health. They found that adolescents with CD were more independent than those with AD. Specifically, only 50% of the adolescents with ASD were able to complete basic self-care activities independently and consistently, in contrast to 100% of adolescents with CD. Furthermore, when the adolescents' parents were surveyed regarding social functioning, 95% of the parents with ASD children stated that their children had difficulty socially with peers. In contrast, only 60% of parents with CD children reported the same. The adolescents with ASD reported more difficulty than CD adolescents in areas such as understanding others' feelings of annoyance, coping with teasing, and dealing with their own feelings of annoyance (Green et al., 2000). Parental responses for both groups paralleled the adolescents' responses. The parental reports indicated that the two groups had similar experiences of chronic sadness, loneliness, anxiety, poor attention, temper tantrums, lying, defiance of parents, and aggressiveness. In addition to these issues, the ASD group reported a greater frequency of sleep issues, obsessions and compulsions, disinhibition, a lower frequency of restlessness outside of the home, and substance abuse.

Intelligence as a Protective Factor

As noted previously, intelligence is generally considered to be a protective factor against offending (Heilbrun et al., 2005). However, there has been some controversy surrounding its application to all populations (Mulder et al., 2010). An unpublished study by Caffero-Tolemy (2012) was conducted to determine if high intelligence was a mediating factor for adolescents with ASD and PDD-NOS. Participants included a sample of 35 adolescents who were diagnosed with Asperger's disorder (n = 22) or PDD-NOS (n = 13). The inclusion criteria included any individuals between the ages of 12 and 18 who completed the WASI (Wechsler Abbreviated Scale of Intelligence) and whose VIQ (verbal intelligence quotient) and PIQ (performance intelligence quotient) scores were included in their reports. Participants from all ethnicities and racial backgrounds were included. Overall, 28 (80%) participants were male and 7 (20%) were female, which is similar to the ratio of male to female diagnoses in the general population (Ehlers & Gillberg, 1993). Additionally, 33 (94.3%) of the participants were given at least one other Axis I diagnosis. Of the given additional Axis I diagnoses, the three most common were an anxiety disorder (n = 16; 48.5%), ADHD (n = 13; 39.3%), and a depressive disorder (n = 12; 36.3%).

Of the 35 participants, 10 (28.6%) did have a history of arrest and were considered to be offenders. Of the offenders, 9 (90%) were male and 1 (10%) was female. The ages of the offenders ranged between 12 and 18 years old (M = 14.78, SD = 1.86). All of the offenders were given at least one other Axis I diagnosis. Of the additional Axis I diagnoses given to offenders, 6 (60%) were diagnosed with a depressive disorder, 3 (30%) with an anxiety disorder, and 2 (20%) with ADHD.

This study sought to determine whether VIQ and/or PIQ had a predictive relationship with offending in juveniles with ASD and PDD-NOS. The results showed that there was no significant difference between the two groups in terms of scores on either the VIQ or the PIQ. However, while the results did suggest a trend toward significance, additional research is needed on this topic using a larger sample size.

The model accounted for approximately 20–28% of the variability in criminal history. There are a few possible explanations for these results. First, it is possible that there really is no relationship between IQ and offending in juveniles with PDDs. Although the results suggest a trend toward a relationship, the relationship was not significant. Second, it is possible that there were not enough participants to detect a significant relationship between the VIQ and PIQ scores, respectively or in combination, and offending. Third, it is possible that there are other intervening factors that were not accounted for in this model. For instance, parents of children with PDDs may provide increased supervision of their adolescents due to the diagnosis. These adolescents may also be supervised by other adults during more of the day and therefore have less unsupervised time than their non-PDD counterparts. This increased supervision may serve as a protective factor that exerts a greater effect than intelligence when predicting offending. While many protective factors apply to both those with and without ASD, the fact that intelligence does not adds to some of the variability in the research and remaining unanswered questions on this topic overall.

Does ASD Lead to Crime?

Intro of Sides

Any questions regarding the relationship between ASD and criminality may seem clear cut. After all, compared to the general population, forensic settings are home to a larger percentage of individuals with PDD (Krisiansson & Sorman, 2008). Specifically, it was found that there is a larger percentage of individuals with ASD in forensic hospitals (1.5–2.3%) than there is in typical community settings (Scragg & Shah, 1994). Additionally, numerous studies have reported strange, unusual, and serious crimes that have been committed by individuals with Asperger's disorder (Baron-Cohen, 1988; Haskins & Silva, 2006; Krisiansson & Sorman, 2008). Such crimes include sexual assaults, threatening phone calls, attempted murder, and murder. Furthermore, in one study by Siponmaa et al. (2001), researchers found that 63% of arson cases involved individuals with AD. This data, along with a tragedy like the Sandy Hook Elementary School shooting, would seem to indicate a relationship between ASD and criminality. As we will see, this is not necessarily the case. In fact, a deeper dive into the data, coupled with a look at the long-term research, seems to portray a very different picture.

Historical Perspective

In addition to the findings mentioned above, some additional research has pointed to a direct relationship between ASD and criminal behavior. Mawson, Grounds, and Tantam (1985) were the first to discuss the relationship between Asperger's disorder and crime, and they were soon followed by Baron-Cohen (1988). Both discussed case reports of individuals with AD who engaged in serious and violent crimes, such as assault, rape, and murder. While these early contributions to the research raised important questions about the topic, it is necessary to note that both studies were based on case reports and minimal statistical inferences can be made.

Perhaps more importantly, one of the first meta-analyses of relevant articles on the topic was completed by Ghaziuddin, Tsai, and Ghaziuddin (1991). These researchers found that there was no more of a relationship between crime and Asperger's disorder than in a typical population. More than a decade later, Ghaziuddin et al.'s (1991) findings were confirmed by Schwartz-Watts (2005). Schwartz-Watts (2005) conducted case forensic studies that identified numerous supplementary factors such as additional mental illnesses, homelessness, and a history of prior interpersonal issues with the victim. From these findings we can infer that, at very least, these additional factors add to the complex relationship between AD and criminal activity.

Newman and Ghaziuddin (2008) attempted to determine to what extent psychiatric factors contributed to offending behaviors in individuals with AD. They reviewed 37 cases in which there was an individual with AD who committed a crime. Of these 37 cases, 11 (29.7%) cases had definitive evidence of psychiatric disorders and 20 (54%) cases had evidence of possible psychiatric disorders. The specific disorders were not listed. In six cases (16.2%), there was no clear evidence of a comorbid psychiatric disorder (Newman & Ghaziuddin,

2008). The primary diagnosis was ASD in 16.2% of the cases. These findings suggest that "impairment of mental health may be an important reason why some persons with Asperger syndrome commit violent criminal acts" (Newman & Ghaziuddin, 2008, p. 1850). The authors did not indicate whether the individuals with ASD experienced any comorbid disorders. As with Ghaziuddin et al. (1991) and Schwartz-Watts (2005), there is an implication that the diagnosis of Asperger's disorder without any other comorbid mental health diagnosis may not be related to criminal activity.

Yet more evidence against a clear relationship between ASD and criminality comes in research from Hare et al. (1999). After screening more than 1,300 patients in English forensic hospitals, the researchers found that only 21 patients had ASD in their clinical record. When these 21 patients were compared to the general forensic population at the hospitals, there was no difference in the conviction rate for homicide and other violent offenses. Interestingly, arson was overrepresented in the ASD group (16% vs. 10%), and sexual offenses were underrepresented (3% vs. 9%).

The findings in the English forensic hospital study is supported by Mouridsen et al. (2008). They conducted a study involving both incarcerated and non-incarcerated adults, half of which had previously received a diagnosis of some form of PDD, including ASD. They found that 18.4% of the adults with PDD had previously been convicted of a crime. This is lower than the 19.6% of adults who did not have a PDD but had been convicted of a crime.

Newman and Ghaziuddin (2008) attempted to determine to what extent psychiatric factors contributed to offending behaviors in individuals with Asperger's disorder. They reviewed 37 cases in which there was an individual with AD who committed a crime. Of these 37 cases, 11 (29.7%) cases had definitive evidence of psychiatric disorders and 20 (54%) cases had evidence of possible psychiatric disorders. The specific disorders were not listed. In six cases (16.2%), there was no clear evidence of a comorbid psychiatric disorder (Newman & Ghaziuddin, 2008). The primary diagnosis was ASD in 16.2% of the cases. These findings suggest that "impairment of mental health may be an important reason why some persons with Asperger syndrome commit violent criminal acts" (Newman & Ghaziuddin, 2008, p. 1850). The authors did not indicate whether the individuals with ASD experienced any comorbid disorders. However, this implies that the diagnosis of AD without any other comorbid mental health diagnosis may not be related to criminal activity.

Im (2016) also conducted a meta-analysis of research published regarding the relationship between ASD and violent behavior. This review explored 65 articles from 1943 to 2014. Across those 65 articles, there were 27 case reports involving 48 individuals with ASD who engaged in a violent act of physical assault, sexual assault, arson, murder, or stalking/violent threats. It was found that individuals with ASD are no more violent than those without ASD. Furthermore, there were three factors that may contribute to the violence seen in individuals with ASD: comorbid psychopathology, deficits in empathy and theory of mind, and difficulty with emotional regulation. In summary, Im (2016) found that it was not ASD that led to violence, but the comorbid features.

The Juvenile Question

Interestingly, research focusing specifically on juveniles with ASD who engage in criminal activity has been, to date, much more inconclusive, given that so many of the risk and protective factors that we explored earlier are established early in life and progress into adulthood.

One study that does specifically address this area of research was conducted by Cheely et al. (2011); however, they included all ASD diagnoses. Their goals were threefold: to gain information about the frequency and type of crimes charged to juveniles with PDD, to determine if cases involving PDD are handled differently by the Department of Juvenile Justice (DJJ), and to determine if there are any predictors of criminal behavior in juveniles with PDD. Cheely et al. (2011) used archival data from the South Carolina Autism and Developmental Disabilities Monitoring Project (SC ADDM), which identifies children who meet criteria for PDD. They also used the South Carolina Office of Research and Statistics (ORS) to obtain information on contact that the children with PDD had with the DJJ.

Of the 609 adolescents that were in the study, 32 (5%) were charged with a total of 103 offenses, averaging 3 offenses per offender (Cheely et al., 2011). The 32 with PDD were compared to other juvenile offenders without PDD. Those with PDD had a lower number of offenses (3 to 4). Additionally, there was a significant difference between the types of crimes that were committed, with the PDD group having a higher percentage of crimes against other people and a lower percentage of crimes against property than the non-PDD group. When the two groups were compared for additional diagnoses, there were no significant differences. In conclusion, Cheely et al. (2011) found that juvenile offenders with PDD are more likely to commit a crime against a person, less likely to commit property crime, and more likely to have their cases handled differently than juvenile offenders without PDD.

What Crimes Are Being Committed?

Despite the fact that there does not appear to be a clear relationship between ASD and criminal behavior, some individuals with ASD do commit crimes. Freckelton (2013) presented a review of the types of crimes that are committed by those with ASD based on a review of literature. The crimes that those with ASD disproportionately commit are: arson offenses, computer offenses, stalking offenses, sexual offenses, violence and neglect offenses, and dishonesty offenses.

The research regarding ASD and crime is often presented with a discussion of arson. This is likely due in part to the case of William Cottrell, who was charged and convicted for eco-terrorism in 2003 when he destroyed 125 SUVs using arson and other means of destruction, resulting in the death of 12 people. In spite of the Cottrell case, according to Freckelton (2013), there are not as many cases of arson as expected given the presentation in the research.

Meanwhile, while the internet can seemingly be a safe place for individuals with ASD to explore their interests, it may also encourage obsessiveness. Specifically, the internet provides these individuals a way to perseverate on things that may otherwise not be accepted in daily life while also not requiring that they engage in the real world. Of course, not all of the internet is harmless, and computer offending (Freckelton, 2013) refers to a diverse and troubling set of crimes ranging from hacking to having child pornography on one's hard drive.

The remaining crimes noted by Freckelton (2013) involve the complex issues surrounding power and relationship dynamics. First, an ASD individual's inability to read social cues, coupled with a tendency toward preservation or perseverating tendencies, may manifest in the form of stalking or harassing behaviors. While inappropriate on behalf of the stalker/harasser, and in no way the fault of the victim, it is not hard to imagine that some ASD individuals might engage in this behavior simply because of their inability to understand situational social mores. Equally troublesome, Freckelton (2013) draws attention to crimes of sexual offending associated with individuals with ASD. It is important to note that there is only a minimal amount of data on this type of crime and ASD. Moreover, judges have displayed a great deal of variability in how they sentence this sort of case in terms of the weight given to autism.

Violence and neglectful offending make up another of Freckelton's (2013) category of crimes associated with individuals with ASD. It is these crimes that are most often found to be due to deficits related to ASD, theory of mind, poor self-regulation, or literal interpretation of a situation. Finally, dishonesty offending may potentially be due to their obsessional thinking, such as stealing of strange items that are their focus of perseveration.

Actus reus is the action or the lack of action that constitutes the crime. The various behaviors that are common with ASD can be used to mediate the *actus reus*. For instance, an individual with ASD who contacts a stranger via email multiple times per day may be perceived as harassment, but it is likely due to their deficit in theory of mind and poor social skills. Also, ASD can be used to mediate *mens rea*, which is the "mental state" of an individual during the crime. If in a stressful, overwhelming situation, an individual with ASD may become upset and unintentionally aggressive when touched.

Interaction with the Justice System

No matter what the underlying relationship between ASD and criminality, the fact remains that some individuals with ASD have or will commit crimes.

Recognizing this, it is necessary to examine how ASD individuals interact with the criminal justice system, from arrest to conviction and beyond.

Arrest

When individuals with ASD do commit crimes, they are more likely to be caught than individuals without ASD due to their lack of sophisticated coping and planning skills. Once arrested, individuals with HFASD are also more likely to make false confessions due to their social naiveté (Lerner et al., 2012). Alley (2015) noted that individuals with HFASD may not be able to effectively deal with the demands of police during and following an arrest or detainment. Many individuals with HFASD are compliant, increasing their risk of agreeing to crimes they did not commit. Additionally, a theory of mind deficit can impair their ability to accurately recall the details of events, particularly related to others' perspectives about the incidents. ASD individuals also may become emotionally distressed due to the interrogation, possibly increasing their risk of making a false confession. This is problematic, because they can then be convicted and charged, forcing them to enter into a criminal justice system that is overtaxed and unprepared to deal with individuals with such complex needs.

Furthermore, it is unlikely individuals with ASD are able to fully understand their *Miranda* rights. This may be because of cognitive deficits that are inherent to many individuals with ASD (Lerner et al., 2012). Sadly, 90% of police officers lack training to specifically address the needs of those with ASD (National Autistic Society, 2008). Since the police are often the first line of the criminal justice system, their lack of training can create an escalation of aggression, potentially leading to additional charges.

Court

According to Freckelton (2013), some characteristics of ASD may negatively impact an individual's ability to understand charges, assist counsel, and submit a plea. As noted above, the courts are not always sympathetic to this concern. Undoubtedly, individuals with ASD would benefit by having an attorney versed in ASD to assist and defend them. However, this is not always an option, as not all attorneys have completed training in the best practices for working with individuals with ASD. Since it can be argued that that training would need to extend to all individuals who come in contact with the defendant, including legal aides, paraprofessionals, court staff, police and correctional officers, it is easy to anticipate numerous barriers standing in the way of this possibility. Additionally, because individuals with ASD are more likely than others to have a comorbid disorder, it is likely that the training would be more complex and more time-consuming. Of course, given the challenges that we noted earlier, it could be argued that higher prevalence of a comorbid disorder in AD individuals is enough of a reason to make training more necessary.

In any event, Browning and Caulfield (2011) found that the difficulties for those with HFASD continue throughout their time in the court room. For all defendants, their conviction and charges lie in the hands of a judge or jury. However, in the case of those with HFASD, the impact that their disorder has on them, and what role it played in the crime, is also decided. This is heavily based on the amount of knowledge that the judge or jury has on HFASD. In recent years this has been demonstrated by the great deal of variance in charges and convictions for similar crimes committed by those with ASD.

As Freckelton (2013) noted, those with ASD may be negatively impacted by two important factors. The first is that they may have a diminished capacity to understand and communicate with others, specifically related to their charges. If an individual cannot communicate effectively, they are less likely to be capable of aiding their attorney in their own defense. Freckelton (2013) also noted that an individual with ASD, in court or during an interview, may present in a way that is not beneficial to them. For instance, limited eye contact or a decreased display of emotion may be misinterpreted by the judge or jury as callous, when it may actually be symptomatic of ASD.

In 2007, the Supreme Court of New Jersey ruled that the intermediate appellate court erred when the defendant was not allowed to introduce evidence that he had ASD when he was tried for second-degree sexual assault and third-degree endangering the welfare of a child (*State v. Burr*, 2008). The Supreme Court found that the defendant was wronged because the jurors were not made aware that his AD kept him from viewing the world as others do in terms of acceptable social interactions. This ruling appears to be accounting for the inherent social deficits that individuals with AD have that may lead to criminal behaviors.

However, in 2009, the United State Court of Appeals ruled on a case involving W. Cottrell, an adult with AD who was convicted of conspiracy and arson (*United States v. Cottrell*, 2009). He initially pled guilty to being the driver for a group of would-be arsonists as they picked up gasoline and then went to various dealerships to set fire to cars. During the 2004 trial, the judge did not allow Cottrell to present evidence of his Asperger's disorder because it did not hinder his ability to foresee his fellow group members' actions. However, in 2009, the 9th U.S. Circuit Court of Appeals overturned part of the decision, upholding only the conspiracy conviction. The court stated that, while ASD does not limit an individual's availability to facts, it does limits the defendant's ability to draw inferences from the facts that they perceive (*United States v. Cottrell*, 2009). Importantly, not allowing an individual with ASD to present evidence that they have a disorder that results in deficits in theory of mind, ability to estimate the thoughts, feelings, and perceptions of others (Haskins & Silva, 2006), would seem to be in direct opposition of the findings of *State v. Burr* (2008).

In an in-depth investigation of individuals with PDD who came in contact with the legal system, Cheely et al. (2011) found that no members of the PDD group were detained, in comparison to 5% of the non-AD group. The PDD group was significantly more likely to have their charges diverted and was less likely to have their cases prosecuted. These findings are interesting given the larger context, and a more in-depth investigation is necessary.

Prison

There has been very little research done investigating how individuals with ASD manage in prison. Prison life presents many challenges to anyone entering, including issues such as hostility, violence, gang activity, and racial tensions (Allely, 2015). These issues can lead to the creation of unwritten rules of conduct that those with ASD are particularly unprepared to deal with. Unsurprisingly, those with ASD are more likely to be the victim of bullying, exploitation, and social isolation, similar, but worse than when not incarcerated. Cottrell reported that he was the victim of harassment by guards due to the label of terrorist (Teetor, 2009). Further, having a developmental disability increases the risk for sexual assault while incarcerated and decreases empathy from guards, likely due to a lack of training. These challenges are worsened by sensory sensitivities often present in individuals with ASD. As a loud and unpredictable place, prison can be especially challenging for those on the spectrum, potentially leading to behavior outbursts and, in turn, additional time on a sentence.

What Needs to Be Done

Despite decades of back-and-forth research regarding the criminal nature of individuals with ASD, a few points seem clear. First, individuals with ASD are no more likely to be the perpetrators of a crime than those without ASD. With that said, there are those who do engage in criminal behaviors. Some of the symptoms associated with ASD, such as lack of theory of mind, poor communication skills, and difficulty managing emotions, does predispose them to engage in criminal acts. More importantly, their risk factors are quite similar to those without ASD. Adolescents who are abused, have parents who engage in crime, and/or live in high-crime areas are more likely to commit crimes regardless of an ASD diagnosis. Further, adults who have comorbid diagnoses, are homeless, or who are abusing substances are also more likely to engage in criminal acts regardless of an ASD diagnosis. So, while ASD individuals' risk and protective factors are not so different from typical individuals, they are still often ill prepared to deal with various aspects of the criminal justice system.

Answering the question of whether or not there is a positive correlation between ASD and criminality may be less important than finding ways to ensure that ASD individuals, guilty of a crime or not, are able to enjoy full and equal protection under the law. Here, Lerner et al. (2012) recommend that attorneys who work with individuals with ASD attend best practices training to better equip them to understand the needs of ASD. Lerner et al. (2012) also recommended that police carry information with them regarding signs of ASD and how to best interact with individuals on the spectrum. Specifically, it was recommended that they turn off lights and sirens (as they can be overly stimulating), avoid touching, model calm behavior, use simple and clear language, allow for a delayed response, and speak with caregivers and others who know the individual with ASD (Allely, 2015).

Lerner et al. (2012) also recommend that legal training for individuals with ASD be conducted using a direct, rules-based approach. This could be similar to the way other skills are taught using applied behavioral analysis, which is the primary method of teaching individuals with ASD.

In conclusion, there have been many changes to the lives of individuals with ASD over the recent decades. Autism went from being an unknown disorder to general vernacular. There are now a variety of evidence-based services and early diagnosis tools. Clearly, we have made significant progress for individuals with ASD, in the general setting. However, we appear to be decades behind in terms of how individuals with ASD are treated by all aspects of the criminal justice system. Given all we know, and all of the progress that we have made in other areas, it is hoped that we are able to make the necessary improvements in this area too.

References

Adam Lanza. (2016, June 13). Adam Lanza. *Biography*. Retrieved July 7, 2017, from www.biography.com/people/adam-lanza-21068899

Allely, C. S. (2015). Autism Spectrum Disorders in the Criminal Justice System: Police Interviewing, the Courtroom and the Prison Environment. *Recent Advances in Autism*. Retrieved from www.smgbooks.com/autism/chapters/AUT-15.02.pdf

American Psychiatric Association. (2013). *Diagnostic and Statistical Manual of Mental Disorders*, 5th ed. Washington, DC: Author.

Andrews, D. A., & Bonta, J. (1998). *The Psychology of Criminal Conduct*, 2nd ed. Cincinnati, OH: Anderson.

Baron-Cohen, S. (1988). An Assessment of Violence in a Young Man with Asperger's Syndrome. *Journal of Child Psychology and Psychiatry*, *29*, 351–360.

Browning, A., & Caulfield, L. (2011). The Prevalence and Treatment of People with Asperger's Syndrome in the Criminal Justice System. *Criminology & Criminal Justice*, *11*(2), 165–180.

Bushway, S., & Reuter, P. (2002). Labor Markets and Crime Risk Factors. In Bushway, S., & Reuter, P. (Eds.), *Evidence-Based Crime Prevention* (pp. 198–222). New York: Routledge. Evidence-Based Crime Prevention (pp. 198–222).

Caffero-Tolemy, A. (2012). Relationship Between IQ and Juvenile Offending in Youth with Asperger's Disorder/PDD-NOS, doctoral dissertation, Alliant International University, California School of Forensic Psychology, Los Angeles.

Cauffman, E., Feldman, S., Steiner, H., & Waterman, J. (n.d). Posttraumatic Stress Disorder among female juvenile offenders. *Journal of the American Academy of Child & Adolescent Psychiatry*, *37*(11), 1209–1216.

Cheely, C., Carpenter, L., Letourneau, E., Nicholas, J., Charles, J., & King, L. (2011). The Prevalence of Youth with Autism Spectrum Disorders in the Criminal Justice System. *Journal of Autism and Developmental Disorders*, *42*(9), 1856–1862.

Chitsabesan, P., Bailey, S., Williams, R., Kroll, L., Kenning, C., & Talbot L. (2007). Learning Disabilities and Educational Needs of Juvenile Offenders. *Journal of Children's Services*, *2*(4), 4–17.

Davies, D. (2004). *Child Development: A Practitioner's Guide*, 2nd ed. New York, NY: The Guilford Press.

Durose, M., Cooper, A, & Snyder, H. (2014). Recidivism of Prisoners Released in 30 States in 2005: Patterns from 2005 to 2010. *Bureau of Justice Statistics Special Report, April 2014, NCJ* 244205.

Ehlers, S., & Gillberg, C. (1993). The Epidemiology of Asperger Syndrome: A Total Population Study. *Journal of Child Psychology and Psychiatry*, *34*(8), 1327–1350.

English, D. J., Widom, C. S., & Brandford, C. (2002). Childhood Victimization and Delinquency, Adult Criminality, and Violent Criminal Behavior: A Replication and Extension. Final report presented to the National Institute of Justice, Grant No. 97-IJ-CX-0017.

Freckelton, I. (2013). Autism Spectrum Disorder: Forensic Issues and Challenges for Mental Health Professionals and Courts. *Journal of Applied Research in Intellectual Disabilities*, *26*(5), 420–434.

Garabedian, P., & Gibbons, D. (1970). *Becoming Delinquent: Young Offenders and the Correctional Process*. Chicago, IL: Aldine Publishing Company.

Ghaziuddin, M., Tsai, L., & Ghaziuddin, N. (1991). Brief Report: Violence in Asperger Syndrome—A Critique. *Journal of Autism and Developmental Disorders*, *21*, 349–354.

Green, J., Gilchrist, A., Burton, D., & Cox, A. (2000). Social and Psychiatric Functioning in Adolescents with Asperger Syndrome Compared with Conduct Disorder. *Journal of Autism and Developmental Disorders*, *30*(4), 279–293.

Hare, D. J., Gould, J., Mills, R., & Wing, L. (1999). A Preliminary Study of Individuals with Autistic Spectrum Disorders in Three Special Hospitals in England. London: National Autistic Society.

Hartup, W., & Moore, S. (1990). Early Peer Relations: Developmental Significance and Prognostic Implications. *Early Childhood Research Quarterly*, *5*(1), 1–17.

Haskins, B., & Silva, A. (2006). Asperger's Disorder and Criminal Behavior: Forensic-Psychiatric Considerations. *Journal of the American Academy of Psychiatry and the Law*, *34*, 74–84.

Hayes, S. C. (2005). Diagnosing Intellectual Disability in a Forensic Sample: Gender and Age Effects on the Relationship Between Cognitive and Adaptive Functioning. *Journal of Intellectual and Developmental Disability*, *30*(2), 97–103.

Hays, J. R., Solway, K. S., & Schreiner, D. (1978). Intellectual Characteristics of Juvenile Murderers Versus Status Offenders. *Psychological Reports*, *43*(1), 80–82.

Heilbrun, K., Sevin Goldstein, N., & Redding, R. (2005). *Juvenile Delinquency: Prevention, Assessment, and Intervention*. New York, NY: Oxford University Press.

Hoge, R. D., Andrews, D. A., & Leschied, A. W. (1996). An Investigation of Risk and Protective Factors in a Sample of Youthful Offenders. *Journal of Child Psychology and Psychiatry*, *37*(4), 419–424.

Howlin, P. (2004). *Autism and Asperger Syndrome: Preparing for Adulthood.* Abingdon/ New York, NY: Routledge.

Huizinga, D., Loeber, R., Thornberry, T., & Cothern, L. (2000). Co-occurrence of Delinquency and Other Problem Behaviors. *Juvenile Justice Bulletin.* Retrieved from www.ncjrs.gov/html/ojjdp/jjbul2000_11_3/contents.html

Im, D. S. (2016). Template to Perpetrate: An Update on Violence in Autism Spectrum Disorder. *Harvard Review of Psychiatry, 24*(1), 14–35. Retrieved from http://doi. org/10.1097/HRP.0000000000000087

Kandel, E., Mednick, S. A., Kirkegaard-Sorensen, L., Hutchings, B., Knop, J., Rosenberg, R., & Schulsinger, F. (1988). IQ as a Protective Factor for Subjects at High Risk for Antisocial Behavior. *Journal of Consulting and Clinical Psychology, 56*(2), 224–226.

Kawakami, C., Ohnishi, M., Sugiyama, T., Someki, F., Nakamura, K., & Tsujii, M. (2012). The Risk Factors for Criminal Behaviour in High-Functioning Autism Spectrum Disorders (HFASDs): A Comparison of Childhood Adversities Between Individuals with HFASDs Who Exhibit Criminal Behaviour and Those with HFASD and No Criminal Histories. *Research in Autism Spectrum Disorders, 6*(2), 949–957.

King, C., & Murphy, G. H. (2014). A Systematic Review of People with Autism Spectrum Disorder and the Criminal Justice System. *Journal of Autism and Developmental Disorders, 44*(11), 2717–2733.

Krisiansson, M., & Sorman, K. (2008). Autism Spectrum Disorders—Legal and Forensic Psychiatric Aspects and Reflections. *Clinical Neuropsychiatry, 5*, 55–61.

Långström, N., Grann, M., Ruchkin, V., Sjöstedt, G., & Fazel, S. (2009). Risk Factors for Violent Offending in Autism Spectrum Disorder: A National Study of Hospitalized Individuals. *Journal of interpersonal violence, 24*(8), 1358–1370.

Lerner, M. D., Haque, O. S., Northrup, E. C., Lawer, L., & Bursztajn, H. J. (2012). Emerging Perspectives on Adolescents and Young Adults with High-Functioning Autism Spectrum Disorders, Violence, and Criminal Law. *Journal of the American Academy of Psychiatry and the Law Online, 40*(2), 177–190.

Mawson, D., Grounds, A., & Tantam, D. (1985). Violence and Asperger's Syndrome. *British Journal of Psychiatry, 147*, 566–569.

Mouridsen, S. E., Rich, B., Isager, T., & Nedergaard, N. J. (2008). Pervasive Development Disorders and Criminal Behaviour: A Case Control Study. *International Journal of Offender Therapy and Comparative Criminology, 52*(2), 196–205.

Mulder, E., Brand, E., Bullens, R., & Van Marle, H. (2010). A Classification of Risk Factors in Serious Juvenile Offenders and the Relation Between Patterns of Risk Factors and Recidivism. *Criminal Behaviour & Mental Health, 20*(1), 23–38.

Murrie, D. C., Warren J. I., Kristiansson, M., & Dietz, P. E. (2002) Asperger's Syndrome in Forensic Settings. *International Journal of Forensic Mental Health 1*(1): 5970.

National Autistic Society (NAS) (2008) Autism: A Guide for Criminal Justice Professionals. Retrieved from www.nas.org.uk/nas/jsp/polopoly.jsp?d=471&a=8528

Newman, S., & Ghaziuddin, M. (2008). Violent crime in Asperger Syndrome: The Role of Psychiatric Comorbidity. *Journal of Autism and Developmental Disorders, 38*(10), 1848–1852.

Patterson, G. R., DeBaryshe, B. D., & Ramsey, E. (1989). A Developmental Perspective on Antisocial Behavior. *American Psychologist, 44*(2), 329–335.

Pliszka, S. R, Sherman, J. O., Barrow, M. V., & Irick, S. (2000). Affective Disorder in Juvenile Offenders: A Preliminary Study. *American Journal of Psychiatry, 157*, 130–132.

Premack, D., & Woodruff, G. (1978). Does the Chimpanzee Have a Theory of Mind? *Behavioral and Brain Sciences, 1*(4), 515–526.

Puzzanchera, C., (2009). Juvenile Arrests 2008. *Office of Justice Programs.* Retrieved from www.ncjrs.gov/pdffiles1/ojjdp/228479.pdf

Sampson, R. J., & Laub, J. H. (2003). Life-Course Disasters? Trajectories of Crime Among Delinquent Boys Followed to Age 70. *Criminology, 41*(3), 555–592.

Satterfield, J. H., & Schell, A. (1997). A rospective Study of Hyperactive Boys With Conduct Problems and Normal Boys: Adolescent and Adult Criminality. *Journal of the American Academy of Child & Adolescent Psychiatry, 36*(12), 1726–1735.

Schwartz-Watts, D. M. (2005). Asperger's Disorder and Murder. *Journal of the American Academy of Psychiatry and the Law, 33*, 390–393.

Scragg, P., & Shah, A. (1994). Prevalence of Asperger's Syndrome in a Secure Hospital. *British Journal of Psychiatry: The Journal of Mental Science, 165*, 679–682.

Siponmaa, L., Krisiansson, M., Jonson, C., Nyden, A., & Gillberg, C. (2001). Juvenile and Young Adult Mentally Disordered Offenders: The Role of Child Neuropsychiatric Disorders. *Journal of the American Academy of Psychiatry and the Law, 29*, 420–426.

Snyder, H. (2012). *Arrest in the United States, 1990–2010.* NCJ, 239423, 26. Retrieved from www.bjs.gov/index.cfm?ty=pbdetail&iid=4515

Snyder, H., & Sickmund, M. (1995). *Juvenile Offenders and Victims: A National Report.* Washington, DC: Office of Juvenile Justice and Delinquency Prevention.

Stahlberg, O, Anckarsäter, H., & Nilsson, T. (2010). Mental Health Problems in Youths Committed to Juvenile Institutions: Prevalences and Treatment Needs. *European Journal of Child and Adolescent Psychiatry,19*(12), 893–903.

State v. Burr, 195 N.J. 119, 948 A.2d 627, 2008 N.J. LEXIS 606 (2008).

Tanner-Smith, E. E., Wilson, S. J., & Lipsey, M. W. (2013). Risk Factors and Crime. In Frances T. Cullen & Pamela Wilcox (Eds.), *The Oxford Handbook of Criminological Theory* (pp. 89–111). Oxford, UK: Oxford University Press.

Teetor, P. (2009, November 24). A Terrible Thing to Waste: Billy Cottrell, Part Deux. *LA Weekly.* Retrieved June 30, 2017, from www.laweekly.com/news/a-terrible-thing-to-waste-billy-cottrell-part-deux-2162703

Teplin, L. A., Abram, K. M., McClelland, G. M., Dulcan, M. K., & Mericle, A. A. (2002). Psychiatric Disorders in Youth in Juvenile Detention. *Archives of General Psychiatry, 59*(12), 1133–1143.

United States v. Cottrell, 333 Fed. Appx. 213, 2009 U.S. App. LEXIS 20123 (9th Cir. Cal. 2009)

U.S. Department of Health and Human Services, Administration on Children, Youth, and Families (2010). *Child Maltreatment 2009.* Washington, DC: U.S. Government Printing Office.

Walsh, Z., Swogger, M. T., & Kosson, D. S. (2004). Psychopathy, IQ, and Violence in European American and African American County Jail Inmates. *Journal of Consulting and Clinical Psychology, 72*(6), 1165–1169.

Wing, L., & Gould, J. (1979). Severe Impairments of Social Interaction and Associated Abnormalities in Children: Epidemiology and Classification. *Journal of Autism and Developmental Disorders, 9*(1), 11–29.

9

MULTICULTURAL PERSPECTIVES ON AUTISM SPECTRUM DISORDER

The Ways in Which Cultural Beliefs Impact Perceptions, Diagnosis, and Treatment Interventions

Diana Osipsov

Introduction

When considering the diagnosis, treatment, and perception of autism as a developmental difference, culture is a concept which is rarely discussed, though the impact can be tremendous. Culture can be understood as the customs, beliefs, social norms, and shared traits of a group of people. For each of us, our culture guides and directs our thoughts, beliefs, values, and perceptions, often without conscious awareness. And, there are collective communities or groups of people with shared cultural beliefs that transcend the individual. People of various ethnic groups share certain customs and traditions that define their culture; different religions hold to different beliefs and practices that make their culture unique; various universities or educational programs hold to different norms, standards, or practices that make their culture their own.

Likewise, clinical practices, schools of thought, theorists, researchers and practitioners maintain different perspectives, shared traits, beliefs, and systems of operation which set them apart from one another as distinct entities—making their culture their own. When considering the various cultural influences of different groups throughout the world, there are many implicit cultural biases. This includes opinions of normal versus abnormal (typical versus atypical functioning) that impact the direction of research, treatment foci, and opinion regarding developmental differences of those with an autism spectrum disorder (ASD). The purpose of this chapter will be to focus on the cultures of different regions of the world, both past and present, and the ways in which the customs, beliefs, and norms of these various people groups impact the perception, diagnosis, and treatment of ASD.

The World Health Organization (WHO, 2011) asserts the following with regard to disability—"Disability is part of the human condition. Almost everyone will be temporarily or permanently impaired at some point in life, and those who survive to old age will experience increasing difficulties in functioning." If, then, disability is to be considered a normal part of the human life, condition, and experience, why is it that certain impairments or difficulties are stigmatized while others are not? How do so many different perspectives, beliefs, and practices with regard to recognizing and treating certain disabilities or differences come to be?

Historical Perspectives

The perceptions on causes of autism or even the presence of autism in different parts of the world have developed and changed significantly in the past several decades. Even as recently as the 1980s, researchers questioned whether autism was a universal developmental difference and whether it existed outside of the Western world (Bakare & Munir, 2011). In fact, the existence of ASD was not recognized in China until the 1980s (Sun & Allison, 2010). Within the Western world, there existed different schools of thought with regard to the origins of autism, its prevalence, whether it exists as a spectrum disorder or not, and which treatment approaches are most effective. Grunya Sukhareva, a Russian child psychiatrist, was one of the first to publish a list of symptoms and characteristics, including eccentric or avoidant behavior with regard to social-emotional engagement or interaction—what we today consider to be the framework of autism spectrum disorder (Manouilenko & Bejerot, 2015). Her original paper was published in Russian in 1925, in German a year later, and then, only in 1996, translated into English by Sula Wolff. Hans Asperger was an Austrian pediatrician, researcher, and medical professor who published a definition of "autistic psychopathy" in 1944, while Leo Kanner, an Austrian-American psychiatrist, published an article on "early infantile autism" in 1943. Though Asperger and Kanner published their writings in close proximity and studied what we consider today to be the same spectrum disorder, their beliefs led them to view and describe the characteristics and symptoms of autism in two very different ways.

Kanner's description of autism focused on the severe impairments possible in the autistic presentation, while Asperger described the high-functioning and potential giftedness of the children with whom he worked. These two very different descriptions of a now diagnostic spectrum demonstrate the fact that autism is a spectrum disorder, but also that the beliefs and perspectives of researchers and medical professionals can frame a particular set of characteristics in individuals.

Current Multicultural Perspectives

It is now generally understood and accepted that autism spectrum disorder (ASD) is defined by a set of symptoms that include deficits in social-emotional engagement and interaction. The *Diagnostic and Statistical Manual of Mental Disorders* characterizes autism spectrum disorder with symptoms, including deficits in social-emotional reciprocity, deficits in nonverbal communicative behaviors used for social interaction, and deficits in developing, maintaining, and understanding relationships (American Psychiatric Association, 2013). When considering the various facets of autism spectrum disorder, cultural norms can play a significant role in the report, identification, and classification of these symptoms.

In highly individualistic cultures, some of these deficits with regard to social-emotional reciprocity, social communication, and developing and understanding relationships, especially in the case of the presentation of high-functioning autism, may not be identified until a child begins to interact with siblings or enters school. Similarly, though limited or restricted engagement with others is one of the commonly accepted indicators of ASD, the ways in which this qualifier is identified can be impacted by cultural expectations and social practices. Since girls are expected to be more shy in Saudi Arabian culture, there is often a later age of diagnosis of ASD in girls than in boys, and because direct eye contact is viewed as disrespectful in Asia, limited eye contact is viewed differently than it is in Western cultures. Socially, disruptive behaviors that are sometimes associated with ASD are reported more frequently than communication challenges in Indian culture because this culture focuses on, and values, social conformity (Council of Europe, 2014).

Another factor to consider is the focus within the culture of medical or human health groups and associations of different countries on health, wellbeing, and potential or on disability, illness, and dependency. The United States Centers for Disease Control and Prevention (CDC) describes developmental disabilities as a group of conditions due to impairment in physical, learning, language, or behavioral areas. The CDC describes that these conditions begin during the developmental period, may impact day-to-day functioning, and usually last throughout the life cycle. The list of some of these developmental disabilities includes: attention deficit hyperactivity disorder, autism spectrum disorder, cerebral palsy, hearing loss, intellectual disability, learning disability, vision impairment, and other developmental delays. It is estimated that 15% of children aged 3 to 7 years have one of these developmental delays (Centers for Disease Control and Prevention, 2016). Given this estimation, focus on the need for clinical treatment and intervention is evidenced in the following statement: "it is especially important for children with developmental disabilities to see a health care provider regularly."

The Canadian Pediatric Society describes developmental disabilities as a set of abilities and characteristics that vary from the norm in the limitations they impose on independent participation and acceptance in society and defines this list of disabilities to include intellectual disabilities, sensory-related disabilities (including hearing and vision), communication and language disabilities, and physical disabilities. The International Classification of Functioning, Disability and Health (ICF) and the World Health Organization note that personal and environmental factors, including culture, share a complex relationship with functional capabilities and participation. And these groups include consideration of medical and biological dysfunction, social aspects, cultural and familial attitudes, availability and accessibility of resources, and social and legal entities that may have an impact on the expression of disability (Canadian Pediatric Society, 2016). Both of these systems, the Canadian Pediatric Society and the United States Centers for Disease Control and Prevention, are in place to promote health and to support the treatment of various illnesses or disabilities. The beliefs and values of the culture of which they are a part evidence themselves even in the wording of their statements regarding developmental disabilities and differences. The CDC takes the perspective of developmental differences existing as a life-long impairment, whereas the Canadian Pediatric Society demonstrates its focus on developmental disabilities existing as variances or differences from the norm in the ways in which they potentially hinder both independence and participation in community. One perspective paints the picture of an isolating and helpless life-long struggle, while the other describes a challenging experience which is only one part of a person's overall being and existence. The former asserts the expertise of solely the clinical or medical professional, while the latter distributes the responsibility for health and functionality between multiple system groups and individuals.

Treatment Approaches and Implications for Practice

Cultural values, beliefs, and systems impact not only the perception among people groups of certain diagnoses or differences in others, but also treatment approaches and interventions—both those available to individuals and families—and the manner in which they are or are not sought out by people in that particular country or community.

Though identification, diagnosis, and effective treatment of autism spectrum disorders in Africa, especially sub-Saharan Africa, is low with regard to the population served, the practices and beliefs which comprise the culture of this region of the world prove promising with regard to efficacy in autism treatment (Bakare & Munir, 2011). The use of traditional healers and herbal remedies is quite common with regard to treatment approaches, and other forms of care and evidence-based practices are limited. In spite of these differences, southern regions of Africa focus on a person's ability to observe social practices and norms and to overcome difficulties: "this cooperative view of social and individual endeavor has been shown to increase social functioning and maturity in intellectually disabled children when compared with more individualistic Western approaches." Some of these Western approaches in North America include outpatient clinical therapy, occupational therapy, speech and language therapy, and physical therapy. Interestingly, in Europe, some countries offer inclusive programs, while others are hesitant to move past institutionalized care. This, too, is reflective of different cultural beliefs and values with regard to the diagnosis and treatment provided to persons with developmental disabilities and mental illnesses.

Some Asian cultures incorporate alternative medicines, including yoga, sensory integration, and acupuncture through the pairing of homeopathy with conventional medicine. Chinese medicine, specifically, integrates the relationship between mind and body as integral to overall health and wellbeing, as it views the mind and body as existing within the same circular system of the central nervous system and organs. Chinese medicine focuses on health in terms of achieving balance through reason and awareness and strives to treat dysfunction or imbalance in a person's health with this mindset. In this manner, both the perspective through which health and disability is viewed, and the practices that are incorporated and utilized in efforts to achieve health and wellness, drive the cultural beliefs and norms of the medical community through which autism is also understood and treated. Two treatment approaches that are considered complementary therapeutic interventions for the treatment of autism include acupuncture and massage.

Acupuncture is believed to address natural opioids, the central nervous system, and neuroendocrine function within the human body, and has reportedly been shown to have success in the treatment of autism spectrum disorders (Pacific College of Oriental Medicine, 2014). One specific form of acupuncture, which has reportedly demonstrated progression with regard to the effective treatment of autism, is tongue acupuncture. Tongue diagnosis and treatment is a central component of the Chinese medical system as it is the only organ that can be seen externally, and as such, its condition with regard to color, thickness, dryness, smell, and superficial growth helps in determining the condition of the heart and treatment approach as a result (Pacific College of Oriental Medicine, 2014). Traditional Chinese medicine also asserts that many health problems are related to imbalances in diet, and offers treatment interventions that include dietary therapy. With regard to autism, food sensitivities are not regarded as a causal factor in yielding the presentation of symptoms, but that the components of certain foods can exacerbate these symptoms (concept of the Leaky Gut Syndrome). As a result, dietary therapy is utilized as part of the intervention approach in treating autism. Although this does not answer the question asked by many who come into contact with autism spectrum disorders (whether through personal experience or in clinical practice or research), regarding the cause of autism, it does shed light on the possibility that a treatment approach which incorporates the perspective of treating the mind and body together can yield more successful results.

Stanley Greenspan was a child psychiatrist who developed the DIR Floortime approach to autism treatment. His approach stemmed from the belief that emotional engagement is key to building relationships. He developed six functional capacities as developmental milestones and theorized that autism treatment should address challenges or disruptions to the development of these functional capacities through play. These functional capacities include: self-regulation and interest in the world, engaging and relating, purposeful two-way communication, complex communication and shared problem-solving, using symbols and creating emotional ideas, and logical thinking and building bridges between ideas (Greenspan & Shanker, 2994). Richard Solomon is a pediatrician who believes in the culture of play and using play as a universal tool to connect and build relationships with all children, including children with autism spectrum disorders. He is the founder of The PLAY Project, an evidence-based autism intervention program which emphasizes the importance of building relationships, engaging and connecting with others, "filling in the gaps" within the functional capacities as outlined by Dr. Greenspan, and using play as the avenue to build these lasting connections. Through his approach, the culture of Dr. Solomon's treatment modality demonstrates its values and beliefs - the value of human connection, the belief that play is the universal language of children, and the belief that there is potential within any and every person (Solomon, 2016).

Autism Speaks is an autism advocacy organization which endeavors to raise awareness and support research related to ASD. The efforts of the organization have included providing support and resources to families, governmental entities, and the public, and in 2008 the organization launched the Global Autism Public Health Initiative (Autism Speaks, 2014). Through this initiative, Autism Speaks has worked with partners in many areas of the world, including Central and South America, the Middle East, Asia, and Africa, to increase public and professional awareness of autism spectrum disorders, to increase collaboration and enhance expertise with regard to research and the provision of treatment services, and promoting efforts which encourage early detection and diagnosis through the training of public health workers and medical professionals (Autism Speaks, 2014). With these types of efforts in place, the diagnosis and treatment of autism and other developmental disabilities can be enhanced by recognizing and incorporating the values, beliefs, and practices of many different cultures and people groups around the world. This much is evident: the need for a composite view of brain–body treatment, as in part of Asian culture; the incorporation of social engagement and belonging, as emphasized in some African cultures; and the understanding that each of these pieces is vital and crucial to treatment, as outlined in the Canadian Pediatric Society's description of treatment interventions for persons with developmental differences or disabilities.

Treatment interventions which recognize the important relationship between mind and body, consider the relevance of early detection and intervention in a manner that builds upon a child's functional capacities, provide support and education to parents and caregivers, recognize that engagement and play are foundational to a child's growth, learning, and development, and encourage this development to take place in the context of social engagement and community participation, can prove tremendously effective in the treatment of autism spectrum disorders in the future.

The Culture of Autism

And so, we must recognize the culture of autism itself: the culture of the people who experience autism spectrum disorder and their desire to connect with other people. We know that engagement and attunement with others is a basic human function. The desire and need to belong is both universal and innate. Donna Williams says it best when she describes her experience of meeting other individuals with autism. She states that

> together we felt like a lost tribe. "Normal" is to be in the company of one like one's self. We all had a sense of belonging, of being understood . . . all the things we could not get from others in general. It was so sad to have to leave.
>
> *(Williams, 1994)*

Even with set diagnostic criteria for autism spectrum disorders, specific attributes as they relate to these criteria or presentation of symptoms may vary across cultures—what is identified as a warning sign or red flag in a Western or individualistic culture, for example, may exist as a desirable attribute in an Eastern or collectivist culture. When we consider fundamental aspects of social-emotional development and functioning, however, we reach a level of interpersonal interaction and engagement that spans across cultural norms and beliefs. The desire and ability to connect with other people is a core aspect and innate need of human nature and functioning that can be found across all cultures and people groups. The desire to be known and understood, to belong, is one which is foundational to human interaction and interpersonal engagement. And it is on the basis of these foundational capacities, including relationship and two-way communication, that we can identify developmental markers, differences, and difficulties within the context of autistic tendencies.

References

American Psychiatric Association. (2013). *Diagnostic and Statistical Manual of Mental Disorders*, 5th ed. Arlington, VA: American Psychiatric Publishing.
Autism Speaks. (2014). *Autism Speaks Global Autism Public Health Initiative.* Retrieved from www.autismspeaks.org/science/research-initiatives/global-autism-public-health
Bakare, M. O., & Munir, K. M. (2011). Autism Spectrum disorders (ASD) in Africa: A Perspective. *African Journal of Psychiatry*, *14*(3), 208–210.

Canadian Pediatric Society. (2016). *Developmental Disability Across Cultures*. Retrieved from www.kidsnewtocanada.ca/mental-health/developmental-disability

Centers for Disease Control and Prevention. (2016). *Facts About Developmental Disabilities*. Retrieved from www.cdc.gov/ncbddd/developmentaldisabilities/facts.html

Council of Europe. (2014). *Human Rights of Persons with Disabilities*. Retreived from www.coe.int/cs/web/commissioner/thematic-work/persons-with-disabilities/-/asset_publisher/DM45YCiuGfnz/news/tags/persons%20with%20disabilities

Greenspan, S. I., & Shanker, S. G. (2004). *The first idea: How symbols, language, and intelligence evolved from our primate ancestors to modern humans*. Cambridge, MA: Da Capo Press.

Kanner, L. (1943). Autistic Disturbances of Affective Contact. *Nervous Child, 2*, 217–250.

Manouilenko, I., & Bejerot, S. (2015). Sukhareva—Prior to Asperger and Kanner. *Nordic Journal of Psychiatry, 69*(6), 479–482.

Pacific College of Oriental Medicine. (2014). *Traditional Chinese Medicine and Autism*.

Solomon, R. (2016). *Autism: The Potential Within, the PLAY Project Approach to Helping Young Children with Autism*. Lulu Publishing Services.

Sun, X., & Allison, C. (2010). A Review of the Prevalence of Autism Spectrum Disorder in Asia. *Research in Autism Spectrum Disorders, 4*(2), 156–167.

Williams, D. (1994). *Somebody Somewhere*. London, UK: Jessica Kingsley Publishers.

World Health Organization. (2011). *World Report on Disability*, 1–349. Geneva: WHO Library.

10

WHEN DO I GET TO BE GOOD ENOUGH?

Rochelle Manor

Goals, Objectives, Grades . . . Educational systems require constant cycles of testing, performance, and passing or failing.

My mom and dad are educators—teachers, administrators. Both spending their adult lives helping other children succeed. But one of their daughters never experienced success the same way their other students did.

My sister Renee was among the first students in Indiana identified under Public Law 94-142 in 1975. The Education for All Handicapped Children Act was enacted by the United States Congress when Renee was 8 years old. Prior to that, she has been bussed to the adjacent county to a school for the deaf. It was the closest place with "special education," but Renee's nervous system was overloaded every day from the deaf children yelling and screaming, so being able to attend the same school that I did, riding my bus, and walking through the relatively quiet hallways, was a blessing.

It was a small rural school, which was another blessing, with a small student body in a primarily Christian community. While bullying was minimal, Renee was clearly misunderstood by most. My friends and I included.

Recess was awkward as she paced the edge of the playground, touching the ground every few steps, talking to herself. Up and down, round and round. She didn't talk to the other kids or play on the equipment. Back in the hallways, she had to walk on the edge, running her hand along the wall of lockers and when there was a doorway/gap on the wall, she would touch the floor . . . then back up when the wall resumed again.

Every school picture was one of Renee with a terrified look on her face and/or tears in her eyes, in anticipation of the impending flash. But she went—day after day—fearful of the possibility of the fire alarm going off or kids screaming on the playground, unable to walk in the middle of the hallway, never smiling.

Individual education plans (IEPs) became a way of life. Renee had her own set of academic goals, and my parents poured all their expertise and passion into helping the teachers understand who Renee was and how to reach her. But, even though she learned to read, do basic math, and even attempted taking French in high school, every day was a struggle.

Graduating from high school at 20 years old was an incredible accomplishment for Renee, which she still brings up on a regular basis. Also, she'll never go to a high school reunion. Little did she know that adulthood would be a never-ending continuation of the sensory overload, inability to manage her body, and lack of happiness she experienced through school.

Living in Overload

Renee was officially diagnosed as having Asperger's when she was 28 years of age, when the DSM-IV and diagnosis of Asperger's first came to the US in 1994. Until then, learning disabilities and attention difficulties were the academic focus of her IEPs, but no one really understood the sensorimotor difficulties, the biggest source of trauma for her. The social difficulties were never part of her educational goals and she had no friends.

In young adulthood, she tried to work in food service (where again the sensory overload caused such anxiety she couldn't continue). She even earned a driver's license and drove for a few years, until too many fender-benders from lack of depth perception became a problem.

After job stress and losing her car, she was placed on anxiety medications. Any dream of functional independence was finally thwarted and she settled into life with case managers, behavioral analysts, and psychiatrists.

This year, Renee turns 50 years old and, still, the sensory issues remain one of the largest stressors. She rushes through the grocery store, throwing anything into the cart, so she can get home quickly. She wears the same outfits repeatedly and hates shopping for new clothes. Her diet is incredibly limited. She leaves food on the plate if she doesn't really like it (regardless of who made or bought the food for her). Socially, she has little interaction with "peers" but lives in an apartment with disabled adults where she knows a few people by name but doesn't do any social activities with them.

But what is even more of a struggle is the "systems" that keep making "goals and objectives" without understanding the sensory overload and social deficits. Her nervous system is aggravated by the very "teachers" there to "help" her that insist managing money and making grocery lists is a life skill she has to master—taking her to the store during peak hours when the lines are long and lots of shoppers are in the aisles. This fits their schedules, not Renee's. The "systems" that insist she not do laundry so many times a week and want her to wear clothes that she deems uncomfortable. But, at least she still is in control of what she will and won't eat . . .

More Goals and Objectives

Her days are filled with sleeping, watching the same shows over and over, and making phone calls to Mom. So, "the system" thought she should try working again. But, rather than meeting with Renee in her apartment or an office to review options and fill out applications, the caseworker scheduled the meeting in a fast-food restaurant and suggested working at Goodwill (a place filled with smells, visual overload, and a physical environment where it would be difficult for her to walk down the aisles in a straight line). Even Renee is able to recognize that she wouldn't be successful working in a restaurant or store. But staff interpret her as "resistant" and didn't follow up on Mom's recommendation that they see about Renee setting tables at a nearby nursing home. Again, the "system" has to put her through trials in established settings first . . . leading to a life of repeated failure.

Over and Over, Again and Again

The other aspect that is just "who Renee is" is her incredible ability (or curse) to perseverate. Once she gets an idea in her mind, she can't stop talking about it. Often this is anticipatory anxiety about events that are coming up (going somewhere, Mom and Dad leaving town, family events, what she's going to eat at the next meal). She also obsesses about her money, what she can or can't buy, and always has a "wish account" where she wants to "save up" for something she wants to buy (related to her special interest areas, but no one understands why she wants it because it will just sit around her apartment after she has bought it).

Psychiatrists have attempted to medicate her obsessive compulsive behavior or "mania." Behavioral analysts have attempted to "reward" her for not expressing her anxiety but have not provided a way to cope differently. There was a behavioral analyst who saw the frequent phone calls to Mom as the "behavior" to reduce, but she clearly didn't understand that Mom is Renee's anxiety management strategy. Mom has always been the interpreter, helping every teacher, caseworker, and professional to understand Renee and helping Renee to relate to them. Thus, restricting Renee's ability to make those phone calls to Mom escalated her anxiety and anger outbursts.

Mom still receives 10 to 15 phone calls from Renee daily, even though she lives in an apartment less than two miles away. She has a camera for staff to monitor her in the apartment and has 15 to 25 hours of one-to-one staffing per week. Regardless of the staff assigned to her, Mom is still Renee's primary anxiety management tool.

And, the staff themselves are often a trigger. If staff are supposed to be there at a set time, they better arrive "on the dot." If someone arrives early one day, Renee will worry every time that staff is scheduled to come that she won't be ready and they will let themselves in without her knowing. If someone is late, she is pacing the floor and calling Mom to "report" that they are late. Renee can't read an analogue clock, but holds us all to the numbers on the digital clock as though they are sacred.

Every few months, there is a change in staffing. Either the number of hours or days of the week are altered, or there is a new staff person altogether. Mom is the primary "trainer"—for the staff and Renee. Mom has had to "interpret" for Renee; when the caseworker is different from what Renee expects such as the gal with the purple hair and multiple piercings. Or the caseworker who kept cancelling on Renee because she had to go bail her own kid out of jail. Or the countless times staff would tell Renee about their own financial troubles, challenges with their health, or consequences of their poor life choices to the point where Renee would feel sorry for them and feel she couldn't ask them to help her. Or feeling she has to "accept" the assigned staff so they would get the paycheck they needed. So many "blowups" and tears Mom would have to calm down after days with those staff.

Recently, Renee fell in her apartment and broke her ankle in two places. After surgery, there was 2–3 months where Renee couldn't live alone. But the agency couldn't find enough staffing, so Renee had to go live with Mom and Dad for that time, – Mom being the only caregiver for all Renee's physical and emotional needs, through pain management and tracking her medications and physical therapy.

Our parents continue to be the educators, trying to navigate and protect her from the very system that is there to help her. But, at 50 years old, the "systems" and "professionals" keep trying to change the very things that are the symptoms of Renee's ASD, setting her up in environments that overload her sensory system and try to medicate away the "stuck thinking" (instead of teaching her coping strategies).

Just Like the Ole' Days:

After years in Special Education, now, at 50 years old, Renee still has figurative "IEP" meetings – she sits in a room every quarter, surrounded by her parents and an army of professionals who repeatedly review what she needs to do differently, setting new goals and behavioral strategies to try to minimize the impact of her autism.

Most of those meetings result in Renee leaving the room (she has been taught to not explode but to seek "time out" when she gets upset).. I'm still not sure what "person centered" goals are in her plans, except that there are certain times she can select the restaurant where she gets to eat or how to spend her "wish account" funds when she has them. But the amount of medications she has or the hours of staffing still seem driven by what the agency or "system" decides. And after every meeting, there is always a plan to change something to try to "make Renee better."

Saving Grace:

Through the years there have been a few who helped Renee know she is valued. Ms. Dewalt was an incredibly dedicated special education teacher who, single-handedly, got Renee through high school and graduation. She still comes around occasionally to take Renee to the movies. Ms. Dewalt is still the person Renee credits with being her best teacher ever.

A few caseworkers along the way have understood Renee well, adapting to her sensory needs, offering more choices of how Renee could do things, and speaking to Renee with respect and dignity. Thankfully, her current one, Gail, is one of the best, going out of her way to sit with or chat with Renee at church, even though she is "off the clock." She recognizes the importance of being on time, honoring your promises, helping map out a plan for after she leaves so Renee knows what to expect, speaking to Renee with calm and respect in your voice.

Renee now has Dr. Gallihugh, behavior analysist, who keeps reminding the rest of the team about what autism is. She has sensory overload and will shut down if you overwhelm her. She is perseverative and obsesses on topics and will keep thinking about it or making phone calls until someone calms her down. She is inflexible and can't just "go with the flow." She can't interpret social situations well and often misunderstands or gets upset when she thinks someone is trying to manipulate her.

But, after 50 years, are those things really going to change? Who among us would welcome that intensity of scrutiny of our choices in clothing, food, activities? What adult at this age would welcome strangers who don't share our values to come into our homes and micromanage what is in our cupboards, closets, and bank account? How is she supposed to keep facing the repeated experience of "failure"?

When does Renee just get to be who she is? When is her life "good enough"? When do professionals stop trying to set goals and change behavior and just let her live the life that is suited for the way she is "wired"?

Living with ASD is hard. But the very systems set up to try to "support" those with ASD need to understand when we become part of the problem. Autism is not the same as cognitively impaired and our systems of care for adults need to reflect that. While the world has come a long way since 1975 and the enactment of PL-94-142, the children who first benefited from those changes in education need to be addressed in the adult worlds as well . . . individually, with a focus on "setting the person up for success."

Understanding autism isn't just about the research and checklists of symptoms. It's about knowing how people are "built" and what we can and can't change.

Yes, in childhood and early adulthood there are a multitude of interventions that have substantial impact. And we all know early intervention is critical. Having lived with someone through the litany of interventions, I have to ask: Where is that point when too much is too much?

What does "person-centered planning" really mean to us as professionals? On the surface, it seems like we are giving them a say in life choices, but it is our responsibility to ensure these choices are actually going to contribute to healthy well-being. First, I believe we need to establish the options based on the person's functioning (strengths and weaknesses) with emphasis on environments and activities that will enhance the personal success. This is critical for individuals with ASD, where the sensory environment can literally "make or break" their anxiety levels. Second, life isn't about getting what you want. Everyone has to live with restrictions (lack of money) and making healthy choices (nutrition), but if we don't have stability in our finances and health everything else feels worse. It is a delicate balance of allowing freedom in decision making, but recognizing when someone can't learn from cause-and-effect consequences. Last, recognizing what is a symptom of the diagnosis, what is a personality style, and what is a personal value all needs to be understood and respected. The responsibility lies on the professionals to be creative, inventive, and advocating for more options.

> Eventually, adults with ASD just need to be accepted and supported. They need to hear that they are "good enough" and valued as people in our communities, symptoms and all . . .
>
> *Rochelle Manor, Ph.D.*
> *Older Sister*

Checklist for Professionals

To understand how to "set a person up for success," it isn't just about their wishes or desires, but also balancing your professional understanding of their symptoms and needs. The following are things to consider:

- *Consistency and Predictability*: Will there be changes in schedule, staffing, expectations? How do we maximize predictability to reduce anxiety?
- *Sensory*: What is the physical environment going to be like during the time the person is there?
- *Nonverbals*: ASD, by definition, means the person has difficulty reading social cues. All staff need to be aware of the nonverbal cues they exhibit that could be misinterpreted or convey lack of respect.
- *Boundaries*: Staff and professionals are here to serve. Balancing "relational approaches" with too much personal information is important.

- *Values*: Staff and professionals are here to serve, not to change, the person's values and beliefs. Working within their personal value system is critical and is a great way to find natural supports.
- *Decision Making*: Executive functioning skills such as planning ahead and making decisions are often impaired in individuals with ASD. This doesn't mean we take away their choice, but rather need to set them up with positive options. They can be either rigid in their thinking or susceptible to suggestion. It is the professional's responsibility to be aware of their power and to guide the person into positive options.

11

LIFE ON THE SPECTRUM

Liane Holliday-Willey

My life is interesting. It can be a bit of a challenge, but it's always interesting. I tend to see, feel and relate to things differently from most people. For example, sensory information doesn't make my world a safer and happier, more informed or easier to navigate place. Sudden noises, busy crowds, background commotion, things that sway, nasally voices, tags on my clothes, click-clacking shoes, mushy foods, warm rubber smells, asymmetrical anything, ice-cream sticks, and light pressure on my skin, wreck my mind like a bowling ball making a strike leaving the pins of my neuro system randomly scattered and out of place. Simple things like driving, playing, shopping, eating, listening, and sometimes even talking, becomes complicated. Then life starts to feel unclear and dangerous and I start to panic. Quirk, by quirk, I start marching toward dysfunction.

If I understood people better than I do, it would be easy enough to ask someone for a helping hand, but reading people isn't my strong suit. People tend to be very confusing. They use language like it's a hot dish of left-overs steaming in a crockpot. They pepper their talk with jokes, sarcasm, idioms and colloquialisms that sit in my brain like fat needing to be skimmed off that crockpot. Their facial expressions, body positioning, gestures and eye contact run circles around my cognition, making most days feel like everyone might as well be wearing a Halloween mask. If I'm going to understand someone, I need lots of context, background experience with the situation at hand, direct language and no passive aggressive behaviors or deceptions. When I was a kid and someone told me it was raining cats and dogs, I couldn't wait to get outside and grab a few to take in and cuddle. Words are crafty and, when used lightly, they can have more levels of meaning than five foreign languages put together. After five decades of listening to people talk, I'm still confused by the crazy ways people twist and turn language. On the surface, people tend to think I'm naïve or overly trusting, or too stupid to figure out people, I'm being duped. While all those suspicions may be a bit accurate, the truth is, I have autism.

I grew up in a time before autism was a large spectrum of challenges. In my youth, autism was stereotyped as a grave debilitating disorder that had no inclusion programs for people close to the tail-end of neurotypical. People diagnosed with autism were sent to special education schools until they turned 18, at which time their parents kept them at home, typically away from the public and any semblance of skill-building support, or in a residential center that served pharmaceutical cocktails and bland meals between arts and craft time and bedtime.

Despite my close-to-normal traits, my parents, community, teachers and doctors knew there was something unique about me. On one hand, they thought I might be a stereotypical indulged only child who is naturally more inclined to make big developmental milestones because I had so much adult attention and a father who was quite brilliant. I started using an above average vocabulary and excellent sentence structure when I was still in diapers. I showed signs of a near photographic memory with an unusually keen ability to see details others missed. I wrote and performed plays with props I made from things lying around the house, while other kids were still cuddling their teddy bears and taking naps. I outsmarted my grandmother at every turn and rarely did I lose a debate with kids anywhere near my own age. I had a deep fascination with all things cowboys and Indians and I could ride a horse better bareback through the woods before I was 4. My parents agreed I was unique, but they were proud I was set to make my own path in whatever way I saw fit.

The folks on our block accepted me for me. They knew to come to me if their dogs were missing, knowing I'd probably taken them home with me after letting myself into their unlocked houses while they were at work or school. Some neighbors were so sure I'd come by, they left cookies out for me, great treasures I'd dunk in water and not milk because of a one-time sip of revolting buttermilk at the Collins' house. My quirks weren't met with weird stares and screams to get off lawns. I was lucky to have gentle and strong support from the people I grew up with. Calls were made to my parents and not the police when I used shrubs for a toilet. Firemen let me ring the truck's bell after they'd rescue me, time and time again, from culverts and water drains. Teachers coaxed me out of the trash containers, rather than calling the principal when I'd be surfing for used teacher's materials for my "classroom" in our basement. The older kids would coach me into tops when I'd wander around in nothing more than my favorite pair of blue stretchy shorts way past the age when girls learn modesty. The adults in the random churches I'd step into on Sundays always let me sit with them in their Sunday school class rather than sending me off to the age-appropriate room. I was a lucky kid, able to romp and roam and be me while a mist of kind people kept me from getting stuck in the abyss.

I made my childhood my normal. But eventually there came a time just after puberty when friendships started to get too taxing. The girls started odd behaviors like shaving, and fixing their hair, and applying lip gloss and a hint of blush. Boys started to want to feel parts of me I didn't want to share. Some authority figures came to think my debates were more rude than clever. The playground got ugly and crowded and scary. The time had come for my supporters to realize my uniqueness was more than some sort of only-child syndrome.

In late elementary school, my dad started to recognize I saw the world like he did and his concern grew. He'd been bullied, beaten up, cast out, and left with no friends but his farm animals, his family, his books and his tractors. That life, he wouldn't have for me. Relying on his engineering scientific background, Dad came up with the idea that he and I to have analysis and debriefing meetings after he came home from work each day at precisely 4:15 p.m. We'd hop in the car and go to the same restaurant we always went to every night for dinner (except on the weekends, when crowds were too big) and discuss my day. Together we'd go through my "reports," including the behaviors of others I could so accurately mimic, and the experiences I had seen or been a part of. Like helping me with my math homework, Dad helped me with the study of human behavior. Like good reporters (he'd say), we would work within the wisdom of this eternally apropos quote "Who, what, and where, by what helpe, and by whose, Why, how and when, doe many things disclose" (*The Arte of Rhetorique*, written in 1560) to figure out how to safely and smartly react to the mysterious nature of human beings.

Here's an example. One day my much-beloved bicycle that helped me wear out my OCD tendencies through 10 miles to the dot rides every day was taken from me by older kids on the school playground. I had no idea how to approach this situation, though I knew full well it was wrong not just because it was my bike, but also because I hadn't finished my 10-mile ride and because the bike, my five-speed named Black Beauty, was my special interest.

The day Dad found out Black Beauty had been kidnaped (stolen were his words), we took a pause on going to dinner. "We can have soup tonight," Dad told me when I asked why we weren't getting in the car for supper. "We have work to do first," and thus began the careful unwinding of the reporter's tools. To begin with I had to stop crying.

Dad: First things first. You need to calm down. Take a deep breath. Crying won't solve anything. Start from the beginning and tell me what happened.

Liane: (after hyperventilating and stimming my way into circles around our living room): These mean kids took her away from me. I was riding down the hill and they told me to get off and when I did, they kidnaped her and rode off.

Dad: Number one: how do you know the kids were mean? Number two: did they take the bike away while you were riding down the hill or when you were at the bottom. By the way, you know it's not safe to ride down that hill. You need to learn that.

Liane: Because they were pushing each other and yelling. I was at the bottom of the hill. How do you know it isn't safe? You don't ride down the hill.

Dad: Don't get smart with me. I know it isn't safe because I know you're an accident waiting to happen. I don't want you hurt. Do you understand?

Liane: Yes. OK, but Black Beauty. We have to find her.

Dad: We will try. Hmm . . . it does sound like the kids were mean. Could you tell how old these kids were?

Liane: Not really. I mean, one is in my grade, and the others were taller, so I'm thinking they are older.

Dad: That's a good thought, but we can't be sure. Some children grow at faster rates than others. Do you have any other clues?

Liane: One was smoking cigarettes. He looked like he was the oldest and not just because he was taller than the girl in my class. No matter how old he was, he was the one who took my bike and the other kids just laughed and followed him. He looked like their leader.

Dad: Cigarettes kill. So, I'm assuming these kids are stupid, as well as bullies. Cigarettes are also expensive, so I'm beginning to think they stole your bike to sell it for cigarette money. Did you see where they went after they took the bike?

Liane: Yes. They rode her back up the hill and over to the houses behind the baseball field.

Dad: Did they keep riding, or did you see them go into a driveway?

Liane: They went into a driveway.

Dad: Can you point it out if I drive you over there?

Liane: I think so.

A short time later, Dad and I stood at the door to the house on the driveway. Politely, Dad knocked. A gaggle of kids came to the door, sneering as their dad met my dad face-to-face. My memory has erased the conversation, but I remember Dad's face was angry. He had the face he used every time he "meant business". Though the monster children swore they didn't have my bike, their dad was persuaded to open the garage where lo and behold, Black Beauty sat. Dad took the bike, loaded it in the car and made one last comment to the other father. I never thought to ask Dad what he said to the man, but I do know the kids never took my bike again. Though I never got an apology, I did get a new lesson from Dad. "The next time you are alone on the playground, I want you to find the biggest person you can and ask them to protect you. That may not work, and if it doesn't, get on your bike and ride away as fast as you can. And, by the way, if I ever catch you riding down that hill again, you and Black Beauty will both be grounded for a month."

A few weeks later, the big person advice worked and the bullying kids left me alone once and for all. No punches were thrown or bodies pushed or shoved, but I like to think the kids knew I wasn't an easy mark anymore. Either that, or they saw what I saw: my Dad's green '67 Cougar driving small, slow circles around the entrance to the parking lot more often than occasion. No doubt they thought he was looking right at them, but I'm pretty sure he was watching them and my proximity to the hill!

These early lessons were really supports of the kind we now know people on the spectrum need: fact gathering, calming and diffusion, analysis help, intervention, direct instruction, comprehension checks and behavioral follow-ups. Dad shared his model of parenting with my doctors, teachers, family, neighbors and a few of my true friends so they could help me apply it. Thinking logically, building hypotheses from observations and applying my building schema helped me become a member of the spectrum who could cognate my way through most things . . . but not all.

When I went off to college, and away from my big support group, it didn't take long for drug abuse, self-harm, bulimia and date rape to collide with my suddenly unsupported executive functioning skills, emotional regulation and social skills. Though I had grown up with the right kinds of intervention and tools for self-development and continued growth, I couldn't manage my life on my own. I needed a new set of skills and supports, and a new framework from which to build my knowledge base. College wasn't my neighborhood. I couldn't escape the sensory violations. I couldn't run away on Black Beauty. I couldn't call Dad to help me find my way to class or help me dissect my university rules and professors' course lectures. As good as I was at fitting in and pretending to be normal, I was no good at fighting off depression, anxiety and the bone-crushing crash to self-esteem that came when I had no one to guide me.

I try not to spend much time outside of my professional counseling sessions thinking about the bad stuff that came my way in college. Instead, I try to focus on what I did to find my way back to a healthier and happier life. Above all else, I returned to square one. I learned how to ask trusted people for help when I knew my abilities were compromised or lacking. I started going through the reporter's formula again with Dad on the weekends when he would come visit. I sought counseling for social skills understanding and self-esteem enrichment. I found safe, quiet spots in the library where I could relax and unwind between classes. I studied the effects of drugs and cutting and bulimia on the mind and body, using that knowledge to self-talk my way into better stress-relieving choices like equine therapy, water therapy, weightlifting and academic classes that helped me study humans. I found ways, old and new, to stop the chaos and help my brain click into a better place.

It's been years since I finished from my 11 years in college. Years since I have sat with my dad and tried to figure life out. Today, I travel the globe talking about my life with autism. I share my past, the supports and interventions that were helpful and those that weren't. I use my unique ability to speak autism and neurotypical to bridge gaps in understanding between those on the spectrum and those who aren't. My goal through each presentation and every book

I write is to stimulate conversation and ideas that help our two communities learn from one another, learn with one another and respect one another.

I still struggle now and then. Some things remain as cloudy for me today as they ever did. I'll never find noise appealing. I won't ever like surprises or sudden movements. Friendships will always be tricky and I'm sure I'll continue to misunderstand jokes, sarcasm and nonverbal communication. I know I will always need help managing financial decisions, health directives and executive functioning. I may never get good control over my emotional regulation and my depression and anxiety will probably be my shadows forever. But overall, I am comfortable with who I am and I know I am not broken or unable, not bad nor a castoff. I'm a member of a community filled with genius originality, wonderful kindness, dependable friendships and honest voices. I wouldn't leave my community for any other. Autism isn't my passion, but it is something I will have to study until my days are over. I finally know how to use my weaknesses to support discussion, education and advocacy. I'm closer to normal than I ever thought I could be, but I am still autistic and that's just fine.

Happily, the media, academics, healthcare and individuals on the spectrum are starting to make advances changing the perception of autism. More and more, people are learning the autism spectrum is vast and deep. We are finally being recognized for the unique insight we bring to science, art, mechanics, architecture, music, friendships, relationship dynamics and humanity. However, while our contributions to the world continue to be discovered, we need to remember the world is still filled with imminent dangers people with autism aren't naturally wired to recognize or deal with.

I fought through this disarray, firm in my belief that an ASD diagnosis can be a precious thing. But, also, firm in the knowledge I'm not naïve to its challenges. I'm not happy with everything my ASD brings to my life. I would change a few things about my neurobiological challenges, if I could. But . . .

12

LIVING FROM THE OCCUPATIONAL PERSPECTIVE

Occupational Therapy and Autism Spectrum Disorder

Susan Cleghorn, Lauren Vetter, and Shaunna Kelder

Occupational therapists (OT) use everyday life activities as a therapeutic means to enhance participation in occupations that support roles, habits, and routines in functional living (AOTA, 2014). The focus of OT services changes over the lifespan depending on individual needs in the areas of life skills, work, and play. Specifically, the focus of OT with young children with ASD may be in developing play, self-care, and social skills through sensory, motor, and social skill development, while OT with adolescents or adults with ASD may address work and behavior skills (Case-Smith & Arbesman, 2008).

History of OT and ASD

Occupational therapy began in 1917, when George Edward Barton, Dr. William Rush Dunton, Jr., Thomas B. Kidner, Isabel G. Newton, Susan C. Johnson, and Eleanor Clarke Slagle gathered to discuss how occupations could be used as a "curative service" (Peloquin, 1991). The early years of OT were influenced by the Moral Treatment movement, Arts and Crafts movement, and two world wars leading to the rehabilitation movement. During this early period, there was surge in the demand for OT (Anderson & Reed, 2017; Reed, 2006; Reed & Peters, 2006).

According to Colman (1988), OTs first began work with children through the Maternal and Child Health (MCH) movement in the 1940s (Reed & Peters, 2006). While the medical community and researchers were debating how to diagnose and support persons with autism, from 1947 to 1981, the *American Journal of Occupational Therapy* included eight articles that specifically addressed autism (as cited in Johnson & Ethridge). Articles reported that OTs were using milieu therapy, behavior modification, play facilitation, crafts, and sensory integration to support children with autism (Bloomer & Rose, 1989).

Throughout the 1950s and 1960s, OT expanded in pediatric therapy, as services grew from working with children with orthopedic conditions to working with a variety of disabilities in rehabilitation and special education programs (Colman, 1998). In the 1970s, the rights of individuals, social climate, and civil rights legislation for children with disabilities impacted OT services (Colman, 1998). Specifically, the Education for all Handicapped Children Act changed the way both typically developing children and children with disabilities received free public education. In addition, the Individuals with Disabilities Education Act (IDEA) allowed OT to provide therapy and assistive technology support. It was during this period that it became mandatory for OT services to be provided in public schools.

After 1980, the *Diagnostic and Statistical Manual of Mental Disorders* (DSM-III) introduced the term "pervasive developmental disorder" (PDD) and autism as a general category. At the same time, A. Jean Ayres began research and innovation in the field of OT and sensory systems through development of the Sensory Integration Theory (Bloomer & Rose, 1989). Ayres recognized children with ASD demonstrated poor sensory processing related to sensory input "not being registered correctly in the child's brain, resulting in hypoactivity and hyperactivity to stimulation," "not [modulating] sensory input well, especially vestibular and tactile sensations," and "brain dysfunction [causing] the child to have little interest in performing constructive and purposeful activities" (p. 15).

The 1980s resulted in an increase in knowledge of the needs of children and adults with ASD by governmental, medical, and educational settings. This increased understanding led to support for ASD across the lifespan. Research in the area of sensory systems and OT was further developed by Dr. Winnie Dunn throughout the 1990s. Expanding on A. Jean Ayres' Sensory Integration Theory, she "proposed a model for sensory processing that accounted for the nervous system's thresholds for acting and responding to sensory thresholds" (Dunn, 2001, p. 611). Dunn's research demonstrated that people with ASD had significantly different sensory processing compared to peers without disabilities (Dunn, 2001). The expansion of sensory processing assessment and intervention models provided structure for OTs to work with children and adults with ASD (Dunn, 2001). Dr. Dunn's research led to a body of research outlining *best practices* for OT with children with sensory issues (Dunn, 2011).

Today, occupational therapists' work with people who have ASD across the lifespan (AOTA, 2014). The intent of occupational therapy is to provide services needed for each person to engage in desired occupational activities. Occupational therapy professionals follow a specific process in providing services to its consumers that is science driven and evidence-based. An overview of this process follows.

Infant/Toddler

Callie is a 3-year-old female was diagnosed with ASD. She was referred for occupational therapy with concerns regarding emotional regulation, social engagement, play, self-care, and communication. Callie was a full-term baby, delivered without complications. Her mother reported that she was a healthy baby, with the occasional ear infection. Motor development was within normal limits for major milestones of sitting, standing, and walking; however, Callie appears clumsy and uncoordinated. Imitation skills are inconsistent and expressive communication is limited to two-word requests.

Callie has been unable to potty-train, refusing to enter the bathroom due to over-responsivity to the sound of the flush. She also is sensitive to tactile input, especially with teeth brushing, hair brushing, and nail clipping. Callie melts down with changes in routine lasting from five minutes to a half-hour.

Callie gravitates toward simple cause-and-effect toys. When introduced to a novel toy, Callie is unable to use the toy functionally, despite modeling from peer or adult. She demonstrates minimal eye gaze and an inconsistent response to her name. Currently, she does not demonstrate any interest in playing with others.

Callie has received OT services at an outpatient clinic once per week for the last three months. Parent education and play-based therapy have been provided to help with engagement, flexibility, and independence in daily occupations. A visual schedule has been provided for home, which has helped Callie. This has led to a reduced number of meltdowns during transitions. A Wilbarger Brushing Protocol was also begun utilizing a therapressure brush and joint compressions four to six times per day to help Callie's sensory system reorganize and calm down and to assist with tolerating tactile input during self-care activities. Systematic desensitization combined with a reward chart has also been used to help Callie tolerate the noise and thought of entering the bathroom. She is now able to flush the toilet without covering her ears or running away. Parents have participated in therapy sessions and trained in basic play techniques, which have helped increase Callie's expressive language and expanded play. She is currently using three- to four-word requests, has increased eye gaze, and an increased affective range while engaging in play with her brother and parents. Therapy is expected to continue to support Callie as she begins transitioning to preschool. Fine and gross motor development, self-care independence, and social interaction/play will continue to be addressed through this developmental period.

Occupational Therapy Process

The occupational therapy process begins with an evaluation/assessment. This initial information gathering and evaluation includes obtaining an *occupational profile*, an analysis of occupational performance, and the determination of related targeted outcomes (Chisholm & Boyt-Schell, 2014). This initial step in the OT process leads to development of goals and objectives that guide the development of a comprehensive intervention plan. Specifically, a combination of quantitative and qualitative baseline data is gathered through standardized and non-standardized methods in order to establish client-centered goals. These goals address identified occupational performance issues (OPIs). Figure 12.1 includes assessment tools that are commonly used by occupational therapists who support individuals with ASD (AOTA, 2017; Children's Hospital of Philadelphia Research Institute, 2015).

Assessment Tool	Area of Assessment	Age
Activity Card Sort, 2nd edition (ACS 2)	IADLS, Social, Leisure	Adults
Adaptive Behavior Assessment System, 3rd edition (ABAS-3)	Behavior	Birth to Older Adult
Assessment of Functional Living Skills (AFLS)	ADLs, IADLs, Community, Work	Adults
Battelle Developmental Inventory, 2nd edition (BDI-2NU)	Behavior, Social, Motor, Cognition, Communication	Birth to Child
Bayley Scales of Infant and Toddler Development, 3rd edition (Bayley 3)	Cognition, Play, Communication, Motor	Infants and Toddlers
Beery-Buktenica Test of Visual Motor Integration, 6th edition (Beery VMI)	Visual Perception Visual Motor	Toddler to Older Adults
Bruininks-Oseretsky Test of Motor Proficiency, 2nd edition (BOT 2)	Motor	Child to Adult
Canadian Occupational Performance Measure (COPM)	Occupational Performance and Satisfaction with Everyday Living Skills	All ages
Children's Assessment of Participation and Enjoyment and Preferences for Activities of Children (CAPE/PAC)	Recreation, Social, Physical, Self-Improvement	Child to Adult
Community Based Skills Assessment (CSA)	IADLs, Community, Work	Adolescents to Adults

Goal Oriented Assessment of Lifeskills (GOAL)	Sensory, Motor, Cognition, Functional Daily Activities	Child to Adolescent
Home and Communities Activity Scale (HCAS)	ADLs Home and Community	Child and Adolescent
Kohlman Evaluation of Living Skills (KELS)	ADLs, IADLs	Adult to Older Adult
Miller Function and Participation Scale (MFUN)	Fine and Gross Motor, Visual Motor	Toddler to Child
Peabody Developmental Motor Scales, 2nd edition (PDMS 2)	Fine and Gross Motor, Visual Motor	Birth to Child
Pediatric Evaluation of Disability Inventory (PEDI)	ADLs, Motor, Social	Infant to Child
Perceived Efficacy and Goal Setting System (PEGS)	ADLs, Leisure	Child
Quick Neurological Screening Test 3 (QNST 3R)	Motor, Sensory	Child to Older Adult
School Function Assessment (SFA)	Social, Leisure, ADLs, Motor	Child to Adolescent
Sensory Integration Praxis Test (SIPT)	Motor, Visual Motor, Sensory	Child
Sensory Processing Measure (and pre- school version) (SPM)	School and Home, Vision, Sensory, Motor	Child to Adolescent
Sensory Profile 2 (Birth to Adolescent Version) (Adult Version)	School and Home, Sensory	Birth to Adult
Social Responsiveness Scale, 2nd edition (SRS-2)	School and Home, Social, Behavior	Toddler to Older Adult
Test of Playfulness (ToP)	Play	Infant to Adolescent
Tool to Measure Parenting Self-Efficacy (TOPSE)	Parenting Skills	Parent Questionnaire
Vineland Adaptive Behavior Scales, 2nd edition	ADLs, Behavior, Communication, Motor, Social,	Birth to Older Adult
Vocational Fit Assessment (VFA)	Work	Adolescents to Older Adults

FIGURE 12.1 Commonly Used Occupational Therapy Assessment Tools

Following data collection, the occupational therapist reviews the results of the comprehensive evaluation and develops an intervention plan (AOTA, 2014; Chisholm & Boyt-Schell, 2014). This plan includes goals that facilitate progression client factors (body functions, body structures, values, beliefs, spirituality) and skills (motor, process, social interaction).

The intervention plan is carried out in a variety of settings (AOTA, 2014). A person with ASD may receive OT services in the home, hospital, clinic, school, industry, or community. Interventions may be provided directly or indirectly, individually or in a group. Discontinuation of occupational therapy services occurs when the person with ASD no longer requires direct skilled intervention to support OPIs. Yet, due to the nature of ASD, a person may require some level of support to participate in occupations indefinitely. The OT may refer the person with ASD to additional services for ongoing support, such as a para-professional in the school setting or a peer support person in a work environment.

At times, a person with ASD may be functioning well without OT intervention; however, the occupational therapist remains part of the care team as a consultant. Using this service delivery method, the OT indirectly supports the person by providing as-needed guidance and support to other care team members. For example, when a student transitions from middle school to high school the OT may not provide direct one-on-one intervention, but they may participate in care team meetings to suggest the use of coping strategies such as a social story to prepare the student for environmental transitions. A referral for OT services can made at any time during the lifespan through a person's primary care physician, teacher, or other service provider, such as a social worker, speech therapist, psychologist, or physical therapist.

Person, Environment, Occupation Model

To understand the unique role of occupational therapy in working with people who have a diagnosis of ASD, the Person-Environment-Occupation (PEO) model will be used to frame the chapter. The PEO model guides occupational therapists in evaluating clients, developing an intervention plan, implementing the plan, and evaluating therapy outcomes. This model describes the transactional relationship between three components when engaging in tasks and activities. These components include the person, the environment, and occupations. Specific to ASD, the person component may consider an individual's interests, values, sensory preference, motor skills, and cognition. The environment component may include the physical and social worlds such as the home, school, work, community, family, and friends. The occupation component includes tasks and activities that a person needs or wants to engage in, such as play, academic work, self-care, and job responsibilities. Each of these components impacts the others, resulting in some form of occupational performance. The occupational performance may be negatively or positively impacted by any or all of the components (Law et al., 1996). Problems in performing tasks and activities are referred to as occupational performance issues.

The Person With Autism as an Occupational Being

Occupational therapy focuses on the individual's engagement and performance of daily activities, personal satisfaction, adaptation, role competence, quality of life, and the needs of the family. With an increased prevalence of ASD, it is important to understand its development through the lifespan, including changes in the individual's habits, routines, and roles. Part of the DSM-5 criteria for a diagnosis of ASD is the age at onset (American Psychiatric Association, 2013). Symptoms must be present early on in infancy or toddlerhood to receive a diagnosis; however, these symptoms manifest uniquely (Coury et al., 2014). Initially, the occupations (daily activities) of an infant or toddler with autism are self-regulation and play. As the child ages, demands increase and more roles are defined. For school-aged children, self-care, motor skills, and social interaction become important in their daily lives. As they enter adolescence and progress through adulthood, the focus shifts to job performance, transition planning, community management, transportation, leisure exploration, and independent living skills. Occupational therapists can help identify triggers and implement calming strategies for dysregulation, provide environmental and equipment modifications to increase school/job performance, address social engagement through play and leisure, and improve gross and fine motor abilities to increase their client's quality of life (AOTA, 2014).

When developing a treatment plan, occupational therapists take into account the following areas that impact the client's occupational performance: client factors, mental functions, sensory functions, motor functions, and body systems functions. These areas are all uniquely affected by a diagnosis of ASD.

Client Factors

Occupational therapists consider the specific capacities, characteristics, or beliefs that reside within their clients and how they influence performance in daily occupations. These are referred to as client factors (AOTA, 2014). A holistic view is taken to assess all facets of a client's life that may be causing barriers in participation.

Mental Functions

The cognitive strengths and weaknesses typically exhibited by a person with ASD include difficulties predicting others' behaviors based on their thoughts and feelings, problems regulating and controlling their behavior, and an aptitude for detecting parts of objects or intricate details. These cognitive skills can vary and change over time (Society for Research in Child Development, 2010). These skills also underlie overall functioning in daily tasks, including sequencing the steps for self-care, time management, interacting appropriately with others, awareness of safety, and attention to initiate and complete a task. Occupational therapists can address cognitive difficulties associated with ASD through individual and group therapy.

Sensory Functions

Occupational therapists also look at the overall sensory functions, including tactile, auditory, visual, gustatory, olfactory, proprioceptive, and vestibular processing. The integration of these senses is physiologically necessary for home-ostasis. An individual's ability to process and integrate sensory information directly impacts their performance in overall quality of life. Sensory processing disorders are common clinical characteristics of children with ASD and are now a part of the diagnostic criteria (McCormack & Holsinger, 2016). The DSM-5 definition of autism, for instance, includes "hyper- or hypo- reactivity to sensory input or unusual interest in sensory aspects of the environment" (American Psychiatric Association, 2013). Families report that sensory impairments significantly restrict full participation in daily activities and create social isolation for the individual with ASD as well as the family, necessitating intervention (Schaaf et al., 2012).

Sensory-integration-based therapy focuses on registering, modulating, and integrating sensory information to increase engagement and participation in occupations across environments (Schaaf et al., 2012). First, the brain can decide which sensory input should be brought to our attention. The brain then decides whether to act in response. The individual with ASD may appear to not respond to auditory or tactile input or to overrespond and withdraw. The brain also oversees modulating the amount of input needed to engage in daily interactions and tasks. This may look like an individual seeking out certain stimuli, such as spinning continuously or crashing into things, while others may reject stimuli, withdrawing from a light touch or refusing to play on equipment or resist an environment. The third area of sensory processing is integration. Without adequate registration of sensory information from the skin, muscles, joints, and vestibular system, the individual with ASD cannot form a clear body percept. This affects motor planning and limits the type and number of physical and social play opportunities, ultimately affecting emotional development (Ayres, 2005). The occupational therapist's job is to use clinical reasoning skills to understand an individual's overall sensory processing through registration, modulation, and integration to guide the intervention process, individualizing the approach to each child's unique sensory profile (Watling & Dietz, 2007).

The central idea of sensory integration therapy is to provide and control sensory input with the individual. Therapy is most effective when the individual directs their own actions and the therapist directs the environment. This is because the brain is designed to seek out experiences necessary for its own development. Sensory-integration-based therapy often looks like play or leisure, as individuals use swings, music, sand bins, and trampolines. However, the therapist is using these tools to activate specific sensory systems for appropriate motor responses through motivational means. Effectiveness of sensory integration therapy is measured by the child's ability to respond effectively to previously difficult or disorganizing tasks (Ayres, 2005).

Motor Functions

While ASD has been categorized within psychiatric symptoms, research is focusing on a neurobiological basis (Rinehart et al, 2006). Evidence has linked ASD with impaired motor performance, including clumsy or unusual gait, impaired coordination, balance, tone, motor planning, and posture (MacNeil & Mostofsky, 2012). Additionally, intrusive and abnormal movements appear in ASD in the form of stereotypies and self-injurious behaviors (Ming, Brimacombe, & Wagner, 2007). This is due to deficiencies in the basal ganglia and cerebellum. The basal ganglia's role is to initiate and mediate movements, while the cerebellum is involved in controlling and terminating actions (Rinehart et al., 2006). Due to the expansion in the neurobiology of ASD, DSM-5 now includes "odd gait, clumsiness, and other abnormal motor signs (e.g., walking on tiptoes)" as part of the clinical description (May et al., 2016).

Individuals with ASD tend to have lower levels of physical activity than their typically developing peers due to hypotonia, muscle rigidity, akinesia, bradykinesia, and poor postural control (Calhoun, Longworth, & Chester, 2011). Not only are motor functions impaired, but interpretation of others' motor performance is impaired as well (MacNeil & Mostofsky, 2012).

Individuals with ASD often exhibit difficulty with perceptual motor integration, the ability to anticipate the actions of other and the consequences of movements (Linkenauger et al., 2012). Perceptual motor integration is a key skill involved in overall motor planning, or praxis. Praxis is the ability to conceptualize, plan, and successfully complete motor actions in novel situations. Praxis develops through interaction with other people and objects through observation, imitation, and exploration (Ayres, 2005). With a lack of opportunity or interest, there is a higher incidence of obesity, and decreased ability to participate in developmentally appropriate activities that lead to reduced social interaction (May et al., 2016). As a result, research has begun to show that motor features of autism may predate the language and social impairment (Rinehart et al., 2006).

Occupational therapists can address the impact of motor impairments on activities of daily living (ADLs) and quality of life through a variety of interventions (Calhoun, Longworth, & Chester, 2011).

Other than sensory integration therapy, occupational therapists may use neurodevelopmental therapy (NDT) to address motor challenges associated with ASD. NDT emphasizes the use of individualized therapeutic handling and loaded somatosensory input to improve postural control, movement, and body awareness (Instructors Group of NDTA, 2016). Gail Ritchie, an occupational therapist and certified NDT instructor, stated that the belief is with functional repetition the body will learn how to accurately recruit muscles for motor performance (personal communication, October, 2014).

Body Systems Functions

Sensory and motor difficulties also impact many different body systems, including the respiratory system and gastrointestinal system. Individuals with ASD may have difficulty with controlling volume, rate, rhythm, and pattern of respiration. The breath is necessary for motor coordination and emotional regulation, two primary areas of difficulty in ASD. It is also common for an individual with ASD to have gastrointestinal impairments, specifically motility issues, reflux, constipation, and food allergies (G. Ritchie, personal communication, October 2014). These symptoms have been found to increase with autism severity (Adams et al., 2011). Based on the correlation between ASD and body system dysfunction, research is currently considering an autoimmune component to ASD that alters these body systems (Valicenti-McDermott et al., 2008).

Child

Trip is a 5-year-old boy with ASD who is an only child. He attended an early childhood special education preschool, where he received speech language pathology therapy and OT, and has recently transitioned into a public-school kindergarten class. Trip has high tactile sensitivity and will only eat chicken nuggets, applesauce, or steamed and mashed vegetables. He is unable to tie shoes or fasten small buttons or snaps; he has a favorite pair of superhero Velcro tennis shoes. Trip becomes very overwhelmed in crowded areas and covers his ears to loud noise. He loves trucks and airplanes and will only initiate parallel play if related items or themes are involved. After much work with parents and his occupational therapist, Trip is able to dress, wearing all seamless lightweight compression-style shirts and (non-string waist) gym shorts independently at home with some extended time, verbal encouragement, and a visual schedule. A token system is currently being used to encourage Trip to engage in play, with others, that is not related to trucks or airplanes, with some success. Trip and his parents attend feeding occupational therapy at an outpatient clinic every other week to expand food choices and oral motor coordination and desensitization.

At school, Trip appears unable to complete any dressing tasks; he refuses and has meltdowns several times each day. The school-based OT completed an assessment of Trip at school. The OT provided education and coaching to parents and the teacher. Adjustment of the schedule and routine for Trip at school allowed him more time, decreased sensory input, and appropriate assistance to dress when needed. In addition, to support this occupation in a different context, the home visual schedule was modified and provided at school, and a reward chart was created to give motivation for Trip in this occupational area.

Environment: Physical and Social

The second component of PEO, environment, refers specifically to the physical and social influences that impact a person's ability to participate in activities. While these environments are in specific contexts, it is important to differentiate between environment and context when identifying barriers and supports to participation in tasks and activities. (AOTA, 2014).

The physical environment includes both the natural and the built environments. The natural environment includes the landscape such as grass, trees, hills, sand, and snow, while the built environment includes roads, paths, schools, grocery stores, homes, objects, and furniture. The DSM-5 (American Psychiatric Association, 2013, p. 56) describes behaviors associated with ASD that are directly related to the physical environment. This includes "stereotyped or repetitive motor movements, use of objects, or speech (e.g., simple motor stereotypes, lining up toys or flipping objects, echolalia, idiosyncratic phrases)," "highly restricted, fixated interests that are abnormal in intensity or focus (e.g., strong attachment to or preoccupation with unusual objects, excessively perseverative interests)", and "hyper- or hyporeactivity to sensory input or unusual interest in sensory aspects of the environment (e.g., apparent indifference to pain/temperature, adverse response to specific sounds or textures, excessive smelling or touching of objects, visual fascination with lights or movement)."

In each of these illustrations, behaviors include the use of objects in the physical environment. For example, an object in the home environment, such as Legos, may become an item of interest for a person with ASD. The behavior may include fixation on the Legos to the extent that other toys, people, and activity opportunities are ignored and refused. The challenge for occupational therapy becomes developing an intervention that increases the person's repertoire of interests, skills, and abilities within the physical environment.

Sensory features of the physical environment also impact a person with ASD. A body of evidence supports the notion that auditory, tactile, and visual features of the physical environment in schools have an impact on academic performance. These physical features combined with individual sensory processing abilities of individual students, determine whether a student will choose to participate in school activities and routines. Furthermore, this combination also determines student success or challenge in activity participation (Fernández-Andrés et al., 2015; LaVesser & Berg, 2011; Martin, 2016; Smith Roley et al., 2015; Tomchek et al., 2014). Studies have determined that sensory input such as auditory stimulation that is difficult for a student to control and filter, unexpected touch or tactile input, and visual stimulation from classroom objects all negatively impact academic participation. Occupational therapy interventions include collaborating with educators to make adjustments to the physical environment by assessing individual student sensory needs, modifying the environment to promote student participation, offering sensory options by grading input higher or lower, and providing human support to monitor participation and modifications (Piller & Pfeiffer, 2016).

The social environment pertains to a person's interpersonal and group relationships with those they need and want to have contact. This includes social expectations that are perceived by the person with ASD and those they interact with (AOTA, 2014). Frequently the person with ASD has maladaptive behaviors that impede his or her ability to effectively and positively interact with individuals and groups during daily routines at home, school, and work. Some of these behaviors may include aggression, social awkwardness, and self-injury (Woodman et al., 2016).

Few studies have addressed the impact of the social environment on people with ASD across the lifespan. A study by Woodman et al. completed a longitudinal study of more than 400 adolescents and adults with ASD. Through naturalistic observation, the study identified improved participation in activities of daily living and decreased maladaptive behaviors when social contexts where provided consistently. Specifically, success in the home environment included improvement in family relationships, communication, and emotional expression. Desired outcomes in daily activities and behavior were also noted through inclusion in academic and social activities. The study correlated successful social contexts in childhood with positive transition to adulthood measured by consistent improvement in activities of daily living and improved behavior (Woodman et al., 2016).

Contexts

Context differs from environment in that it is less concrete. Context in occupational therapy literature considers the cultural, personal, temporal, and virtual influences (AOTA, 2014).

Cultural Context

A person's culture includes beliefs, behavior expectations, and customs commonly understood and accepted by a particular group. These cultural influences impact a person's preferences for daily activities. Occupational therapists must be aware of both individual and group cultural influences throughout the therapy process in order to collaboratively develop appropriate goals and interventions (AOTA, 2014).

Views of health and disability as well as approaches to healthcare treatment are impacted by culture and vary from families, communities, and countries. It is critical to develop an understanding of how different cultures perceive disability and causes for illness. Beliefs about causes can significantly influence the client, healthcare provider, and the community's attitudes toward the evaluation and intervention process. These beliefs will in turn impact the investment in time and financial resources that a client, family, or community is willing to commit to the therapy process (Groce & Zola, 1993). OTs are charged with developing an evaluation and intervention plan that includes client, family, and community education with cultural considerations (Ravindran & Myers, 2012).

For example, in occupational therapy, when working with a child with ASD, cultural influences impact the manner in which parents and caregivers perceive and participate in therapy interventions (Mandell & Novak, 2005). These interventions are widely varied in focus and include sensory, motor, behavioral, cognitive, pharmaceutical, and nutritional or dietary approaches (Christon, Mackintosh, & Myers, 2010; Goin-Kochel et al., 2007). As a result, parents and caregivers play a large role in deciding what to do for their child. Cultural beliefs about autism influence a family's' decisions in terms of initiating and supporting intervention. Occupational therapists need to be culturally aware of parent and caregiver intervention preferences in order to manage family stress. In turn, this open communication provides an avenue for education and more efficient care for the child (Ravindran & Myers, 2012).

Personal Context

The World Health Organization defines personal context as including aspects of the individual that are not part of a diagnosis or conditions including influences such as socioeconomic status and age (WHO, 2001). In 2013, the Centers for Disease Control & Prevention (CDC) estimated that 1 in 88 children had ASD, with the incidence in boys to girls to be 5:1 (CDC, 2018). Today, that number has increased to 1 in 68, based on a representational sample of 8-year-olds according the Autism and Developmental Disabilities Monitoring Network (ADDM) (CDC, 2018). Furthermore, ASD knows no racial, socioeconomic, or ethnic boundaries with equal distribution across each category. Males are

4.5 times more likely to have a diagnosis of ASD than females. For occupational therapists, personal context considers where the person lives, the financial supports and challenges, education level of client and families, chronological and developmental age, and gender.

Temporal Context

The temporal context refers to time and rhythm of activities as well as stage of life (AOTA, 2014). People with ASD have difficulty with the temporal context as it relates to transitioning between tasks and routines. The DSM-5 describes behaviors associated with autism spectrum disorders that are directly related to the temporal context. Specifically, the DSM-5 illustrates "inflexible adherence to routines, or ritualized patterns of verbal or nonverbal behavior (e.g., extreme distress at small changes, difficulties with transitions, rigid thinking patterns, greeting rituals, need to take same route or eat same food every day)" (American Psychological Association, 2013, p. 50).

This rigidity with patterns and routines impacts a person's ability to move fluidly and flexibly between required, expected, and desired daily activities. The temporal context of the person with ASD may be mismatched with those around them. For example, rigidity in routines may interfere with the success of a family's cohesiveness. Examples of such family occupations include eating dinner, preparing for work and school, and completing bedtime routines. The meaning and practice of these family rituals contribute to a family's cohesion and connectedness. If a child's rigid behaviors impact a family's ability to successfully participate in routine occupations, then the family is at risk for dysfunctional routines and unhealthy connections (Rodger & Umaibalan, 2011).

Virtual Context

Virtual context refers to "interactions that occur in simulated, real-time, or near-time situations absent of physical contact (AOTA, 2014, p. S9)." As the virtual world grows in terms of technology use, both clients with ASD and occupational therapists must consider both the support and barriers imposed by the virtual context. Access to virtual contexts are readily available through technology tools including smartphones, videogames, and computers. These tools may be used by clients with ASD to complete preferred activities and daily routines (AOTA, 2014).

Literature is just now beginning to explore the impact of virtual context through technology use with people who have ASD. Evidence has shown that some screen based social media technologies can improve social functioning among adults in the general population; however, few studies have explored the application to those with ASD. One study with 108 adults with ASD used self-report of social networking sites (SNS) and found that 79% of participants identified using SNS for developing relationships and close friendships (Mazurek, 2013).

The use of virtual contexts in education is emerging and relevant for professionals concerned about the educational needs of students with ASD. Literature indicates an increase in parent request for technology-supported education for students with ASD. Specifically, parents are advocating for students to have access to mobile tools and applications such as laptop computers, tablets, and iPad due to student high interest in these tools as well as the decrease in cost for technology (Nally, Houlton, & Ralph, 2000). In addition, recent literature has identified that students with ASD prefer to learn via mobile technology and have demonstrated increased ability to learn concepts and skills via technology (Ayers, Mechling, & Sansosti, 2013).

Occupations and ASD

The following section provides an overview of common OPI areas for people who have ASD (see Figure 12.2). Although an intervention plan will look different for each individual with ASD, the examples provided allow the reader to understand approaches that occupational therapists use to support this population. For a full summary of interrelated constructs that describe the scope of occupational therapy practice, please refer to the third edition of *Occupational Therapy Practice Framework Domain and Process* (OTPF3) (AOTA, 2014).

Activities of Daily Living (ADL)

As defined by the OTPF3 (AOTA, 2014, p. S19), ADLs are "activities oriented toward taking care of one's own body . . . [and] fundamental to living in a social world, they enable basic survival and well-being." Such activities include, bathing and showering, toileting and toilet hygiene, dressing, swallowing/eating, feeding, functional mobility, personal device care, personal hygiene and grooming, and sexual activity. Occupational therapists provide interventions related to these occupational areas if there are any occupational performance issues.

OPIs related to ADLs will vary greatly depending on the presence or absence of the symptoms associated with ASD. Intellectual and language impairments and coexisting sensory, psychiatric, and motor deficits can all have significant implications on the degree in which the person can engage in ADLs (Atchison & Dirette, 2017). Assessment related to ADLs would follow the OT process noted above. Observation would occur either in the natural ADL environment, for example at the sink for grooming tasks or by a hallway locker for dressing for recess, or through other structured activity in which the OT can observe any intellectual, behavioral, sensory, and/or motor skill difficulties that are limiting performance in ADLs.

Occupations	Tasks/Activities	Client Factors and Performance Skill Examples					
		Body Functions and Structures	Sensory Processing	Motor Skills	Cognitive Processing	Social Interaction	Emotional Processing
ADLS	Bathing, Showering	Muscle strength, coordination, dexterity during washing.	Tactile sensitivity to water pressure, temperature. Auditory input of closed space overwhelming.	Dyspraxia—unable to wash hair.	Difficulty with routine and sequencing tasks for thorough washing.	Parent/caregiver bonding time during bath limited or absent due to fears or sensory related OPIs. Social stigma of poor hygiene and grooming.	Activity of bathing/ showering causing distress, leading to delay or disengagement in other occupations, including sleep.
	Toileting and Toilet Hygiene	Associated medical diagnosis related to bowel control can contribute to routines that interfere with play, school, and other occupational engagement. Muscle strength, coordination, dexterity for handling toilet tissue or other hygiene items.	Auditory sensitivity to toilet flushing, fear. Tactile sensitivity to hygiene after bowel movement or urination.	Dyspraxia—unable to motor plan accessing toilet paper and wiping.	Difficulty with routine and sequencing tasks for toileting. Inability to generalize skill to public toilet.	Disrupting other students in school bathroom with outbursts or fear-related behaviors. Missing out on other occupations due to bowel or other related toileting occupation difficulties.	Distress with urgency for bowel movements or urination. Loss of privacy.
	Dressing	Muscle strength, coordination, dexterity for donning and doffing clothing items and doing fasteners and ties.	Over-responsiveness to sensations of clothing: tags and seams feel "painful" or are distracting. Inability to wear standard-made clothing due to seams and tags. Need for pressure or weighted garments that increase time in dressing. Inability to wear socially acceptable clothing due to sensitivities.	Dyspraxia—difficulty donning and doffing any or all clothing. Unable to coordinate and tie shoes.	Lack of ability to sequence dressing leading to extending time for tasks. Unable to quickly undo fasteners or change when needed for recess or P.E. class. Morning routine extended due to required help for setup and sequencing of dressing tasks.	Missing out on peer interactions due to extended time required for dressing tasks, ex. recess or changing boots to shoes to enter classroom.	Frustration, social isolation due to extended time required for tasks.
	Swallowing/Eating	Muscle strength and coordination for mastication and swallowing without aspiration of food or liquids.	Gagging, aspiration due to oral sensitivity to foods.	Aspiration of liquids or food.		Gagging, aspiration limited social interactions during mealtimes.	Fear of gagging, aspiration, choking.

Feeding	Muscle strength, coordination, dexterity for handling utensils and dishes during feeding.	Food refusal, food selectivity, and ritualistic eating patterns.	Dyspraxia—difficulty opening packages, using utensils, bringing food to mouth.	Decreased sequencing and problem solving to complete a meal.	Inability to eat and socialize at the same time or required adult for task making typical child social interactions awkward. Inability to eat foods peers are eating. Decreased opportunities to build on needed social and interactions skills that are natural during group meal times due to sensory, motor, or other OPIs.	Frustration with inability to feed independently. Fear of foods, textures, and smells. Fear of common eating contexts such as cafeteria.
Personal Hygiene and Grooming	Muscle strength, coordination, dexterity for handling personal care items such as toothpaste tube, hair brush, deodorant, etc.	Unable to brush hair due to tactile sensitivity. Aversion to brushing or flossing teeth due to oral sensitivity.	Dyspraxia—difficulty opening toothpaste, squeezing appropriate amount onto brush.	Difficulty completing grooming tasks in appropriate order, forgetting steps such as zipping, applying deodorant, etc.	Grooming routines taking extended time and impeding on social plans.	Frustrations or distress during personal care tasks, such as brushing teeth or hair. Relationship strain when a parent or caregiver is required to complete these tasks understress.
Sexual Activity	Muscle strength, coordination, and endurance for sustaining activity.	Inadequate self-care, deficits in physical boundaries, and repetitive patterns and sensory fascinations related to sexuality due to hypo/hyperresponsivity to sensory input.	Difficulty with motor planning, grading force/speed.	Difficulty with planning, initiating, sequencing steps, problem solving.	Poorly developed theory of mind can lead to undressing or masturbating in public areas, misinterpreting relationship boundaries, skipping steps toward intimacy, making improper comments.	Relationship strains, frustrations during sexual activity if unable to reach satisfaction.

IADLS						
Care of Pets	Muscle strength, coordination, dexterity. for handling food supplies, leashes, kennels.	Sensitivities to pet food smell, to the pet, texture of food, tactile input from pet.	Gross and fine motor uncoordination and motor planning issues.	Difficulty with planning, initiating, sequencing steps, problem solving.	Ability to interact with other pet owners when encountered in public.	Tolerance for behavior of pet, flexible with changes in pet routines.
Communication Management	Fine motor strength, coordination, and dexterity for using communication devices.	Sensitivities to sound, volume during communication face to face or with technology.	Motor control for manipulation of devices such as smart phones, computers, and augmentative communication devices.	Difficulty with initiating, interpreting, and responding to face-to-face and technology-supported communication.	Ability to interpret and respond appropriately to social encounters.	Ability to regulate and manage emotions when frustrated with use of communication devices.
Community Mobility	Endurance, strength, and coordination for navigation and movement through the community.	Sensitivities to movement in cars, public transportation. Difficulty tolerating noise, sounds, smells encountered on public transportations, such as buses, trains.	Motor planning when navigating through streets, sidewalks, on public transportation.	Difficulty planning routes, choosing modes of transportation.	Ability to use etiquette such as moving out of the way of another pedestrian's path, asking for directions as needed.	Ability to regulate and manage stress associated with learning new routes and community areas.
Money Management	Fine motor strength, coordination, and dexterity for handling money/credit card.	Ability to tolerate textures of money, identify differences in coin sizes, shapes.	Manipulation of coins, paper money, credit cards, in wallet, purse, backpack.	Challenges with budgeting and planning spending.	Ability to ask about prices, interact with sales people.	Ability to manage excitement over purchases, delay gratification and adhere to budget.
Home Management	Endurance, strength, coordination for cleaning, yardwork.	Sensitivities to smells of cleaning products, stimulation from outdoor yardwork.	Gross and fine motor strength and coordination to use equipment needed to maintain home and yard such as vacuum, broom, rake, lawnmower.	Ability to identify need for cleaning, initiate, and ask for assistance when needed.	Ability to contact appropriate support persons and communicate needs related to home maintenance, such as calling a plumber or the landlord and expressing concerns.	Ability to manage frustrations over home maintenance problems and seek support in a calm and effective manner.
Meal Preparation	Fine motor strength, coordination, and dexterity for handling cooking supplies and utensils.	Sensitivities to food smells and textures.	Fine motor coordination and planning for use of kitchen utensils, able to pour, stir, mix.	Ability to follow directions, such as a recipe or instructions on a box, ability to sequence steps in making a sandwich.	Ability to work with others in meal preparation, such as family members. Communicate needs, ask questions, coordinate roles and tasks.	Ability to delay gratification, such as waiting until a meal is fully prepared before tasting.

	Spiritual Activities	Endurance, coordination, dexterity for sustaining position during services, manipulating spiritual materials (hymnals, candles, readings from a book).	Tolerance for crowded rooms, smells present in nature or in religious settings.	Motor planning and coordination needed to access spiritual activities such as sitting in meditation, walking a nature trail, sitting/standing/kneeling as needed through a religious ceremony.	Ability to follow written or oral procedures for participation, ability to pay attention.	Ability to verbally respond and interact as needed in religious services or ceremonies. Ability to interact with others during service, charity, or mission work, including asking questions.	Ability to manage emotions during long services, such as feelings of restlessness, boredom, or excitement.
	Safety	Reflexive responses to noxious or dangerous situations, heat, fire, smoke.	Ability to recognize noxious from safe smells, such as identify spoiled foods. Difficulty tolerating loud sounds in emergency situations, such as fire and tornado sirens at school and in the community.	Motor planning and coordination needed to exit unsafe situations, including being approached by a bully at school, seeking shelter during a thunderstorm.	Ability to recognize, identify, and act appropriately in the case of emergencies, such as calling 911 when there is a health crisis.	Ability to communicate unsafe situations to law enforcement officers in the community or ask a teacher for assistance at school.	Ability to manage emotions and remain calm during dangerous situations such as hearing a fire alarm and exiting the building.
	Shopping	Fine motor strength, coordination, and dexterity for managing and transporting items.	Ability to tolerate busy visual environments, such as grocery stores with bright lights, crowded aisles, fully stocked shelves.	Motor planning and strength needed to gather items, and transport home, such as reaching, grasping, bagging, and carrying grocery items.	Ability to plan shopping by identifying needs, choosing necessary items from the appropriate store, and identifying/using payment method such as cash or credit card.	Ability to ask store employees questions, such as where an item is located.	Manage feelings of frustration when unable to locate items needed at a store.
Rest and Sleep	Rest	Cognitive diagnoses may interfere with ability to identify the need for rest before exhaustion occurs.	Sensitivities to light, sound, tactile features of the environment impact ability to rest, such as rough fabric on a chair, prevent comfort and rest.	Difficulty with ability to relax muscles and assume a restful position.	Ability to determine a need for rest, recognize the physical and mental signs of fatigue.	Ability to communicate the need for a break or rest with family members, teachers, employers.	Ability to manage emotions experienced, during fatigue and delay rest if necessary.
	Sleep Preparation	Fine motor strength, dexterity, interfere with ability to engage in sleep preparation activities such as brushing teeth, setting temperature controls.	Ability to accommodate sensory preferences for types of sheets in bed, temperature of room, amount of light in sleep environment.	Motor planning abilities to prepare sleep space, such as making the bed.	Identifying sleep routines that facilitate restfulness, such as listening to calming music and turning off lights.	Ability to communicate sleep preferences with caregivers.	Ability to manage emotions when sleep routine needs to be altered, such as sleeping at a friend's house.
	Sleep Participation	Medical conditions such as sleep apnea interfere with full night's sleep.	Recognizing and adjusting sleep environment as needed, such as closing window if outside sounds awake the person during sleep cycle.	Motor coordination needed to safely navigate bedroom to bathroom areas if mid-sleep toileting is needed.	Recognizing the best time of day or night to go to sleep and wake up. Ability to recognize alarms and wake from sleep as needed.	Interacting with others in the sleep environment, such as pets, siblings, and caregivers.	Ability to self-calm if anxious or disrupted sleep occurs.

Category	Sub-category						
Education	Formal Education	Muscle strength, coordination, dexterity for handling books, electronics, supplies, etc. needed for education. Delays or struggles in psychological functions required for learning.	High or low thresholds to sounds, textures, etc. Inability to participate in school assembly, refusal to use glue, inability to sit on carpet during circle time.	Dyspraxia—difficulty in handwriting, fasteners for dressing/toileting, reading a book.	Low or high IQ leading to difficulties or frustrations related to content.	Difficulty with peer interactions, play, engagement in group learning activities due to social limitations or missing social cues.	Being overwhelmed by expectations, lacking friendships, being made fun of for differences in behaviors.
	Informal Personal Education and Participation	Muscle strength, coordination, dexterity for handling books, electronics, supplies, etc. needed for education. Delays or struggles in psychological functions required for learning.	Inability to participate in community-offered learning experiences, such as children's museums, due to auditory sensitivities.	Interest in sports or music with inability to motor plan for equipment or instrument use.	Inability to engage in family learning opportunities.	Difficulty engaging with others and learning during a group activity, such as a community painting and crafting fair.	Being overwhelmed by expectations, lacking friendships, being made fun of for differences in behaviors
Work	Employment and Volunteer Seeking	Physical limitations may interfere with pursuing specific types such as jobs requiring walking, standing for long periods of time, balance, coordination.	Sensitivities to sound and noise may limit some work prospects, such as factories, stores.	Motor limitations that limit ability to visit potential work sites to get an application, have an interview.	Ability to identify skills and select corresponding work opportunities.	Ability to effectively ask questions, inquire about work or volunteer opportunities.	Frustration experienced from difficulty locating work opportunities that match skill and interest areas.
	Job and Volunteer Performance	Physical limitations may interfere with ability to perform jobs that require manual tasks, such as tool use or use of heavy equipment.	Difficulty tolerating noisy work environments, such as factories.	Difficulty with motor coordination when using tools such as screwdrivers, hammer/nails, brooms, meal prep utensils/equipment.	Challenges following sequence of work, such as assembly work at a factory. Negotiating benefits, salaries, and work schedules.	Ability to effectively communicate with co-workers, supervisors, and community members.	Ability to manage emotions during conflict at work with co-workers or customers.

Play and Leisure	Exploration	Over-responsiveness to environment (tactile, auditory, visual input) can limit exploration of toys, activities, and tools.	Dyspraxia—difficulty manipulating tools/toys to explore different types of play.	Difficulty with problem solving and sequencing leads to more exploratory behaviors than in direct/purposeful play.	Withdrawal from others restricts exploration of play.	Being overwhelmed by demand tool/toy places on the individual in relation to their actual skill level.
	Participation	Over-responsiveness to environment (tactile, auditory, visual input) can limit participation in activities.	Dyspraxia—difficulty imitating motor actions to participate in activity.	Difficulty with abstract thinking limits play participation with others, especially with imaginative or cooperative play.	Difficulty reading and responding appropriately to social cues restricts engagement in play with others.	Difficulty with regulating emotion during competitive play in regards to winning/losing.
Social Participation	Community	Over-responsiveness to environment (tactile, auditory, visual input) can limit interaction outside familiar spaces.	Difficulty with community mobility, driving, taking public transportation.	Difficulty generalizing skills to various environments.	Difficulty with flexibility limiting appropriate interactions with others across environments and situations.	Being overwhelmed by demand of the environment in relation to their actual skill level to cope.
	Friends/Family	Limited participation in social meals due to sensory sensitivities in regards to food.	Dyspraxia—difficulty participating in family games/activities due to difficulty with motor planning.	Difficulty with expressive and receptive communication can limit conversations with others and overall interaction.	Difficulty with flexibility limiting appropriate interactions with others across environments and situations.	Being overwhelmed by demand of the environment in relation to their actual skill level to cope.

FIGURE 12.2 Typical Occupational Performance Issues Experienced by Children and Adults With ASD

Instrumental Activities of Daily Living (IADLs)

Instrumental activities of daily living (IADLs) can be described as complex activities that an individual engages in within home and community environments. These IADLs are more complex than ADLs in that the tasks and activities require the person to use higher level skills in all domains of functioning, including physical, cognitive, social, and emotional. Specific examples of IADLs include caring for others, cleaning the house, shopping, meal preparation, and driving (AOTA, 2014). In addition, key informants are needed to fully gather evaluation data including the person with ASD, parents/caregivers, and teachers (AOTA, 2014; Tomchek & Case-Smith, 2009).

People with ASD are at risk for decreased participation in home and community IADLs than their counterparts without ASD thereby limiting diversity in experience, exposure to different environments, and opportunity to develop skills and adaptive behaviors (Little, Sideris, Ausderau, & Baranek, 2014). Specific examples of OPIs may include challenges with successful completion of academic work at school, safely preparing a meal at home, accessing community mobility (including using public transportation), and managing money.

Rest and Sleep

Rest and sleep are identified in the OTPF-3 as "activities related to obtaining restorative rest and sleep to support healthy, active engagement in other occupations" (AOTA, 2014, p. S20).

These occupations include tasks and activities such as restful breaks from physical activities, sleep preparation including completing grooming, dressing, and cultural routines, and sleep participation, which includes discontinuing physical activities, addressing toilet and hydrations needs during sleep, and assisting others with meeting their sleep needs (AOTA, 2014).

Occupational therapists need to consult with parents and caregivers to identify rest and sleep routines and needs. Therapists evaluate rest and sleep by gathering an occupational profile, interviewing parents/caregivers, and observing the person with ASD (AOTA, 2014). Disruption in rest is a common issue. Sleep-related OPIs have been reported as high as 87% among children with ASD, with almost 60% of families reporting sleep routine problems. Typical sleep-related issues include ability to acknowledge the need for rest or sleep and maintain a state of rest or sleep through the night. The implications for decreased rest and sleep impact the person with ASD. Persons with ASD may experience decreased attention, disruptive behavior, and anxiety. Families report a higher level of stress and lower quality of life as a result of disrupted sleep routines (Cavalieri, 2016).

Adolescent

Jake is a 16-year-old male high school sophomore, and was diagnosed with Asperger's syndrome at age 10. He has difficulty communicating, socializing with family members, peers, and people in the community, and reading nonverbal body language. His parents describe social interaction as awkward, often resulting in frustration or anger. For example, Jake is very interested in weather and often discusses this topic with everyone. He has difficulty seeing when others become disinterested in the topic and, as a result, has made few friends and been bullied. Jake has limited leisure and social interests, as he spends most of his free time watching the weather channel and documenting in a dedicated weather notebook. Jake does well in school with a structured routine that includes a daily agenda and frequent verbal reminders to stay on task, organize work, and self-monitor his mood. He is interested in science and wants to pursue a career in meteorology. Jake receives support through an Individualized Education Program (IEP) that includes a transition plan with support from social work and OT services.

Jake and his OT meet once a week to develop skills and review progress. The OT used the Canadian Occupational Performance Measure (COPM) to help Jake identify his areas of strength and needs related to emotional management, social interaction, and vocational training. The results of the COPM indicate that Jake is most interested getting a job in weather but is dissatisfied with his skills related to working with others. Together, the OT and Jake developed a plan to learn about working in meteorology. As part of Jake's OT intervention, he researched the meteorologist's job description, learned about the functions of the news station, and developed a social story about expected behaviors at work, including how and when to discuss weather. In addition, Jake practiced using his Alert Program at school to monitor his mood and frustration levels and accessed his artillery of sensory solutions. After two months of practice with the OT, Jake was able to begin job shadowing at the news station two afternoons a week as part of his vocational skills class. Jake's OT and a support staff member went with him for support initially with a plan. In addition, the OT referred Jake and his family to a summer camp for adolescents interested in meteorology at the local community college.

Education

The occupational area of education is defined as "activities needed for learning and participating in the educational environment" (AOTA, 2014, p. S20).

Occupational therapists view education in three ways, formal educational participation, informal personal educational needs or interests exploration, and informal personal education participation (AOTA, 2014). Formal education includes participation in academic areas such as math and reading, nonaca-demic activities such as recess and lunch, extracurricular activities like sports and band, and vocational training. Informal education can include a person being able to identify topics and methods for gaining further information or skills. When a person engages in any type of learning environment—for example, a community painting class—occupational therapy considers this education participation.

OPIs related to education typically align with difficulty in memory functions for learning and socialization skills (Atchison & Dirette, 2017). In addition, due to the motor aspects associated with learning, especially in earlier years, motor deficits can impede on educational engagement.

Work

Christiansen and Townsend (2010) defined work in the OTPF-3 as "labor or exertion; to make, construct, manufacture, form, fashion, or shape objects; to organize, plan, or evaluate services or processes of living or governing; committed occupations that are performed with or without financial reward" (p. 423). Work occupations that impact people with ASD include selecting and seeking work, job performance, seeking volunteer opportunities, and per-forming volunteer tasks (AOTA, 2014). The U.S. Department of Education has identified an increase in the number of working age students with ASD as 514% in ages 14–17 and 317% in ages 18–21. This significant increase in the number of working age individuals with ASD sheds light on the fact that children who were first diagnosed in the 1990s are transitioning to work-ing ages. The benefits of work for the person with ASD include increased financial independence, self-esteem, dignity, and sense of purpose, while the benefits to society and families include decreased financial dependence on fam-ily resources and government programs and funding. Despite the benefits of work, this population has and continues to be under-employed (Chen, Sung, & Sukyeong, 2015). Few studies have researched the barriers to employment but some skill areas contributing to under-employment include difficulty seeking employment through phone calls and interviews as well as job skills such as social interaction and communication (Lorenz, Frischling, Cuadros, & Heinitz, 2016).

Occupational therapy evaluation of work should begin prior to age 16 for stu-dents with ASD is identified as an area of need and service in the Individualized Educational Program as mandated by the 2004 Individuals with Disabilities Education Improvement Act (IDEA):

Beginning not later than the first IEP to be in effect when the child turns 16, or younger if determined appropriate by the IEP Team, and updated annually thereafter, [the IEP must include] the following: appropriate measurable postsecondary goals based upon age-appropriate transition assessments related to training, education, employment and, where appropriate, independent living skills, [and] the transition services (including courses of study) needed to assist the child in reaching those goals.

(IDEA, 2004)

Data collection should be client-centered and consider the strengths and needs of the person with ASD, including interests, physical abilities, social and communication skills, and community resources. Some tools used by OTs to evaluate work include the Transitional Planning Inventory (TPI-2) and the Reading Free Vocational Interest Inventory (R-FII-2). In addition, the advocacy organization Autism Speaks has created a tool, Employment Toolkit, for parents, students, transition planners, vocational rehabilitation staff, families, and business to use when exploring work options (Autism Speaks, 2013).

OPIs in work tasks are grounded in the key characteristics of ASD identified in the DSM-5, including social communication, social interaction, and repetitive or restricted patterns of behavior (APA, 2013). OPIs include seeking employment, securing employment, and performing job duties. The performance skills needed to successfully engage in work include cognitive ability and social communication skills needed to interact. Specific examples include difficulty presenting oneself in a positive manner in an interview, asking for help when needed, listening and attending to customers, and cooperating with coworkers. Despite these challenges, a new body of evidence supports the use of task and environmental modifications to improve work skills among those with ASD. These approaches include use of assistive technology for video prompting of work tasks and video modeling of desired behaviors (Rosen, Weiss, Zancanaro, & Gal, 2017).

Play and Leisure

Individuals with ASD experience lifelong barriers to full participation in play and leisure. The lack of participation in play and leisure is directly related to overall health and functioning (Tanner, Hand, O'Toole, & Lane, 2015).

Parham and Fazio (1997) defined play as "any spontaneous or organized activity that promotes enjoyment, entertainment, amusement, or diversion" (p. 252). Children with autism often have significant difficulties with play, as they appear to engage with objects in repetitive ways and fail to develop creative and symbolic ideas. Limitations in play development affect other areas of life, including: language, emotional, and cognitive development (Freeman & Kasari, 2013).

Leisure is defined as "nonobligatory activity that is intrinsically motivated and engaged in during discretionary time" (Parham & Fazio, 1997, p. 250). Researchers have found that people with disabilities show improved adjustment, self-determination, and quality of life when participating in leisure activities. Participation in leisure activities is influenced by environmental and individual/ personal characteristics. These include services received, educational inclusion, parental participation, independence in ADLs, reciprocal social interaction, and motor functioning (Hickerson, Finke, & Choi, 2014). Individuals with ASD tend to prefer activities that can be done in a solitary or sedentary manner, such as playing videogames or watching television, so as not to challenge their limited interest in social interaction (Eversole et al., 2015).

Occupational therapists can address limitations in play and leisure by taking into account individual processing differences, motor skill development, social relationships, and functional emotional capacities. An intervention technique that has been used by occupational therapists working with children with ASD is the Floortime Approach. Occupational therapists work with parents and their clients on building reciprocal play interactions and developing relationships. Researchers have found children who participate in play-based therapy become more empathetic and creative with decreased maladaptive behaviors and emotional dysregulation (Dionne & Martini, 2011).

Social Participation

Social participation is defined as "desired engagement in community and family activities" (AOTA, 2014). In comparison with typically developing peers, children and adolescents with ASD are less likely to participate in activities outside of the home or school. Their social network is mainly restricted to family members, classmates, and paid service providers. However, the lack of participation in social activities does not reflect a lack of desire to participate (Taheri, Perry, & Minnes, 2016). Family and caregiver stress is higher in families of children with ASD often due to financial stress, mental health concerns, and perceived social isolation. It is the role of the occupational therapist to address barriers to social participation to help increase opportunities for full participation in occupation. Occupational therapists may address this deficit via group-based social skills training programs, activity-based interventions, sensory-motor interventions, and social story narratives, all with the goal of increasing social communication, increasing positive interactions, and decreasing maladaptive behaviors (Tanner, Hand, O'Toole, & Lane, 2015).

For people with ASD, intervention includes facilitation of skill acquisition and improved functional performance for all OPI areas (Weaver, 2015). The occupational therapist tailors each intervention and strategy to each person in each environment and context. The following case examples demonstrate this distinct approach to OT intervention for OPIs related to occupational areas across the lifespan.

Adult

Brittany is 30 years old and lives with her mother and grandmother. After many social and behavioral issues in primary school, she was diagnosed with high-functioning autism at 12 years old. At that time, she was provided an Individual Education Plan (IEP) and received occupational therapy and social work services through high school. Brittany has struggled with depression since her mid-20s, and after graduating from college (with a degree in engineering) she moved home. She works 30 hours per week at a local civil engineering firm. Her mother works and cares for Brittany's grandmother, who recently moved into the home after nearly burning down her home due to dementia. The family's church community is supportive. Brittany has experienced high levels of anxiety since her grandmother moved in and with the addition of visitors. She has been demanding regular reassurance from her mother that she will not have to "go to another funeral" and becomes very upset when her grandmother's needs "mess up the day." Brittany has begun engaging in head banging and picking at her arms over the past few weeks and has called in sick to her job several times. These behaviors also happened for a period of time after Brittany's father died. Brittany's mother requested a referral for support and the family psychiatrist ordered home occupational therapy.

After collecting Brittany's occupational profile and history, the occupational therapist determined that Brittany's routine had been significantly changed and her role(s) in the home increased to meet new dynamics. The OT also discovered that Brittany had stopped using a weighted blanket due to the home temperature being raised per her grandmother's needs. Working with Brittany and her mother, the OT created a social story including new routines and roles associated with the family home changes. The story was written in Brittany's high literacy level and used some civil engineering terms—these analogies being helpful for Brittany to apply. Using Brittany's smartphone, she and the OT put new routine items in her calendar. They also discovered an app that played calming music with a steady beat and a math game that kept her focus for periods of time. Brittany found that the tools helped her to better anticipate changes, balance the increase in noise in the home, and gave her a quick tool for focusing on something of interest when she became overwhelmed and was tempted to self-harm. The OT additionally contacted the family church to inquire if a window air conditioner unit could be borrowed. Her sleep improved once she began using her weighted blanket.

Occupational Therapy Outcomes

Occupational therapists consider several categories of intervention outcomes: occupational performance (improvement and enhancement), prevention, health and wellness, quality of life, participation, role competence, well-being, and occupational justice. The outcomes for a person who has ASD will vary greatly based on individual needs and wants. For example, when an occupational therapist considers appropriate outcomes related to *occupational performance*, outcomes can include *improvements* such as the child with ASD engaging in cooperative play with another child, participating in classroom routines, or tolerating a bath at home.

Outcomes related to *prevention* are also grounded directly related to individual needs. Goals related to prevention may direct OT services to use education or health promotion to support the client and caregivers. Examples can be found in four case boxes. In general, this outcome is focused on the person with ASD and/or caregivers gaining knowledge and skills required to participate in healthy living habits and opportunities (AOTA, 2014). This outcome relates also to *health and wellness*, where the occupational therapy ensures that the person with ASD and/or caregivers have ample resources for everyday life.

Occupational therapists consider the outcome of *quality of life* with all clients. This outcome can be measured via the dynamic appraisal life satisfaction of the person with ASD and his or her caregivers (AOTA, 2014). An example of a specific outcome in this area for a person with ASD, or caregivers, could include the person fully and activity engaging in family rituals such as holidays, or other traditions in which family bonds and engages in a variety of chosen activities. This outcome also relates to *participation, role competence,* and *well-being*. For the person with ASD to engage in said family rituals, outcomes in these areas could include things such as the person preparing a treasured family bread recipe using gloves to decrease tactile input and therefore achieving the role of the family member who contributes the traditional bread.

The final outcome area that occupational therapy considers is *occupational justice*. A person with ASD will likely want to engage in occupations that may be difficult to participate in due to many factors. When this is the case, the occupational therapist will work to achieve the outcome of the individual, or caregiver, having full access and participation in a full range of opportunities that satisfy personal, health, and societal needs (AOTA, 2014).

Summary

Occupational therapists have a long history of providing evidence-based services to persons with ASD. The evidence from research in the fields of occupational therapy, medicine, social sciences, and psychology guides the OT process that includes a comprehensive, client-centered evaluation, development of goals and intervention plan, and outcome-oriented results. Occupational therapists use a lens in this process that captures the unique attributes of the person, the environment in which the person needs to function, and the occupations (tasks and activities) that the individual needs and wants to participate in. The intersection within the transaction between person, environment, and occupation is where OTs provide interventions that are key in improving performance in everyday occupations. For a person with ASD, this may include getting dressed, playing with friends, completing job tasks, and eating dinner with the family. Each of these seemingly simple activities is an occupation that contributes to the health and well-being of individuals with ASD. Facilitating opportunities for occupational engagement in these tasks is the role of occupational therapy.

References

Adams, J. B., Johansen, L. J., Powell, L. D., Quig, D., & Rubin, R. A. (2011). Gastro-intestinal Flora and Gastrointestinal Status in Children with Autism-Comparisons to Typical Children and Correlation With Autism Severity. *BioMed Central Gastroenterology*, *11*(22).

American Occupational Therapy Association (AOTA). (2014). Occupational Therapy Practice Framework: Domain and Process (3rd ed.). *American Journal of Occupational Therapy*, *68*(Suppl. 1), S1–S48. doi:10.5014/ajot.2014.682006

American Occupational Therapy Association (AOTA). (2017). *Frequently asked Questions (FAQ): What is the Role of Occupational Therapy in Serving Individuals With Autism Spectrum Disorders (ASD)?* Retrieved from www.aota.org/~/media/corporate/files/secure/practice/children/faq-what-is-the-role-of-occupational-therapy-in-serving-individuals-with-autism-spectrum-disorders.pdf

American Psychiatric Association. (2013). *Diagnostic and Statistical Manual of Mental Disorders*, 5th ed. Arlington, VA: American Psychiatric Publishing.

Anderson, L. T., & Reed, K. (2017). *The History of Occupational Therapy. The First Century*. Thorofare, NJ: Slack.

Atchison, B., & Dirette, D. (2017). *Conditions in Occupational Therapy: Effect on Occupational Performance*, 5th ed. Philadelphia, PA: Lippincott, Williams & Wilkins.

Autism Speaks National Autism Conference. (2013). *Current Problems in Pediatric and Adolescent Health Care*, *44*(2), 26–47. doi: 10.1016/j.cppeds.2013.12.002

Ayers, K. M., Mechling, L., & Sansosti, K. J. (2013). The Use of Mobile Technologies to Assist with Life Skills/Independence of Students With Moderate/Severe Intellectual Disability and/or Autism Spectrum Disorders: Considerations for the Future of School Psychology. *Psychology in the Schools*, *50*(3). doi:10.1002/pits.21673

Ayres, A. J. (2005). *Sensory Integration and the Child: Understanding Hidden Sensory Challenges*, 25th anniversary ed. Los Angeles, CA: Western Psychological Services.

Bloomer, M.L., & Rose, C.C. (1989). Frames of Reference: Guiding Treatment for Children with Autism. *Occupational Therapy in Health Care*, *6*(2–3), 5–26.

Calhoun, M., Longworth, M., & Chester, V. L. (2011). Gait Patterns in Children with Autism. *Clinical Biomechanics*, *26*, 200–206. doi:10.1016/j.clinbiomech.2010.09.013

Case-Smith, J., & Arbesman, M. (2008). Evidence-Based Review of Interventions for Autism Used in or of Relevance to Occupational Therapy. *American Journal of Occupational Therapy*, *62*, 416–429.

Case-Smith, J., Weaver, L. L., & Fristad, M. A. (2015). A Systematic Review of Sensory Processing Interventions for Children With Autism Spectrum Disorders. *Autism*, *19*, 33–148.

Cavalieri, A. (2016). Sleep Issues in Children With Autism Spectrum Disorder. *Pediatric Nursing*, *42*(4), 169–188.

Centers for Disease Control (CDC). (2018). *Data & Statistics*. Retrieved from www.cdc.gov/ncbddd/autism/data.html

Chen, J. L., Sung, C., & Sukyeong, P. (2015). Vocational Rehabilitation Service Patterns and Outcomes for Individuals with Autism of Different Ages. *Journal of Autism and Developmental Disorders, 45,* 3015–3029. doi:10.1007/s10803-015-2465-y

Children's Hospital of Philadelphia Research Institute. (2015). *Elements of an Evaluation for Autism Spectrum Disorder.* Retrieved from www.carautismroadmap.org/elements-of-an-evaluation-for-an-autism-spectrum-disorder/?print=pdf

Chisholm, D., & Boyt-Schell, B. A. (2014). Overview of the Occupational Therapy Process and Outcomes. In B. A. B. Schell, G. Gillen, & M. E. Scaffa (Eds.), *Willard and Spackman's Occupational Therapy,* 12th ed. (pp. 266–280). Philadelphia, PA: Lippincott Williams & Wilkins.

Christiansen, C. H., & Townsend, E. A. (2010). *Introduction to Occupation: The Art and Science of Living,* 2nd ed. Cranbury, NJ: Pearson Education.

Christon, L. M., Mackintosh, V. H., & Myers, B. (2010). Use of Complementary and Alternative Medicine (CAM) Treatments by Parents of Children with Autism Spectrum Disorders. *Research in Autism Spectrum Disorders, 4*(2), 249–259. doi:10.1016/j.rasd.2009.09.013

Colman, W. (1998). The Evolution of Occupational Therapy into the Public Schools: The Laws Mandating Practice. *American Journal of Occupational Therapy, 42*(11), 701–705.

Coury, D. L., Swedo, S. E., Thurm, A. E., Miller, D. T., Veenstra-VanderWeele, J. M., Carbone, P. S., & Lounds, T. J. (2014). Treating the Whole Person With Autism: The Proceedings of the Instructors Group of NDTA (2016, May 27). The NDT/Bobath (Neuro-Developmental Treatment/Bobath) Definition. Retrieved from www.ndta.org/whatisndt.php

Dionne, M., & Martini, R. (2011). Floor Time Play With a Child With Autism: A Single-Subject Study. *Canadian Journal of Occupational Therapy, 78*(3), 196–203.

Dunn, W. (2001). The Sensations of Everyday Life: Empirical, Theoretical, and Pragmatic Considerations, 2001 Eleanor Clarke Slagle Lecture. *American Journal of Occupational Therapy, 55,* 608–620.

Dunn, W. (2011). *Best Practice Occupational Therapy in Community Services with Children and Families.* Thorofare, NJ: Slack.

Ethridge, D. A, & Johnson, J. A. (2012). *Developmental Disabilities: A Handbook for Occupational Therapists.* New York, NY: Routledge.

Eversole, M., Collins, D. M., Karmarkar, A. et al. (2016). Leisure Activity Enjoyment of Children With Autism Spectrum Disorders. *Journal of Autism and Developmental Disorders, 46*(1), 10–20. doi: 10.1007/s10803-015-2529-z

Fernández-Andrés, M. I., Pastor-Cerezuela, G., Sanz-Cervera, P., & Tárraga-Mínguez, R. (2015). A Comparative Study of Sensory Processing in Children With and Without Autism Spectrum Disorder in the Home and Classroom Environments. *Research in Developmental Disabilities, 38,* 202–212. doi:10.1016/j.ridd.2014.12.034

Freeman, S. & Kasari, C. (2013). Parent-Child Interactions in Autism: Characteristics of Play. *Autism, 17*(2), 147–161. doi: 10.1177/1362361312469269

Goin-Kochel, R. P., Myers, B., & Mackintosh, V. H. (2007). Parental Reports on the Use of Treatments and Therapies for Children With Autism Spectrum Disorders. *Research in Autism Spectrum Disorders, 1*(3), 195–209 doi:10.1016/j.rasd.2006.08.006

Groce, N. E., & Zola, I. K. (1993). Multiculturalism, chronic illness, and disability. *Pediatrics, 91(5 Pt 2),* 1048–1055.

Hickerson, B., Finke, E. H., & Choi, Y. (2014). Enduring Leisure Involvement and Children With Autism Spectrum Disorder: Validation of a Parent-Reported Involvement Scale. *Therapeutic Recreation Journal, 48*(1), 31–45.

Individuals with Disabilities Education Act, 20 U.S.C § 300.320 [b] (2004). Retrieved from: https://sites.ed.gov/idea/regs/b/d/300.320/b

LaVesser, P., & Berg, C. (2011). Participation Patterns in Preschool Children With an Autism Spectrum Disorder. *OTJR: Occupation, Participation and Health*, *31*, 33–39. doi:10.3928/15394492-20100823-01

Law, M., Cooper, B., Strong, S., Stewart, D., Rigby, P. & Letts, L. (1996). The Person-Environment-Occupation Model: A Transactive Approach to occupational performance. *Canadian Journal of Occupational Therapy*, *63*(1), 9–23.

Linkenauger, S. A., Lerner, M. D., Ramenzoni, V. C., & Proffitt, D. R. (2012). Perceptual-Motor Deficit Predicts Social and Communicative Impairments in Individuals With Autism Spectrum Disorders. *Autism Research*, *5*, 352–362. doi: 10.1002/aur.1248

Little, L.M., Sideris, J., Ausderau, K., Baranek, G.T. (2014). Activity Participation Among Children With Autism Spectrum Disorder. *American Journal of Occupational Therapy*, *68*(2), 177–185.

Lorenz T., Frischling C., Cuadros R., & Heinitz K. (2016). Autism and Overcoming Job Barriers: Comparing Job-Related Barriers and Possible Solutions in and Outside of Autism-Specific Employment. *PLoS ONE 11*(1). doi:10.1371/journal.pone.0147040

McCormack, G. L, & Holsinger, L. (2016). The Significance of Comforting Touch to Children With Autism: Sensory Processing Implications for Occupational Therapy. *Open Journal of Occupational Therapy*, *4*(2). doi: 10.15453/2168-6408.1133

MacNeil, L. K., & Mostofsky, S. H. (2012). Specificity of Dyspraxia in Children With Autism. *Neuropsychology*, *26*(2), 165–171. doi:10.1037/a0026955

Martin, C. S. (2016). Exploring the Impact of the Design of the Physical Classroom Environment on Young Children With Autism Spectrum Disorder (ASD). *Journal of Research in Special Educational Needs*, *16*(4), 280–298. doi:10.1111/1471-3802.12092

Mandell, D. S., & Novak, M. (2005). The role of culture in families' treatment decisions for children with autism spectrum disorders. *Mental Retardation and Developmental Disabilities Research Reviews*, *11*, 110–115.

May, T., McGinley, J., Murphy, A., Hinkley, T., Papadopoulos, N., Williams, K. J., . . . Rinehart, N. J. (2016). A Multidisciplinary Perspective on Motor Impairment as an Early Behavioural Marker in Children With Autism Spectrum Disorder. *Australian Psychologist*, *51*, 296–303. doi:10.1111/ap.12225

Mazurek, M. O. (2013). Social Media Use Among Adults With Autism Spectrum Disorders. *Computers in Human Behavior*, *29*, 1709–1714.

Ming, X., Brimacombe, M., & Wagner, G. C. (2007). Prevalence of Motor Impairment in Autism Spectrum Disorders. *Brain & Development*, *29*, 565–570. doi:10.1016/j.braindev.2007.03.002

Murray, C., & Doren, B. (2012). The Effects of Working at Gaining Employment Skills on the Social and Vocational Skills of Adolescents with Disabilities: A School-Based Intervention. *Rehabilitation Counseling Bulletin*, *56*(2), 96–107.

Nally, B., Houlton, B., & Ralph, S. (2000). Researches in Brief: The Management of Television and Video by Parents of Children With Autism. *Autism*, *4*(3), 331–337.

Parham, L. D., & Fazio, L. S. (1997). *Play in Occupational Therapy for Children*. St. LouisM, O: Mosby.

Piller, A., & Pfeiffer, B. (2016). The Sensory Environment and Participation of Preschool Children With Autism Spectrum Disorder. *OTJR: Occupation, Participation, and Health*, *36*(3), 103–111. doi:10.1177/1539449216665116

Ravindran, N., & Myers, B. J. (2012). Cultural Influences on Perceptions of Health, Illness, and Disability: A Review and Focus on Autism. *Journal of Child and Family Studies*, *21*, 311–319.

Reed, K. L. (2006). Occupational Therapy Values and Beliefs, The Formative Years: 1904–1929. *OT Practice*, 21–25.

Reed, K. L., & Peters, C. (2006). Occupational Therapy Values and Beliefs, Part II The Great Depression and War Years: 1930–1949. *OT Practice*, 17–22.

Rinehart, N. J., Tonge, B. J., Iansek, R., McGinley, J., Brereton, A. V., Enticott, P. G., & Bradshaw, J. L. (2006). Gait Function in Newly Diagnosed Children With Autism: Cerebellar and Basal Ganglia Related Motor Disorder. *Developmental Medicine & Child Neurology, 48,* 819–824. doi:10.1017/S0012162206001769

Rodger, S., & Umaibalan, V. (2011). The Routines and Rituals of Families of Typically Developing Children Compared with Families of Children With Autism Spectrum Disorder: An Exploratory Study. *British Journal of Occupational Therapy, 74*(1), 20–26.

Rosen, R., Weiss, P.L., Zancanaro, M., & Gal, E. (2017). Usability of a Video Modeling Computer Application for the Vocational Training of Adolescents With Autism Spectrum Disorder. *British Journal of Occupational Therapy, 80*(4), 208–215. doi:10.1177/0308022616680367

Schaaf, R. C., Benevides, T. W., Kelly, D., & Mailloux-Maggio, Z. (2012). Occupational Therapy and Sensory Integration for Children with Autism: A Feasibility, Safety, Acceptability and Fidelity Study. *Autism, 16*(3), 321–327. doi:10.1177/136236131 1435157

Smith Roley, S., Mailloux, Z., Parham, L. D., Schaaf, R. C., Lane, C. J., & Cermak, S. (2015). Sensory Integration and Praxis Patterns in Children with Autism. *American Journal of Occupational Therapy, 69,* 1–8. doi:10.5014/ajot.2015.012476

Society for Research in Child Development. (2010, September 16). Cognitive Skills in Children with Autism Vary and Improve, Study Finds. ScienceDaily. Retrieved from www.sciencedaily.com/releases/2010/09/100915080429.html

Taheri. A., Perry, A., & Minnes, P. (2016). Examining the Social Participation of Children and Adolescents With Intellectual Disabilities and Autism Spectrum Disorder in Relation to Peers. Journal of Intellectual Disability Research, *60*(5), 435–443. doi: 10.1111/jir.12289

Tanner, K., Hand, B. N., O'Toole, G., & Lane, A. E. (2015). Effectiveness of Interventions to Improve Social Participation, Play, Leisure, and Restricted and Repetitive Behaviors in People with Autism Spectrum Disorder: A Systematic Review. *American Journal of Occupational Therapy, 69*(5), 1–36A.

Tomchek, S. D., Huebner, R. A., & Dunn, W. (2014). Patterns of Sensory Processing in Children With an Autism Spectrum Disorder. *Research in Autism Spectrum Disorders, 8,* 1214–1224. doi:10.1016/j.rasd.2014.06.006

Valicenti-McDermott, M. D., McVicar, K., Cohen, H. J., Weshil, B. K., & Shinnar, S. (2008). Gastrointestinal Symptoms in Children With an Autism Spectrum Disorder and Language Regression. *Pediatric Neurology, 39*(6), 392–398. doi:10.1016/j. pediatrneurol.2008.07.019

Watling, R. & Dietz, J. (2007). Occupational Therapy Intervention on Children With Autism Spectrum Disorders. *American Journal of Occupational Therapy, (61)*5, 574–583. doi:10.5014/ajot.61.5.574

Weaver, L. L. (2015). Effectiveness of Work, Activities of Daily Living, Education, and Sleep Interventions for People With Autism Spectrum Disorder: A Systematic Review. *American Journal of Occupational Therapy, 69*(5), 1–11. doi:10.5014/ajot.2015.017962

Woodman, A. C., Smith, L. E., Greenberg, V. S., & Mailick, M. R. (2016). Contextual Factors Predict Patterns of Change in Functioning Over 10 Years Among Adolescents and Adults With Autism Spectrum Disorder. *Journal of Autism Developmental Disorders, 46,* 176–189. doi:10.1007/s10803-015-2561z

13

THE COMMON SENSE OF LIFE

Knowing Is Not Doing

Bradley Bridges

Introduction

An autism spectrum disorder (ASD) is largely a set of challenging behaviors that make it difficult to relate and share meaning with others. Previous chapters in this text have explored neurological and psychological aspects of these social interactions, along with how to assess and diagnose when an autism diagnosis is appropriate. The following will explore practical implications for how these symptoms might be expressed in everyday life, along with strategies for adjusting to the social world.

Learning Skills and Rules Deliberately vs. Automatically

Assuming an adequate level of cognitive functioning and family support, many people with moderate to high functioning ASD demonstrate an ability to acquire necessary skills for developing relationships and independence. Unfortunately, ASD seems to create a barrier to the intuitive development of such skills. Whereas most people find that many skills develop rather automatically, things that are often considered "common sense" can require explicit teaching, modeling, and reinforcement for individuals with ASD.

Difficulty acquiring "commonsense" skills can result in a predictable narrative with some practical effects on daily life. A primary challenge is difficulty intuitively learning appropriate social skills. Social interactions are characterized by near-constant nonverbal cues regarding tone of voice, facial expressions, body language, etc. Some communication (such as sarcasm) might convey the same voice tone and visual cues regardless of whether the comment is sarcastic or not, with only the context of the situation to identify the speaker's meaning.

The ability to intuitively understand the gist of the conversation and respond quickly and appropriately can be a monumental task for those with ASD.

Many individuals find that these skills can be learned, although the process is more intentional—as one might learn skills for math or science. Developing plans for the individual to learn these skills can require explicit teaching, rather than natural social consequences to teach skills. It can also require identifying and understanding skills that many people might not even think about because they happen naturally and breaking down these processes into specific and teachable steps. There are a multitude of strategies for developing these skills. It can be useful to observe and discuss videos or pictures of people with a trusted friend, family member, or therapist to understand how others might interpret an interaction. The individual can be recorded to review his/her own interactions for self-evaluation. Development of acting skills or participation in theater or performing arts can be valuable for communicating more deliberately. Regardless of the strategy chosen, there are often options for overcoming difficulties with automatic social learning.

Information vs. Experiences

The ASD brain seems to be functionally primed to sharing facts and information rather than more subjective experiences and personal stories. A person with ASD might see relationships or conversations as very practical and feel that having a conversation is most enjoyable when there is a clear purpose, such as sharing facts about a particular area of interest. The less practical and more relational aspects of relationships and conversation might seem useless or even bothersome. "Neurotypical" individuals often see value in making small talk or chitchat emphasizing the relation to other people and sharing stories and experiences to help build a sense of closeness. These are two very different ways of thinking about relationships and conversations that can lead to frustration and misunderstanding on both sides.

Conversations involving a person with ASD can often gravitate toward one of two extremes: the ASD person can inundate the listener with a plethora of facts about a particular topic; or respond in brief or one-word responses as the other member(s) of the conversation attempts to extract more personal information. Each party can become frustrated as they experience different motivation and goals for the conversation, and each can find the other's tendency to be boring, irritating, and pointless.

Idealized vs. Effective Thinking

Neurological differences in the ASD brain result in some differences in ways of thinking about and perceiving the world that can create advantages and barriers, depending on the situation. This way of thinking can be overly practical/idealized, with difficulty recognizing the more emotional and irrational expectations of society and relationships. Many people with ASD exhibit a tendency toward idealized thinking by focusing on events as they should be in an ideal world. It can thus be tempting to ruminate on injustices and unfairness in the social world, which often functions in a less than logical and ideal way. This can be a challenging change in mindset to focus on understanding and adapting to the world as it is, rather than trying to change it to what it should be.

Unfortunately, society often expects behaviors that are not the most ideal or practical. Several years ago, I worked with a young man who presented this dilemma quite clearly. This was a young man around age 18, with stated goals to: (1) make friends, (2) get a job, and (3) move out of his parents' house. As it was, he also happened to refuse to shake hands. This did not appear related to a fear of germs or a phobia per se, and indeed he did not demonstrate a fear of germs that would obstruct other behaviors, such as touching doorknobs. Yet, he would repeatedly refuse to shake hands with people he was meeting for the first time—strangers, family, or anyone else. Each time this was brought up, he shared the same response about how impractical handshaking is, how it contributes to spreading germs, and alternative greetings that would be more ideal. In fact, he was probably right that there could be more sanitary alternatives that might make more sense. And yet, he became so focused on the problems with a conventional greeting typically expected in society that he could not compromise his ideals and shake hands. Being that many social contacts are initiated with this greeting, his first impression to nearly everyone he met was characterized by this odd and often offputting behavior. He always demonstrated this behavior, even in job interviews, to the point of sabotaging his two primary stated goals. The last I knew, he continued to live alone with no job and few friends, several years later.

Being successful in a social world means people must sometimes act in ways that do not seem ideal in order to reach goals. There are advantages for those who can effectively read social cues and use this information to navigate social situations. For those who do not do so easily, it can be helpful to develop trust in others who are better able to read social cues and learn how to improve these skills. These skills can involve learning nonverbal and situational cues that help recognize expectations, actively using observation in social situations to assess the behavior of a majority of people, recognizing one's own tendencies for different situations, identifying socially acceptable ways of coping, and visualizing and planning ahead for situations.

Areas of Skill Deficit

Focusing on a subset of life experiences can result in deficits of a variety of skillsets. Many neurotypical children automatically focus on the social world and observe how other people behave, communicate, and interact with the world around them. Meanwhile, children with ASD can fail to recognize many of these skills in others. Failure to learn as effectively through modeling and observation thus can yield an increasing gap in skill acquisition as the child ages.

Executive Functioning

A primary set of skills that can be problematic for individuals with an autism spectrum disorder are referred to as executive functioning skills (Hill, 2004). These are skills that help people advance from childhood to adulthood—from acting based on impulse and feelings to being able to incorporate thinking and logic. Executive skills help people draw on past experiences, anticipate consequences to their actions, and evaluate a variety of possible responses to a situation. They are involved in problem solving, thinking about another person's point of view, and inhibiting impulses. Executive skills are critical for setting goals, making plans to reach those goals, being able to follow through with plans, and evaluating and modifying the plans along the way. In short, executive skills help people figure out where they want to get in life and how to overcome obstacles to get there.

While most people experience challenges in developing at least some executive skills, there can be even greater challenges for those with autism (Craig et al., 2016). There is a myriad of neurological and experiential reasons for this explored in previous chapters, and the skill deficits are exacerbated by additional life challenges faced by those with ASD. This combination of underdeveloped executive skills and additional life obstacles indicate a significant need for direct development of executive skills for those with ASD.

Rather than viewing executive functioning as a single broad skillset, it can be useful to identify skills according to relative areas of strength and weakness. This allows the individual to take advantage of existing strengths while focusing on a few specific skills to target. For example, if organization is considered a primary skill deficit preventing goal completion, the focus can be put specifically into developing a system of skills such as using a planner, calendar, alarms, etc. to help prompt and organize oneself.

Communication

Human communication is highly nuanced. The meaning of a single sentence can change completely by emphasizing a different word, changing the pace or intonation of the sentence, altering the facial expression or body language, or changing any number of other variables. In many instances, the actual words themselves could be one of the least important parts of conveying a message.

Yet, for people with ASD, the words that are used might be the *most* important part of the message. This can lead to profound misunderstandings with others and frustration on the part of both the speaker and the messenger. People with autism tend to struggle with understanding sarcasm, idioms, figures of speech, and many common elements of social language.

They can also be more prone to speaking in ways that others view as socially inappropriate. For example, at one extreme many with ASD will speak with a monotone and pedantic speech pattern. There tends to be little variability in the pace or intonation of speech, sounding almost robotic. Emotion tends to be reflected through increasing volume, rather than facial expression or more subtle speech changes. At the other extreme, some individuals with ASD will chronically use a tone of voice that others perceive as condescending, rude, childish, or in some other was socially inappropriate. One might be oblivious to how this tone is perceived and can persistently communicate messages that are not intended. Others can react automatically to these speech patterns, making character assumptions and feeling irritated or upset with the individual, such as believing the speaker is being disrespectful.

Emotion Regulation

As noted in Chapter 4 in this volume, ASD consists of neurological differences within both the limbic system and the cortex. Both factors can contribute to challenges with emotion regulation. It has been proposed that individuals with ASD can experience differences with functioning of the amygdala, a limbic system structure related to processing fear (Baron-Cohen et al., 2000; Schultz, 2005). This can result in individuals with ASD tending to experience more significant intense feelings across the board (Brigham Young University, 2012). As a result, feelings of anxiety, boredom, anger, sadness etc. might feel more intense than what many neurotypical people experience. Many life challenges and mental health issues result from managing these emotions in response to life circumstances. This challenge can then be magnified than for individuals with ASD, who may experience the same emotions as everyone else, but on a more extreme scale.

The primary pathway for connections from the limbic system to the neo-cortex occurs through the prefrontal cortex (Haznedar et al., 2000). The prefrontal cortex then plays a large role in receiving messages from the limbic system, understanding and recognizing the emotions, and figuring out what to do with them. The prefrontal cortex is strongly associated with executive skill development, such as the ability to set goals and develop and follow plans to reach those goals (Ozonoff, Pennington, & Rogers, 1991). A critical aspect of working toward goals is being able to understand emotions and decide how to act on them. Deficits in this area can lead to reacting on a highly emotional basis in ways that can be counterproductive toward long-term goals. Individuals with deficits in this area can repeatedly struggle to achieve goals, ultimately leading to a higher likelihood of mental health issues or depression as they struggle to achieve the things they would like in life.

ASD is commonly associated with delayed development of frontal lobe functioning (Baron-Cohen et al., 1999). This means that for many individuals with autism, there is a combination of experiencing more intense feelings (differences in the limbic system) and impaired development of the prefrontal cortex that could help to manage these emotions. More intense emotions and reduced capacity to identify, express, and manage these emotions can often be overwhelming. As a result, there is a higher rate of secondary mental health issues for individuals with ASD. This can lead to a higher likelihood of avoidance of situations that might provoke uncomfortable emotions. When such situations cannot be avoided, there can be a greater likelihood of anger, aggression, or attempts to control the situation to remove the trigger to the undesired emotions. Ultimately, these efforts at controlling the situation could be perceived as further attempts at avoiding situations that are creating strongly uncomfortable or overwhelming emotions.

Empathy/Social Perspective Taking

ASD can lead to challenges with theory of mind and genuine empathy (Ozonoff et al., 1991; Vollm et al., 2006). While many people with ASD can intellectually consider another person's point of view, this often does not include an automatic emotional response to another person's emotions. Differences in mirror neuron functioning are proposed to play a role in this process (Hamilton, 2013; Perkins et al., 2010). Seeing another person experience an emotional event, or even reading a news article or seeing a commercial about a traumatic event, can produce intense emotions for many people. Yet, many people with ASD will find these emotional responses to others' experiences to be much more muted or absent. If asked to identify how others might feel in that given situation, many autistic people can identify reasonable thoughts and emotions that others might experience. However, there tends to not be the same emotional connection, and others might view their responses as overly practical and insensitive. This can be especially true with some of the subtler emotional experiences of day-to-day life, such as dealing with the stress or frustration of having a job, raising children, maintaining a home, etc. Because there are not obvious singular events that would trigger extreme emotions, the individual with ASD can struggle to recognize and understand the buildup of emotions related to these experiences in their friends and family. This can result in a disconnect and feelings by those friends and family members that their emotional needs are not met in such a relationship.

Unwritten Social Rules

Recognition and adaptation to unwritten social rules might be one of the most challenging aspects of daily life for many persons with ASD. Unwritten social rules include all the nuanced expectations that people are expected to follow to avoid undesirable consequences. Individuals with ASD tend to do very well with recognizing and understanding written rules. These consists of laws, rules for school or work, or other situations where there are an explicit set of rules with defined consequences for breaking them. However, society also has expectations to follow unwritten social rules. These unwritten rules are so numerous and evolving as to be impossible to define the expectations and consequences in a written format.

Countless variables influence written rules, including where, when, and with whom a person is interacting. Take, for example, a group of friends who occasionally meet to play cards and have fun. A set of unwritten rules will develop as far as how to interact, what to talk about, how much to joke, whether it is okay to swear, and if so how much. Rules will develop regarding where to sit, how and when to eat, how much to joke and/or be serious, etc. Even for a single situation the rules could be too numerous to name. Yet, in one of these interactions a person might suddenly go from laughing and joking to appearing more quiet and serious. Immediately, some of the unwritten rules will change. If the friend then discloses that there is a very difficult situation in his/her life, such as relationship problems, financial or work problems, or illness or death in the family, the unwritten rules change again. There are now new expectations for how much to talk, how much to joke, or what to say to this friend. Failing to recognize these changing rules can hurt feelings and appear insensitive, potentially leading to conflicts or the loss of friendships if the responses are considered to insensitive.

There is no way to name *all* unwritten rules. Society expects that people are constantly monitoring each situation and helping to understand and accommodate the rules in real time and without instruction. This presents a major challenge for people with autism, who can do well with learning and following static rules but can have significant struggles with reading more fluid rules. Some unwritten social rules do not change frequently and can remain static for a certain situation. For example, in the United States it is common in many situations to shake hands when greeting a person. There is a set of rules for how and when to do this that tends to remain consistent over time. There can also be rules for covering one's mouth when sneezing or not picking your nose in public, which are expected in most or all situations. These tend not to be difficult rules for people with autism to learn and follow (although autistic children do often have difficulty with these rules and might be delayed in skill development). But, it is the more fluid rules that tend to create the biggest problems with socializing and relationships.

People with ASD are likely to do well with understanding concrete unwritten rules that hold true over time. The degree to which an individual struggles with more nuanced and flexible unwritten rules can vary greatly depending on the individual. While some have no difficulties with appropriate eye contact, others can be overly intense or avoidant with eye contact. While there is high variability as to how naturally each person learns these rules, the ability to do so can have a significant impact on life. Those who can understand and follow social norms are significantly more likely to develop relationships and succeed in academic and employment opportunities that require such skills. Thus, for those who struggle to naturally develop these skills, developing and understanding and display of unwritten social norms should often be a priority in treatment.

Sensory Processing

Differences in connectivity between brain regions can contribute to atypical sensitivity to various sensory processes (Wigham et al., 2015). A person with ASD can be more likely to experience hypo- or hypersensitivity to primary senses such as touch, taste, smell, light, and sound. This sensitivity can also impact other critical functions such as balance, proprioception, temperature regulation, sleep, appetite, and other aspects of self-regulation. The individual can experience a higher or lower than normal threshold for awareness of these senses either individually or as a whole. Additionally, an individual can experience high sensitivity to some senses and low sensitivity to others.

Challenges with the brain's ability to automatically regulate sensory inputs can be a significant contributor to difficulties with concentration, communication, and emotion regulation (Wigham et al., 2015). Hypersensitivities can cause so much stimulation that the brain must divert additional attention to managing the overload of information. The individual can then have less energy to allocate in other ways and can be more overwhelmed by other tasks of everyday life. Experiencing high levels of stress can worsen these sensitivities, as the brain becomes preoccupied with managing emotions and can become overwhelmed by extraneous stimuli.

Under-responsiveness can also create challenges, as the brain experiences a higher threshold for registering important sensory information. As the individual focuses on a specific task, the brain can be slow to recognize internal functions—such as decreasing blood sugar, fatigue, or bathroom needs. The brain can also be slower to register external information, such as a family member attempting to communicate or gain the person's attention. Failure to register this communication can cause conflicts by not recognizing important nonverbal cues.

Adjusting to the Social World

Education

Education of autism both for the individual and for the family members is often a critical aspect of treatment. The ASD brain has different ways of understanding and thinking about experiences. Learning to live effectively in a world that has been largely influenced and optimized for more neurotypical individuals creates unique challenges. It is often helpful for people with ASD to understand how different situations could be perceived by different people, and to use this information for decisions and actions. Conversely, it is helpful for those relating to the individual with ASD to also understand the different ways of thinking to build healthy relationships and effective communication. These unique perspectives can lead to each person in a relationship becoming frustrated and feeling like the other is illogical or lacking common sense. Understanding that the other points of view are influenced by different neurological processes and working to do so without judgment can be extremely valuable.

Planning

While a range of neurodevelopmental differences can inhibit the development of automatic processes to living optimally in a social world, many higher functioning individuals find that they can deliberately learn important skills. Planning and developing an organized system for identifying and working toward skills to achieve goals are critical steps in this process. This planning stage is ideally a recurring pattern through daily life, helping the individual engage in purposeful and meaningful behaviors that work toward life goals. Planning is not only useful for work or unpleasant tasks, but also for hobbies, relationships, and self-care.

Building Trust

Building trust with a support system of friends, family, and/or professionals who can provide accurate and helpful feedback is critical. Frequently, efforts by people intending to offer support can feel like a personal attack and be met with defensiveness. This is a common and natural response to being told that a person's natural and instinctive way of interacting is ineffective. It is a challenging process for most people to understand that their way of viewing the world is not the same as others, and that following their gut instinct can be counterproductive. In other words, in some situations it is more helpful for a person with ASD to learn to trust others than to trust their own gut.

As an example that most people can probably relate to, think of visiting or moving to a new country with an unfamiliar culture. While intuition might result in using gestures and behaviors that feel natural, a different culture might have different rules for communication, personal space, and behavior expectations. In such a situation it would be important to actively observe and understand the rules of the culture and how best to adapt, rather than relying on one's own intuition and inadvertently alienating oneself. In this situation it could also be invaluable to have a trusted person who is a part of the culture and familiar with the expectations, who can also provide feedback and teach skills for adapting more effectively.

This process involves identifying supports who can clearly be trusted, who have the ASD individual's best interest in mind, and who are willing to listen and support and not merely command. Ideally, the individual will begin to seek feedback from others rather than waiting for feedback to be provided. This creates a more empowering dynamic where the individual is leading the change in his/her life. It can be helpful to think of this as a coaching relationship, where the coach has some valuable information and tools and can provide teaching and feedback. Success can be impacted by the quality of coaching and the individual's reception to coaching. If each participant works to be the best at their role, the entire team is more likely to experience success.

Skill Development and Practice

Much of this chapter has been about recognizing brain differences between autistic individuals and neurotypical individuals, and the impact these differences have on ways of thinking about and experiencing the world. The different perceptions and life experiences result in different skillsets, so that those with ASD can have more difficulty in situations that require a separate skillset. Overcoming such barriers can be aided by recognizing the different skill sets, learning skills that could be beneficial in different life situations, and improving mastery of these skills.

At its core, managing the variety of characteristics of autism that can create challenges in a social world is about identifying and mastering the appropriate skills for each person's unique situation. There is a variety of skills that can be useful depending on the person and situation. Regardless of the skills identified, mastery tends to include explicit teaching, modeling, reinforcement, and practice of the desired skills. Continually revisiting this concept is an important part of intervention to focus on tangible strategies that can be practiced daily, to normalize the experiences in ways that others can relate to, and to reduce judgment about the diagnosis.

Prognosis

In my experience there seem to be three critical factors that can be assessed for evaluating prognosis (likelihood) for change. The first is whether the individual can accept this diagnosis as a way of explaining and helping to understand their symptoms and life experiences. Accepting the diagnosis should not be done in a way of being defeated or defined by it, but as understanding it as a neurological pattern that can lead to experiencing and understanding the world in ways that are sometimes different from other individuals. Accepting the diagnosis means a willingness to understand both the individual's and neurotypical ways of perceiving to adapt in purposeful and deliberate ways that can be more effective. Doing this in a manner that is not judgmental, and not viewing autism as either right or wrong, is invaluable. Being able to view the diagnosis as "a thing about me" but not as a defining characteristic is also critical.

The second factor for assessing prognosis is the cognitive capacity for effective learning and understanding. Many of the strategies for building independence center around improving understanding, developing skills, and implementing cognitive processes to overcome automatic impulses that have been ineffective. Individuals with cognitive or developmental limitations that impair the ability to engage in these processes can experience severe limiting factors to change.

The third factor affecting prognosis is having a support system of individuals who understand the diagnosis and use this to better educate and support the individual. Just as the individual benefits from better understanding the diagnosis and developing skills accordingly, so do the family members and broader support system. Approaching an individual with ASD and attempting to create change through punishments, ultimatums, or other consequences will be counterproductive.

References

Baron-Cohen, S., Ring, H. A., Bullmore, E. T., Wheelwright, S., Ashwin, C., & Williams, S. C. R. (2000). The Amygdala Theory of Autism. *Neuroscience & Biobehavioral Reviews*, 24, 355–364.

Baron-Cohen, S., Ring, H. A., Wheelwright, S., Bullmore, E. T., Brammer, M. J., Simmons, A., & Williams, S. C. (1999). Social Intelligence in the Normal and Autistic Brain: An fMRI Study. *European Journal of Neuroscience*, *11*, 1891–1898.

Brigham Young University. (2012, November 29). Autism Severity May Stem From Fear. *ScienceDaily*. Retrieved October 29, 2017, from www.sciencedaily.com/releases/2012/11/121129143537.htm

Craig, F., Margari, F., Legrottaglie, A. R., Palumbi, R., Giambattista, C., & Margari, L. (2016). A Review of Executive Function Deficits in Autism Spectrum Disorder and Attention-Deficit/Hyperactivity Disorder. *Neuropsychiatric Disease and Treatment*, *12*, 1191–1202. Published online May 12, 2016.

Hamilton, A.F. (2013). Reflecting on the Mirror Neuron System in Autism: A Systematic Review of Current Theories. *Developmental Cognitive Neuroscience*, *3*, 91–105.

Haznedar, M. M., Buchsbaum, M. S., Wei, T. C., Hof, P. R., Cartwright, C., Bienstock, C. A., & Hollander, E. (2000). Limbic Circuitry in Patients with Autism Spectrum Disorders Studied with Positron Emission Tomography and Magnetic Resonance Imaging. *American Journal of Psychiatry*, *157*, 1994–2001.

Hill, E. (2004). Executive Dysfunction in Autism. *Trends in Cognitive Sciences*, *8*(1), 26–32.

Ozonoff, S., Pennington, B. F., & Rogers, S. J. (1991), Executive Function Deficits in High-Functioning Autistic Individuals: Relationship to Theory of Mind. *Journal of Child Psychology and Psychiatry*, *32*, 1081–1105.

Perkins, T., Stokes, M., McGillivray, J., & Bittar, R. (2010). Mirror Neuron Dysfunction in Autism Spectrum Disorders. *Journal of Clinical Neuroscience*, *17*(10), 1239–43.

Schultz, R. T. (2005). Developmental Deficits in Social Perception in Autism: The Role of the Amygdala and Fusiform Face Area. *International Journal of Developmental Neuroscience*, *23*, 125–141.

Vollm, B. A., Taylor, A. N., Richardson, P., Corcoran, R., Stirling, J., McKie, S., . . . Elliot, R. (2006). Neuronal Correlates of Theory of Mind and Empathy: A Functional Magnetic Resonance Imaging Study in a Nonverbal Task. *NeuroImage, 20*, 90–98.

Wigham, S., Rodgers, J., South, M., McConachie, H., and Freeston, M. (2015). The Interplay Between Sensory Processing Abnormalities, Intolerance of Uncertainty, Anxiety and Restricted and Repetitive Behaviours in Autism Spectrum Disorder. *Journal of Autism and Developmental Disorders, 45*(4), 943–952.

14

UNDERSTANDING HOW THE SPECIAL EDUCATION SYSTEM WORKS FOR STUDENTS WITH AUTISM SPECTRUM DISORDER

Mary S. Rozendal and Nalova Westbrook

Alex is a 5-year-old boy diagnosed with an autism spectrum disorder (ASD). He has participated in intensive therapy through a local autism therapy clinic and has had home-based early intervention services since his diagnosis at age 3. Alex has developed some basic language skills, although there are ongoing concerns with socialization, visual stimming during transitions, and aggressive behaviors when he is unable to communicate effectively to meet his needs. Alex's parents have many questions as they prepare for him to enter the school system. Will he be eligible for special education? Will he be able to attend the local school with the children in his neighborhood? What services are available to help Alex navigate and learn in the school setting? Will Alex have support services to assist him with making friends? Will outside therapy still be needed in addition to attending school? How will the school handle his aggressive behavior when it occurs?

When a family receives a diagnosis of autism spectrum disorder (ASD), or when a child with an ASD diagnosis is getting ready to start school, there are often many questions. The special education program in the public schools is a federally mandated system that provides free education with support services to children who are defined as having a disability by the federal and state special education laws. However, because it is a legislated system that differs in some ways from the understanding of disability put forth by professional organizations such as the American Psychological Association, problems may arise without a clear understanding of these differences.

The focus of public schools is to provide opportunities for children to learn academic content and skills. Schools' efforts to provide services to address autism-related factors are centered around the goal of academic learning. Clinicians working with families who have a child with autism need to understand the federally mandated special education system, as it is typically a central part of a child's life. Understanding the system will also better equip clinicians to work with families and coordinate services with schools. This chapter provides an overview of the special education law for clinicians working with families of children with an autism spectrum disorder.

An Overview of Special Education Law

In 1975, the Education for All Handicapped Children Act, also known as Public Law 94-142, became law in the United States. This law mandated free and appropriate public education (FAPE) for all children in the public school system, established procedures for identifying children eligible for special education services, and created guidelines for providing education and related services specific to children's unique learning needs. In addition, the law provided protection for the rights of children with disabilities and their parents, helped states and local districts provide educational services for any child with a disability, and provided a means to assess the effectiveness of these educational efforts for students with disabilities. Prior to the passage of PL 94-142, there were over 1 million children who were excluded from receiving a public education due to a disability. In addition, an estimated 50% of all children in the US with disabilities had only limited access to public education (Office of Special Education Programs, 2012). PL 94-142 required that states provide programs and services for children ages 3–21, but the amendments in 1986 expanded the programs and services to birth through 21.

In 1996, there was a reauthorization of the special education law which was renamed the Individuals with Disabilities Education Act (IDEA). The 2004 version of IDEA was officially called the Individuals with Disabilities Education Improvement Act, but it continued to be identified as IDEA. The most recent revisions (2004, finalized in 2006) have brought the special education law in line with other education laws such as the No Child Left Behind Act of 2001 (NCLB; U.S. Department of Education, n.d.) and Elementary and Secondary Education Act (ESEA, 1965). In addition, legal decisions over the years have helped to shape the implementation of the laws on both federal and state levels.

There are several responsibilities set out in IDEA. First, states and districts are obligated to locate and evaluate students with disabilities. Districts must conduct "child find" activities to identify students with special needs, including autism, who might be in their district boundaries. Second, each child with a disability is entitled to FAPE (Free Appropriate Public Education) in the least restrictive environment (LRE). The definition of LRE is:

> To the maximum extent appropriate, children with disabilities, including children in public or private institutions or other care facilities, are educated with children who are not disabled, and special classes, separate schooling, or other removal of children with disabilities from the regular

educational environment occurs only when the nature or severity of the disability of a child is such that education in regular classes with the use of supplementary aids and services cannot be achieved satisfactorily.

(20 U.S.C. 1412 a(5)(A))

It is the IEP team's (often referred to as a Child Study Team) responsibility to determine what is an appropriate education and what the least restrictive environment is for a particular student. Both are not supposed to be based on the available services in the district, but the *reality* is available services and programs often do factor into the decisions. Many self-contained classrooms, for example, that provide targeted intervention services for students who are not able to participate in a general education classroom are not maintained in the local school district. Teachers in resource rooms often do not have the specific training needed to teach a child on the autism spectrum, even when the child is higher functioning. That being said, schools are expected to provide the education and support services that the IEP team determines are needed for the particular student. This may include providing additional training for the teachers and staff, adding teacher aides or paraprofessionals to provide more one-on-one support, or providing a location where a child with autism can be safe if they are experiencing a meltdown or having behavior challenges due to their autism. Parents should be an integral part of the discussion about what is best for their child in these meetings, but a good parent advocate may also help navigate the process and present the needs of the child to the IEP team.

Whereas previous amendments extended the range of services to age 3, IDEA Amendments of 1997 (PL 105-17) provided guidelines for transition services from high school to adult living. Starting at age 14, each student's IEP must include a transition plan that includes identifying appropriate employment and adult living goals for the student. The transition plan is the point at which students are referred to local community agencies and resources, and the IEP must specify who will be responsible for the transition activities (Office of Special Education Programs, 2012).

As with any legislated system, the special education system has its challenges because no two students are alike. The process involves adhering to the procedures set forth by the federal government and the individual states, and on occasion that process seems to overshadow the needs of students. It is important for parents and non-school clinicians to understand the IEP process to better advocate for the needs of students with autism spectrum disorders.

The Individualized Education Plan (IEP) Process

The special education process can be daunting to parents, clinicians, and medical professionals, so it is helpful to understand the process to make strategic recommendations. The IEP process involves two steps: the determination of eligibility for special education services, and the educational plan if a student is found eligible. Every student recommended for special education must have an initial evaluation to establish eligibility for special education, and re-evaluations every three years to continue or discontinue services. If eligible, an IEP team makes decisions about educational placements and the development of an individual education plan (IEP). The IEP establishes the education and support services for the student for one year. Education goals are written out with specific benchmarks and criteria to determine when they are met. Accommodations are also determined for state and district testing and for when the child is participating in general education, if applicable. Decisions about transportation and extended school year options are also included on the IEP.

Special Education Eligibility

Before a child can be considered for special education, the local education agency (LEA), typically the school district, is responsible for conducting an evaluation of the child. Parents or guardians, the State, or the LEA can request an IEP evaluation; however, parents give final permission for the evaluation to be conducted. The notice to parents of the evaluation must describe the evaluation procedures. The evaluation window is 60 calendar days from the date of parental consent to complete the evaluation and hold the eligibility meeting and IEP meeting if eligibility for special education is determined. The evaluation must include a variety of assessment tools to obtain a thorough understanding of the child and his/her strengths and needs. The assessments must be given in the language most likely to enable the child to demonstrate what s/he knows academically, developmentally, and functionally. When the evaluation is completed, the evaluation team meets to determine special education eligibility. That team must include the parent, except in cases where the school attempts to contact parents, documents those attempts, and is unsuccessful at getting parents to attend. Parents must be given an evaluation report and documentation of the eligibility decision.

To qualify for special education services under IDEA, two conditions must be met. First, a student must meet the eligibility criteria in one or more of the special education categories or be identified as having a developmental delay if they are in early childhood programs. Second, the student must demonstrate a need for special education and related services as a result of his/her disability. The 13 eligibility categories in the most recent (2004) IDEA reauthorization include autism, deaf-blindness, deafness, emotional disturbance, hearing impairment, intellectual disability, multiple disabilities, orthopedic impairment, other health impairment, specific learning disability, speech or language impairments, traumatic brain injury, and visual impairment, including blindness (Section 1401 of the IDEA law). Despite several categories having similar names as diagnoses found in the DSM-5, the eligibility criteria for the special education categories is not necessarily consistent with clinical diagnoses bearing the same label. The autism definition in IDEA is:

> (c)(1)(i) Autism means a developmental disability significantly affecting verbal and nonverbal communication and social interaction, generally evident before age three, that adversely affects a child's educational performance. Other characteristics often associated with autism are engagement in repetitive activities and stereotyped movements, resistance to environmental change or change in daily routines, and unusual responses to sensory experiences. (ii) Autism does not apply if a child's educational performance is adversely affected primarily because the child has an emotional disturbance, as defined in paragraph (c)(4) of this section. (iii) A child who manifests the characteristics of autism after age three could be identified as having autism if the criteria in paragraph (c)(1)(i) of this section are satisfied.
>
> *(Individuals with Disabilities Education Act, 2004)*

The second requirement, the educational need for special education services, may keep some students from being eligible for special education. In other words, it is possible that a child is diagnosed with autism by a psychologist or clinical team and meets the eligibility criteria established by IDEA, but the school does not identify him/her as a child with a disability because they determine there is no educational need for special education. Court cases highlighted later in the chapter have affirmed the IDEA educational definition of disability, but states differ on how they interpret "educational need."

Purpose of an Evaluation

The purpose of an evaluation of a disability at school is to identify if a student, like Alex in the opening vignette, meets the eligibility criteria in any of the 13 special education categories. A student who has a clinical diagnosis of autism spectrum disorder may be eligible for special education services in the autism category, but this is not guaranteed. The school evaluation team may decide the student is eligible in a different category such as Emotional Impairment, Learning Disability, or Other Health Impaired. The evaluation team may also decide the student is not eligible for special education services based on the federal and state criteria. The eligibility category is not supposed to determine the specific educational plan developed later because, regardless of the eligibility category, students are supposed to have their specific needs addressed in the IEP programs and services. Therefore, even if a child with a clinical diagnosis of autism spectrum disorder based on the DSM-5 is found eligible for special education services in a category other than autism, such as Other Health Impaired, if the IEP team determines that child would benefit from placement in an autism program, s/he would be able to receive that service. Conversely, a child who is found eligible for services under the ASD category does not have to be placed in an autism program if his/her least restrictive environment is determined to be in the general education program with specified support services. In other words, the eligibility category does not predetermine the services and educational plan created for the child in the IEP.

Individualized Education Plan (IEP)

If a student is found to be eligible for special education, then the Individual Education Plan (IEP) team must create an education plan specific to any educational need the student may have. Schools are not supposed to offer the child only the services they have in their district, but the needs of the student are supposed to determine the best individualized educational plan for each individual student. This must be in the least restrictive environment, meaning students should be educated as much as possible in the general education setting, with as much independence as is appropriate for their age and disability. Students' IEPs are updated on a yearly basis. Every three years the student's IEP must be re-evaluated. Re-evaluations are typically similar to initial evaluations, but a review of the child's progress on the previous IEP goals will be included. If the child continues to meet eligibility, then he/she will continue receiving the services.

Parent Consent

Parent consent must be given before the evaluation is started. If the child is found eligible for special education services parents must then give their consent for the IEP to be implemented. Parents can request an IEP meeting at any time; however, if those requests become excessive, the school district is not obligated to meet every time. Re-evaluations are limited to once a year if parents request a re-evaluation, but are generally required every three years. If parents and the school decide a re-evaluation is not necessary, a program review is conducted instead of testing. This is typically done when the eligibility for services is not in question and the student is making expected progress. If there are any questions about development or changes in knowledge and skills, then the re-evaluation testing can be targeted toward just those questions.

IEP Participants

After the evaluation team has determined a child is eligible for special education services, the IEP team develops the Individualized Education Plan document. This may take place at the same meeting to determine eligibility, or at a later date. IDEA specifies that the following people must be included in the IEP meeting: (1) parents of the child found eligible for services, (2) at least one general education teacher if the child is participating in any general education classroom, (3) at least one special education teacher or special education provider, (4) a representative of the local education agency (school district) who knows the general and special education programs and services and knows about the availability of resources in the school district, (5) an individual who can interpret the evaluation results and their instructional implications (may overlap with the person in 2–4 above), (6) other individuals who have knowledge of/special expertise regarding the child's disability (this is at the parents' or LEA's discretion), and (7) the child with the eligible disability, when appropriate. If one of the above IEP team members is not able to be at the meeting, s/he may be excused with the consent of the parent and LEA as long as the member submits their input regarding the IEP in writing prior to the meeting. If an LEA has made the special education referral and the student's parent(s) refuse or cannot for some reason give their approval for the evaluation or re-evaluation, the school may still conduct the evaluation, and hold the eligibility and IEP meetings if the school has made and documented reasonable efforts to obtain the parent's permission.

IEP Components

IDEA requires that the IEP team consider the strengths of the child, any parental concerns about the education of their child, results of the most recent evaluation of the child, and the academic, developmental, and functional needs of the child. The IEP document consists of the following:

1. A description of the child's Present Levels of Academic Achievement and Functional Performance (the PLAAFP).
2. Annual measurable goals including academic and functional goals.
3. The manner in which the individual goals will be measured and when parents will receive periodic reports of the student's progress.
4. A statement of the special education and related services to be provided (i.e., departmentalized autism program, speech and language services, social work services, resource room), the supplementary aids and services to be provided (i.e., assistive technology provided, paraprofessional aide), the program modifications (i.e., tests read aloud, reduced assignments, use of visual schedule), and supports for school personnel that will be provided (i.e., OT consultation, Autism Teacher Consultant).
5. An explanation of the extent to which the child will not participate in the regular classroom setting with non-disabled peers.
6. Identification of testing accommodations and/or modifications for state and district-wide assessments.

The projected date for the beginning of services, and the anticipated frequency, location, and duration of the listed services and modifications—typically covers a calendar year, but if a child transitions to a different building (i.e., elementary to middle school), each program duration is listed.

An IEP is *valid* for one calendar year. It can be amended or revised at the request of the school or parents more frequently if there are concerns, program changes, or new information to be included. It is the responsibility of the school to ensure that all school personnel working with the child know what is on the child's IEP.

Early Intervention Services and Transition Plans

In addition to the above requirements, there are provisions for the younger and older students. For children from the ages of 3 to 5, an Individualized Family Service Plan (IFSP) may be developed instead of an IEP. These plans often include early intervention services provided in the child's home or early childhood center rather than the school setting. For a student between the ages 14 and 16, a plan must be developed and put in place by age 16 that transitions the student into post-school life. This may include post-high-school education, community living experiences, employment skill development, adult living objectives, daily living skills and a functional vocational evaluation. A "statement of the interagency responsibilities" is included in the transition plan to identify which government agencies will provide the funding for the transition services. Representatives from these agencies must join the student, parent(s), special education teacher/service provider, and regular education teacher (if appropriate) to develop the transition plan.

IEP Disagreements

If a parent disagrees with the results of the eligibility determination, or any component of the IEP, the IDEA establishes procedures for resolving these conflicts. Negotiations to resolve the differences are strongly recommended and may include an Independent Educational Evaluation (IEE) paid with public funds. An IEE is "an evaluation conducted by a qualified examiner who is not employed by the public agency responsible for the education of the child in question." 34 C.F.R. 300.502(a)(3)(i). In addition to academic and/or cognitive skills evaluations, an IEE may include the evaluation of any skill related to the child's educational needs including, but not limited to "neurological functioning, adapted physical education, sensory needs, behavior, aquatics, even music therapy" (Steedman, n.d.). An IEE may be obtained by parents at their own expense or at public expense under specific circumstances such as when a district is not able to provide an appropriate evaluation, or when parents disagree with the district's evaluation and request an IEE at public expense. In the case of a parental IEE request due to a disagreement with the school's evaluation, the district may instead request a due process hearing, but must prove their evaluation was sufficient. 34 C.F.R. 300.502(b)(2). If a parent obtains an IEE, the IEP team is mandated to consider it. The team does not have to accept the evaluation findings, however, only "consider" it. 34 C.F.R. 300.503(c) If negotiations between parents and the school district do not resolve the differences, IDEA specifies procedures for mediation, due process (presenting the case to special education administrative judges), and civil action. If parents feel that they need to utilize the due process system due to a disagreement with the IEP process, it is important that they understand the rules and timelines established by the states. This should be outlined in the Special Education Policies and Parental Rights materials provided by the school at the time of the IEP, but any disagreements should be given to the IEP team and school and noted during the IEP meeting.

Variation Across States

Clinicians who work with families to address the needs of a child with autism, like Alex in the opening vignette, should be aware that the legal framework for providing autism services in schools has considerable variability across states. Individual states are able to further define the eligibility criteria for special education in their state beyond the federal government guidelines in IDEA, so a child may be eligible for particular special education services in one state, but not in another. Barton et al. (2015, p. 838) observe: "*Each state* establishes their own ASD eligibility criteria, although the criteria must meet or exceed the criteria outlined by the federal regulations." Furthermore, although IDEA indicates that all children with disabilities ages 3 to 21 have access to free and appropriate public education, states can create their own educational eligibility assessment policies as long as they meet the minimum requirements set by the federal government (Barton et al, 2015). It is important that clinicians and parents become familiar with the specific state laws regarding autism. This information is typically provided by the state's Department of Education. In addition, it may be helpful to review recent court cases in your state to more fully understand how the state special education laws are being interpreted.

Variability across states appears to be unavoidable given the need for broader definitions in the federal IDEA that make possible different state interpretations of the law. Despite a 1992 mandate that "school districts provide appropriate services for children with ASD" (Barton et al., 2015, p. 215), each state establishes their own ASD eligibility criteria. In other words, states may develop their own policies of assessment for ASD insofar as such state policies comply with basic federal mandates. The reality, then, is that state interpretations of IDEA mean that states may develop special education programs that extend beyond the federal government directives and be inconsistent with those of other states. Citing a Conderman and Katsiyannis (1996) survey, Barton et al. (2015) observed that 23 of 42 states used the federal definition of autism, but nearly half have opted to use their own definition. They also found state policies regarding eligibility criteria and required assessments varied widely. Further, some but not all states included autism as an eligibility category for early intervention services. As a result, some of the variation of eligibility across states may stem from difference in identified age of early intervention services (Barton et al., 2015).

> Forty-four states included autism as a specific eligibility category or dis-ability for infants and toddlers to receive early intervention services. Seven states did not specify ASD as an eligible disability, covering under other categories or under the Developmentally Delayed category. However, all of these states provide early intervention services for children with ASD if they meet their respective eligibility criteria.
>
> *(Barton, 2015, p. 741)*

Beyond this,

> 17 states plus Washington D.C. used the exact wording in the federal regulations. The remaining 33 states, however, used a variety of different criteria including for determining eligibility: (a) the use of the DSM-IV-TR (APA 2004), (b) mentioning ASDs, and (c) requiring medical diagnoses.
>
> *(Barton et al., 2015, p. 738)*

Ostensibly, eligibility for ASD services across states will be inconsistent when there is room for states to develop their own definitions and criteria for what constitutes a child with autism within the scope of federal regulations.

In particular, states may also differ in eligibility for services based on their attention to education-related spending or healthcare services. Typically, according to Barton et al. (2015), eligibility for special education is based on a medical diagnosis or an educational evaluation. As mentioned, either DSM-5 evaluations or impact of a service on a child's education determines whether a child with autism will receive services to support his/her development or not. Only two states specifically referred to the use of the DSM-5—Maine and West Virginia. As a result, most states use non-standard measures to evaluate a child, which means the reliability of evaluation across states will be compromised. Moreover, because school psychologists often identify children with ASD in educational settings, despite availability of medical professionals upon request, eligibility is determined by a group of professionals that may have little knowledge of the best ways in which to use evaluation tools that would provide reliable and valid diagnosis of a child with ASD. Accordingly, while school psychologists are well intentioned, they may lack some of the necessary skill to identify children who are in need of autism services. Lack of skill plays a role in initial diagnosis and treatment, which increases the inconsistency in diagnosis of ASD.

There are also provisions in place for school districts across states to accept a non-school district evaluation and factor in family input. "Twenty-five states indicated that they accepted non-district evaluations to determine eligibility for special education services under the autism category" (Barton et al., 2015, p. 741) from pediatricians and clinicians; "Twenty-four of these states had specific requirements. Fourteen states indicated that a group of qualified professionals conducted the ASD evaluations within each school" (p. 741); and "Twenty-four states specifically stated they required the evaluation team to gather input from the child's family during the autism evaluation process" (p. 742). Family input must be distinguished, though, from parent notification for the initial evaluation to take place. Family input means that parents or guardians play an active role in the development of an IEP for their child. IDEA specifies that parents or guardians will be notified about eligibility for, evaluations of, educational placement in, and FAPE and meetings designed to address the needs of a child with ASD. Put another way, the only consistency across states with regards to parental involvement is notification by states that their child may receive a number of services to which parents must consent. However, states differ on whether they require parental ideas and feedback on the services a child of parents will receive.

The take-away message for clinicians is this: there is so much variability across states and school districts for eligibility of ASD services for children that warrant continued education and treatment of each case on a case-by-case basis. One must become familiar with the particular eligibility policies, procedures, and assessments of a school district and state for a child who shall be serviced for ASD. In particular, one needs to learn about school psychologist practices and be able to explain to parents the difference between school psychologist and clinical practice on evaluation of ASD and why, in ideal situations, parents should request for both. The reality is, while unintentional, school psychologists, and even special education teachers as part of the IEP team, tend to carry out their evaluations in a manner that may be far different from best practices among clinicians and medical professionals for determining eligibility for ASD interventions. However, such circumstances do not warrant competition among stakeholders when all concerned must keep the best interests of the child with ASD front and center. The implications are that all stakeholders—federal government, states, clinicians, school psychologists and teachers—need to find enough common ground to support Alex and all of those children with ASD like him.

Legal Considerations of ASD and Special Education

There were several landmark court decisions that laid the foundation for special education in general, and ongoing legal cases continue to shape the implementation of special education services across the country. While it is beyond the scope of this chapter to review all cases, key decisions are provided as examples to show how questions about the intent and implementation of IDEA continue to be raised. For example, the *Pennsylvania Association for Retarded Citizens v. Commonwealth* (1971) and *Mills v. Board of Education of the District of Columbia* (1972) placed the responsibility for educating children with disabilities on the states and localities. It was determined that the right of every child with a disability to be educated is grounded in the equal protection clause of the 14th Amendment to the United States Constitution (Office of Special Education Programs, 2012). Prior to these landmark court cases, various laws had been enacted to provide job training and some educational services to select populations with disabilities. Notable examples include the Training of Professional Personnel Act of 1959 (PL 86-158), which helped train leaders to educate children with mental retardation; the training provisions for teachers of students with mental retardation (PL 85-926); and the Teachers of the Deaf Act of 1961 (PL 87-276), which mandated specific training for instructional personnel teaching children who were deaf or hard of hearing.

The laws that were needed to provide education for so many children who had been excluded from receiving a public education at times created a situation where there is disagreement over what that education includes or excludes. IDEA and the special education laws that preceded it provided for the rights of family to be maintained throughout the process. Procedures for due process when parents disagreed with an aspect of the IEP process were established to help parents maintain their voice in the special education process.

Special education is a system set up by rule of law; therefore, disagreements between parents and the LEA over eligibility, IEP implementation, and educational obligations of schools to provide services are challenged in the courts if resolutions are not found through mediation or due process. These rulings affect the way IDEA is implemented, but different state rulings may also seem to contradict. For example, IDEA does not define "educational performance," so individual state laws must guide the eligibility decisions. "Educational performance" is often defined as academic performance, but some states allow non-academic areas such as "communication" to be included in the definition as long as the qualifying disability, such as autism, has some negative impact on the educational performance. In *Mr. I and Mrs. I ex rel.L.I. v. Maine Sch. Administrative District No. 55* (2007), the courts ruled that even though a sixth-grade student had good grades and was not disruptive in class, Maine was obligated to provide special education for direct social skills training because her Asperger's syndrome adversely affected her ability to communicate and interact with her peers. In contrast, in *C.L.J, and C.J. v. Board of Educ. E. Islip Union Free Sch. Dist.* (EDNY 2010), the New York court supported the school district's denial of special education services for a boy with a diagnosis of Asperger's syndrome but above average academic performance. Parents were requesting an IEP to address his struggles with social skills and behavior. Unlike the broader

Maine interpretation, the New York court stated that educational performance was defined as academic performance.

As mentioned above, a diagnosis of autism spectrum disorder in a clinical setting based on the DSM-5, does not necessarily mean a child is automatically eligible for special education. Several cases like the one in West Virginia (SEA WV 2011) have upheld the criterion that academic need for special education is a factor to be considered. The West Virginia court determined that a school district did not err in denying special education eligibility to an elementary student with an autism diagnosis by a private psychologist. The student's grades and classroom performance were in line with his average intellectual abilities. Despite the fact that the student's school assistance team recommended eligibility, his behavior challenges could be managed with supports that did not qualify as specialized instruction. Therefore, a medical diagnosis of autism alone did not qualify him for special education, because he did not demonstrate academic difficulties (LRP Publications, 2012).

One area where court cases have increased in the past two decades is regarding Free Appropriate Public Education (FAPE) (LRP Publications, 2012). IDEA does not require that a school district provide the best possible educational services to maximize the student's potential. Unless a state establishes a maximum potential standard, districts are obligated only to provide an "appropriate" education at public expense. However, it would be impossible for a federal law to specify what "appropriate" means, thus opening the door for questions about FAPE to be brought before state and federal courts. Court cases involving autism have primarily centered on three issues: (1) educational methodology, (2) amount of benefit, and (3) generalization outside of the school setting. In the most recent U.S. Supreme Court ruling about FAPE, *Endrew F. v. Douglas County School District Re-1*, the Court determined a child with autism was entitled to an educational program that provides "merely more than *de minimis* [minimal] educational benefit" (i.e., more than trivial) (U.S. Department of Education, 2017, p. 3). In its ruling, the Court said a school *must* offer an IEP that is "reasonably calculated to enable a child to make progress appropriate in light of the child's circumstances" (p. 3). This decision about what constitutes the amount of benefit students and parents should expect from the individual education program will enable future parents to insist that schools provide an educational plan that will enable their children to make gains in their learning. Schools will not be able to be satisfied with minimal progress.

Legal challenges to the implementation of IDEA for children on the autism spectrum will continue to refine the way educational and related services are provided. The best way to avoid these problems, however, is to strive to work as a multifaceted treatment team to creatively address the unique needs of each child with autism. Being realistic about the mission of public schools to provide academic learning and finding ways to partner with outside therapists and service providers is likely to afford children the best opportunities to grow and develop.

Conclusion

Education for children with an autism spectrum disorder is mandated by IDEA, a federal law providing free and appropriate education in the least restrictive environment. The special education laws vary by state as long as the minimum requirements of IDEA are upheld. The IEP process involves determining eligibility through an evaluation of the disability and the child's need for special education services. Once eligibility is determined, schools are expected to provide services to support academic learning with the goal of transitioning either to a college level educational program, an adult employment or other appropriate programs. Clinicians working outside of the school setting can provide guidance to parents as they navigate the special education system and may have a role as an external evaluator or service provider who may provide helpful information to the IEP team and special education personnel.

References

38th Annual Report to Congress on the Implementation of the Individuals with Disabilities Education Act, 2016. (2016). Retrieved March 24, 2017, from https://sites.ed.gov/idea/2016-annual-report-to-congress

Barton, E. E., Harris, B., Leech, N., Stiff, L., Choi, G., & Joel, T. (2015). An Analysis of State Autism Educational Assessment Practices and Requirements. *Journal of Autism and Developmental Disorders*, 46(3), 737–748. doi:10.1007/s10803-015-2589-0

Elementary and Secondary Education Act (ESEA). (1965). Retrieved March 214, 2018 from www2.ed.gov/documents/essa-act-of-1965.pdf

Individuals with Disabilities Education Act, 34 C.F.R. 300.8 c(1) 2004

Individuals with Disabilities Education Act, 34 C.F.R. 300.502(a)(3)(i) 2004

LRP Publications. (2012). *Autism Case Law: A Desktop Reference to Key Decisions*. Palm Beach Gardens, FL: LRP Publications.

Office of Special Education Programs. (2012). *HISTORY Twenty-Five Years of Progress in Educating Children with Disabilities Through IDEA*. Retrieved from www2.ed.gov/about/offices/list/osers/idea35/history/idea-35-history.pdf. doi:10.4324/9780203120804

Steedman, W. (n.d.). Independent Education Evaluations: What? Why? How? Who Pays?

United States Department of Education. (n.d.). *No Child Left Behind Act of 2001*. Retrieved from www2.ed.gov/policy/elsec/leg/esea02/index.html

United States Department of Education. (2017). *Questions and Answers (Q&A) on U.S. Supreme Court Case Decision on Endrew F. v. Douglas County School District Re-1*. Retrieved January 16, 2018, from https://sites.ed.gov/idea/files/qa-endrewcase-12-07-2017.pdf

INDEX